The Challenge of Achievement

by
Everett Biggs

edited by
Richard Mitchener

The Ontario Milk Marketing Board's first 25 years of operation - 1965 to 1990

The Ontario Milk Marketing Board gratefully acknowledges the individuals and organizations that contributed the photographs used in this publication.

Cover photograph by Dave Barr.

Design and production by Bill Mitchell.

Published by The Ontario Milk Marketing Board, Mississauga, Ontario, Canada, L5N 2L8

ISBN 1-895410-04-5

Printed in Canada.

Contents

Foreword		5
Chapter One:	The Stage is Set	7
Chapter Two:	Point of No Return	30
Chapter Three:	The Die is Cast	51
Chapter Four:	A Presence Felt	77
Chapter Five:	Authority Tested	103
Chapter Six:	Settling In	122
Chapter Seven:	Supply Management	144
Chapter Eight:	The Channel Islands Saga	167
Chapter Nine:	Achievements Challenged	180
Chapter Ten:	The 1990s and Beyond	212
Epilogue		240
Appendix One:	List of Board Members	250
Appendix Two:	List of Achievers	252

FOREWORD

As the Ontario Milk Marketing Board approached its twenty-fifth anniversary of service to the milk producers and the dairy industry in this province, its board members decided that this important milestone should be marked by the publication of a book on the organization's history to date. The tasks of selecting an author and overseeing the project were assigned to a board committee made up of board members, a few staff personnel and chaired by past chairman Grant Smith.

One of the early decisions made by the committee was that the history should be written in a very readable and folksy style, while at the same time documenting the considerable number of challenges and achievements that were met and accomplished over a quarter of a century.

The committee also wanted the author to be one who was personally knowledgeable about the problems in the industry prior to the formation of the board; one who knew and was respected by leaders and personalities in the industry past and present; and one who could write with insight about developments in milk marketing as they unfolded over the years.

In its search for an author who could meet these criteria, the board was particularly fortunate in securing the services of Everett Biggs. As a former dairy commissioner and subsequently deputy minister of the Ontario Department of Agriculture when the Milk Act was passed in 1965, Mr. Biggs had himself made major contributions to creating the opportunity for major change in the way milk was to be marketed in Ontario in the future. Following his selection by the board's committee, he made it clear that he was so interested in taking on the project that he would do so without remuneration, other than for his out-of-pocket expenses.

Everett Biggs, who for the past 13 years has been a consultant to the agriculture and food industry and to government, has given freely of his time and talents in the preparation of this book. He has spent countless hours, weeks and months over the past two years researching the challenges to and achievements of the board. During this period he interviewed many industry participants throughout Ontario to seek out their perspectives on the performance and evolution of the board down through the years. This combination of careful and exhaustive research, along with insights gleaned from interviews with industry participants past and present, has resulted in a very readable, informative and interesting history of one of Canada's most notable and successful marketing boards.

Not only did the board obtain the extensive, knowledgeable and dedicated services of Mr. Biggs, but those of his experienced and talented wife Irene as well. Mrs. Biggs provided secretarial services in the preparation of Challenge of Achievement, including the typing of Everett's taped interviews and the initial drafts of the chapters of the book.

Irene Biggs also played a key role in a related undertaking. She served as producer and set director at Rogers Cable 10 TV in Brampton, where Everett conducted fifteen half-hour interviews, which were recorded on videotapes. These interviews were carried out with prominent people in government and the dairy industry who had intimate knowledge of the need for the creation of a single milk producer marketing board and the establishment of its policies and programs to bring order out of chaos in the marketing of milk in Ontario.

These videos were shown on Rogers Cable TV as part of its programming over a period of several months in 1989-90. They were produced without charge to the board, and Rogers also provided the board with copies of them. The videos will make a most valuable addition, along with Challenge of Achievement, to the board's archives. The board wishes to express its sincere appreciation to manager Craig Cole at Rogers for making this project possible and so successful.

In the last few months leading up to the publication of the book, the board engaged the services of an editor to assist Everett in putting the final touches to his manuscript. The board wishes to acknowledge Richard Mitchener's professional contribution to this undertaking.

Finally, the board wishes to extend its deep appreciation to the numerous individuals who agreed to be interviewed by Everett, and, in many cases, to have their views quoted in the manuscript. These individuals helped immensely in giving this historical publication a great deal of authenticity and a personal orientation that makes for most interesting reading.

On a personal note, as one who has known Everett Biggs since he was dairy commissioner in Ontario back in the '50s, and who has followed his career ever since, I should say here that he has made an enormous contribution to the well-being of agricultural marketing in Ontario and in this country for more than four decades, and especially to milk marketing and to dairy policy in particular. The dairy industry has had reason to be indebted to Mr. Biggs in the past, and it is now indebted to him for writing Challenge of Achievement and for bringing this project to a successful completion—a significant achievement in itself. Our warmest thanks go out to Everett Biggs for all he has done.

Lorne Hurd
General Manager, 1966-90
The Ontario Milk Marketing Board
Mississauga, Ontario
September 19, 1990

CHAPTER ONE

The Stage is Set

In which we remember

- Colonel Tom Kennedy
- Jack McArthur, the bank manager
- The production survey
- The North Shore Co-operative
- Dirty milk
- Toronto surplus milk plant
- The Milk Industry Act of 1954
- Fluid milk pricing formula
- First Dairy Queen competition
- Milk Industry Act of 1957
- Jug milk and Becker's stores
- Watered-down milk
- August 19, 1965

Bill Stewart swung his legs over the side of the bed. He was alone in his usual room in Toronto's Royal York Hotel, number 10-165. Pausing for a moment,he glanced out the window and took a deep breath. To himself he muttered, "This looks like a hot one coming up."

It was August 19, 1965, the morning he would be calling together for the first time his selections for the new Ontario Milk Marketing Board.

Out loud he said ruefully, "Today may be hot, but some of the days to come will no doubt get a lot hotter."

As Ontario's minister of agriculture, Bill Stewart had worked late the previous night in his office on the fourth floor of the Whitney Block at

Queen's Park. He had tried to clear his desk, but that was just something to occupy his hands. He was actually deep in thought about the creation of Ontario's new milk marketing board.

Earlier that day he had met with me and George McCague, chairman of the Milk Industry Board, for a final chat. McCague and I had agreed with Stewart that it was vital to maintain the momentum of the milk policy that was recently established. Any slackening or indecision would be fatal. There was real opposition out there, people who eagerly awaited, like vultures, any sign of weakness on Stewart's or the government's part.

As Stewart shaved, he mulled over the general situation in the dairy industry. There was no doubt that the vast majority of milk producers wanted workable and significant changes in milk marketing. But many producers were confused, and as a group they were virtually rudderless. Some of the opponents of the proposed changes, producers of milk, generally were successful farmers. In the vast majority of cases they had aggressively pursued preferred fluid milk markets and had built good, solid operations.

Many producers were the kind of individuals who come out ahead under most circumstances. Such people typically don't take kindly to interference in their affairs from anyone, particularly anyone in the government. They believe they're sufficient unto themselves. On the other hand, many had received favoured treatment from a trucker or a distributor, treatment that wasn't readily available to most milk producers. Most had earned it through hard work but, again, there generally wasn't equal opportunity out there for the rank and file of producers. With milk distributors, extensive protection, provided under existing milk legislation, had created a large number of what could almost be called fiefdoms.

Getting dressed, Stewart pondered: "How many separate distribution areas are there for fluid milk? Something like 200 strictly regulated areas, I think. If a distributor isn't licensed for a particular area, he can't cross the boundary line into that area. Each concentrated milk plant regards its shippers as personal property. The Cheese Producers' Marketing Board is something else! Hector Arnold makes sure he keeps it on a tight rein."

The minister of agriculture shrugged on his jacket, glanced in the mirror and straightened his tie. He smiled to himself as he thought of Hector Arnold, chairman of the Ontario Cheese Producers' Marketing Board. Arnold was from Northumberland County. With some success he had been aggressively engaging in a virtual one-man show, marketing Ontario cheese in the United Kingdom. Arnold was chairman, sales manager and practically the whole cheese board rolled into one—and his board knew it!

Bill Stewart thought of the many encounters he'd had with Arnold. He smoked a straight, black pipe that was often empty. He tended to point it, to jab with it to emphasize his statements. Arnold was one of those who didn't like interference. He'd gotten away with a deceptive show of interest and concern regarding the overall changes that were needed in the milk marketing picture. He had even signed the cheese producers' brief that was written in support of a new milk marketing plan.

In reality, however, Arnold was really interested only in cheese, and to all appearances, in retaining his own authority and position. He had made a significant contribution to the cheese industry, but some government officials obviously thought changes were needed nevertheless. The Hennessy Inquiry, in an investigation of the cheese board's activities, had recommended that "...the authority and control presently exercised by the chairman and directors of the Ontario Cheese Producers' Marketing Board be suspended immediately and replaced by an interim Board of Administration."

This was something Arnold wouldn't easily live with; he would lose his domination of the board. One of the directors of the cheese board, for example, under questioning by the Hennessey Inquiry regarding the board's marketing activities, didn't know the answers to a series of questions. Increasingly frustrated, he had given up, and in a state of consternation said, "You'd better ask Mr. Arnold."

Among its conclusions the inquiry stated, "The board's affairs are dominated by one man. There is a serious lack of objective recognition of the economic implications of many acts such as price setting and allocation of available supplies of cheese."

The final report of the inquiry had been hard on Arnold, perhaps too hard. But as the minister of agriculture, Stewart reasoned, "Hector Arnold didn't go out of his way to assist the inquiry, and he's been critical of it ever since."

Arnold had angrily attacked the report during the March 15 meeting of the Milk Producers' Co-ordinating Board and again during the 1965 annual meeting of the cheese producers. He had met with Stewart and presented a very critical "analysis" of the Hennessey report.

"This isn't a one-man board," Arnold protested adamantly. "If the Hennessey recommendations are accepted, our producers will lose all the advantages in marketing they've gained over the past fifteen years. Our board can't and won't accept that, nor will our producers accept it."

One thing was certain: Bill Stewart wouldn't be able to count on Arnold for much help in getting the new milk marketing plan put into place.

Bill Stewart, Ontario Minister of Agriculture from 1961 to 1975, was the most influential person involved in creating The Ontario Milk Marketing Board in 1965.

There was no question that August 19, 1965, would indeed be a day in which temperatures soared. Striding down the hotel corridor to the elevators, Bill Stewart was heading toward a monumental meeting, one that would forever change the future of the dairy industry in Ontario, even throughout Canada. Not only would the dairy industry be affected, but other agricultural pursuits across the country, emulating the Ontario Milk Marketing Board, would follow its example. Farmers, truckers, dairy operations, retail outlets and consumers alike, for decades to come would feel the effects of this far-reaching meeting. Many businesses and individuals would react to the results of the meeting with great antagonism, for they would perceive a loss for themselves. Others, however, would sense value in the changes brought about. Still others, many others, would gain long-term benefits without even having known of the meeting and its widespread effects throughout Canadian society.

There were many groups and individuals adamantly opposed to what he was about to do - milk producers, some distributors and others, many through personal concerns and misunderstandings. But as Stewart neared the elevator, he stopped to consider. There were reasons for what he was doing. Damned good reasons! Serious problems and inequities had been rampant in the entire dairy industry for as long as anyone could care to imagine.

The dairy industry was as old as Canada itself. From the time of its origins in this country it had been evolving gradually - in its economic and social structure; through rising costs; through changes in technology, including the switch to farm bulk tanks; in the marketing of products, especially in light of the introduction of margarine; even in the increasing demand for improved quality of milk products. But many farmers, often not understanding the forces affecting them from the outside, tried to resist these changes over the years. Most producers and processors of dairy products were fearful of some of the changes, which were questioned by many, including some politicians. Each plateau of major change in the industry could almost be measured in terms of a generation. It had been sped up by new technology and knowledge, feeding, management, breeding, artificial insemination and the innovation that had brought about the biggest changes in farm life, electricity.

Colonel Tom Kennedy had been primarily responsible for the electrification of rural Ontario. Colonel Tom, as he was affectionately known, was minister of agriculture in the 1930s, and except for the interruption of the Mitch Hepburn Liberal government, he had continued on through the war years and into 1953.

Kennedy also had introduced the first Milk Control Act in 1934 in an attempt to give some protection to the dairy farmers and others involved in producing milk products. At that time the producers were completely at the mercy of the milk distributors. In Ottawa the farmers were being told to accept ninety cents per hundredweight for their milk or they wouldn't have a market. The Milk Control Board was intended to bring some order into the marketing of fluid milk and, for the first time, give the provincial government a real presence in Ontario agriculture. The cheese producers were the first group of milk producers organized under the Farm Products Marketing Act; cream and concentrated milk producers were covered later.

The Colonel felt really at home in the high-echelon business gatherings of Toronto with his dark suit and black homburg. He left no doubt where he stood on agricultural matters when his piercing glance swept an audience as he spoke, eloquently and persuasively. Partly because of his outstanding communication skills and partly due to force of personality, Kennedy's impact on rural Ontario was remarkable. He was at his best in the barnyard and at farm meetings. Admittedly, he left the black homburg at home, loosened his tie and wore an older, rumpled suit on those occasions. He had a complete empathy with rural Ontario, and the people loved him.

After a rain storm, for the benefit of the Toronto press - and always good for a front-page headline - he could accurately estimate in dollars how much a day's rain would mean to farmers. Some said that he was the one who had coined the phrase, "a million-dollar rain."

During a drought his great ability with mental calculations and his intimate knowledge of Ontario agriculture allowed him to confidently state the great losses farmers had suffered and what it would mean to the economy of the province. No one ever dared question his figures.

I well remember the morning of Saturday, November 18, 1950. I was a Department of Agriculture representative in Peel County. The Colonel had called from his office on Friday, the day before: "I'd like to see you at my house tomorrow morning, Ev!"

It's a clear memory because the minister's call came quite unexpectedly.

The sun was attempting to shine on that Saturday morning, and I had planned to attend the Royal Agricultural Fair after my meeting with the Colonel. He lived in Dixie in the south end of Peel County.

I had some difficulty finding the entrance to his place and then had to drive up the long lane leading to his unimposing brick bungalow. It was around 9:45 a.m. The Colonel was still in his dressing gown and slippers, but he wasn't wearing socks. He asked me to sit down and went back to his stuffed chair in the corner of the living room. The partly opened door to his bedroom was visible over his left shoulder. Without speaking, he stared at me for what seemed an eternity.

I had met Tom Kennedy only once beforehand, and that was only briefly, at a gathering arranged by farmers in the Junior Farmers' Building in Brampton at the time of Bruce Beer's retirement as Department of Agriculture representative. As the incoming ag rep, I had to give a little speech. The Colonel had written to me afterwards, making some kind remarks about my talk.

Without any preliminaries the Colonel finally spoke.

"I think you have a future with the Department of Agriculture, Ev. We have two fairly senior positions we want to fill in the next few months. This is confidential, but one of them is the appointment of a dairy commissioner. I promised the milk producer leaders last year I'd create the position of dairy commissioner to coordinate all aspects of the industry in Ontario. They're pressing me now, and I want to fill the position by the first of April 1951.

"I understand an advertising agency has been talking to you," he continued, "so I thought you should know there's a possibility of a good future in the Department of Agriculture. Don't rush into anything in the next little while. You'll know my decision within three or four months."

That pretty well ended the conversation. I didn't see the Colonel again until I reported to Queen's Park as dairy commissioner on April 1, 1951.

I had a problem, however. As of March 31st I wouldn't have a government car, since field staff were the only ones supplied with a vehicle. Nor did I own a car personally. I'd have to get one. I decided that since I'd always banked with the Royal, I might as well go to the local branch for a chat with the manager, whose name happened to be Jack McArthur. As it turned out, I had met and casually spoken with him at farm gatherings from time to time. Little did I realize then the significant role McArthur would play in the future of the dairy industry as a most influential member of the Hennessey Inquiry.

In any case, Jack McArthur gave me a loan, without my having to put up any collateral, to buy a new Chevrolet. I appreciated that because I didn't have any collateral anyway.

Jim Baker, who eventually became dairy commissioner for Ontario, and I often discussed those early days and the early decisions that were made. It was agreed, for example, that a production survey was needed to give an overall picture of the provincial dairy situation. By 1951 certain markets in the United States, particularly Boston, had fluid milk pricing formulas. We decided this could very well be the answer to the price increase squabbles that were making newspaper headlines. Charlie Meek, the administrator on the Milk Control Board, agreed that it would be worth a try. He had been experiencing a great deal of controversy with producer price arbitrations and retail price increases.

As a result, two projects were started, the first of which was a production survey. Forms were drafted for a special survey of farm milk and cream deliveries to plants. Meetings were held with the processor associations. The producer groups were advised at their headquarters at 409 Huron Street, Toronto, as to our intentions. At that time, in 1951, there were 244 creameries in Ontario with 60,272 cream producers. There were 356 cheese factories, 13 combined plants, 56 manufacturing plants, and 582 regular distributors of fluid milk. Fluid milk was also sold by 119 producer distributors and 74 peddlers. As the name implies, the peddlers just bought the milk from some licensed distributor and peddled it door to door.

Altogether in Ontario there were 17,477 cheese milk producers, 15,464 manufacturing milk producers and more than 20,000 fluid milk producers. The survey forms were sent with a letter of explanation to all creameries, cheese plants, milk processors and distributors.

The survey response was excellent. Information came back providing raw data on more than 40,000 milk shippers.

In those days the computer was in its relative infancy. IBM was most anxious to be part of the survey, and so they prepared a special card. The information on the survey returns was transposed manually by magnetic pencil to these cards. They were sorted and analyzed by IBM according to our instructions.

Much information came out of the survey. One point that stands out in my memory was that in certain areas of eastern Ontario, producer plant tests for milk were as low as 2.8 percent in butterfat. Production and shipments of milk in most cases were very low in volume as well.

Regarding the low butterfat findings that surfaced, no one was ever sure whether this was due to some skimming, low-testing cows or, as Sarsfield O'Connor of the OMMB field staff suggested many years later, "...companies frigging around with the butterfat tests."

The survey did give information that hadn't been available previously. The information may have been crude and basic, but it did supply data that was broadly based. It was useful in the sense that it was new knowledge in an area where very little work had been done. The survey was also the first activity that covered the whole breadth of the industry, and the results had some common interest for everyone involved.

Fluid milk pricing was a political issue with both consumers and politicians at municipal and provincial levels. The Milk Control Board included a consumer representative who, in 1951, was Hiram McCallum, mayor of Toronto. With fluid milk prices hitting the headlines of the city newspapers with irritating regularity, it was hard to rationalize why any government would appoint the mayor of Toronto to such a board, which had as a major responsibility the arbitration and setting of prices for fluid milk. McCallum, a very fine gentleman in any case, lived in Guelph until his death in 1990.

In order to gain some acceptance of price changes to producers, a new method of pricing fluid milk was needed; and a formula looked like the answer.

Trips were made to the United States, therefore, and particularly to Boston. At the office and on the kitchen table - and sometimes late at night - using a basic handle-operated mechanical calculator, attempts were made to develop a pricing formula.

Colonel Kennedy had decreed, "It will never be accepted because it's too complicated and nobody will understand it."

Staff reaction was: "That means we'll have to find one that isn't complicated, one that the producers and consumers will understand."

This was eventually accomplished.

Orm Coon, chairman of the Cheese Producers' Marketing Board, was keeping us advised on problems facing that group and the cheese marketing situation in the United Kingdom, which he had viewed first hand. I was maintaining contact with the U.K. trade and with government people whom I had met during my own milk marketing studies in England.

Changes were taking place in the dairy industry, albeit slowly. In 1951 a regulation was passed requiring "trucks to be constructed so as to protect milk and cream from excessive heating and freezing." Several surveys had been made of trucking, and the very discerning conclusion reached contained the following statement: "In every survey the only milk and cream arriving in a frozen state were already frozen when picked up at the farm. In the great majority of open trucks all milk or cream was frozen on arrival. The value of the closed trucks during freezing weather has been definitely proven."

Considering the industry response to any suggested change at that time, this really was a very important conclusion.

The fluid milk industry had developed on the basis of markets having individual market organization. Fluid milk producers, however, in many cases were unhappy with their treatment in the marketplace.

The Toronto Milk Producers' Association and the equivalent Hamilton association had applied for agency powers to market milk, but a vote had indicated they didn't have the necessary sixty-six percent approval to carry.

Some markets were more aggressive than others. The Algoma milk producers were thinking of getting into the milk distribution business. And wheels were set in motion to organize the North Shore Co-operative. In May 1958 the co-op bought a dairy in Thessalon and another in Elliot Lake.

In the late 1950s, producer briefs were being submitted to the Honourable William A. Goodfellow, minister of agriculture for Ontario.

The dairy situation was also a continuing subject in the annual briefs of the Ontario Federation of Agriculture presented to the Ontario cabinet.

Richard Trehane, who had been elected chairman of the Milk Board of England and Wales in 1958, had visited with Bill Goodfellow and me in May 1961. Farmers were looking at retail prices and farm gate prices and making comparisons. They were not happy.

There were presentations made to the royal commission on price spreads of food products in the fall of 1957.

But change was slow in coming. Some pride was being taken that retail sales of milk in the majority of markets in Ontario were now on six-day home delivery, with no delivery on Sundays. In some cases, however, the milk control board had to pass a regulation to enforce compliance. Old habits, it seems, die slowly, and a few bottles of milk sold on a Sunday meant a lot to some of the small dairies, particularly if it meant keeping a customer.

During the period of the '50s the industry was divided in many ways. Administratively it was fragmented. Some aspects were not even under the Department of Agriculture but under the Department of Health and the various municipalities. Legislation emphasized the divisions within the producers and within the processing industry. A study was made of the legislation affecting the dairy industry with the idea of administrative coordination. In the early '50s there were at least nine different pieces of legislation concerned with the production and marketing of milk and cream. The marketing of cheese, cream and concentrated milk came under the Farm Products Marketing Act.

The quality of milk intended for manufacturing into dairy products was downright poor. Much manufacturing milk was just plain dirty. Literally. It contained real dirt and, likely, other assorted foreign substances as well.

Clearly, there was a problem with milk inspection. But high standards were difficult to maintain and enforce. In addition, this difficulty was compounded to some extent by the fact that certain inspectors in eastern Ontario had gained their positions through the benevolence of the local MPPs. This situation usually involved former cheesemakers. There were some faked reports on the cleanliness of cheese factories and other matters. The solution was simple, but the choice was a little difficult for some who had been used to being part of the local patronage system.

Many farmers and truckers didn't have a sense of responsibility or an understanding of milk quality. Flies and rats in cheese factories were tolerated. A report stated, "One of the more serious problems is the returning to the plants and acceptance by them of previously rejected milk. Milk haulers are the greatest offenders. It is recommended that all rejected milk be coloured."

The story is told of a Department of Agriculture inspector who was on the receiving stand at a plant in eastern Ontario. He suddenly noticed some similarity in the cans that were coming through. Had he seen these before? Scratching his head, he squinted his eyes as he gave the matter thought. He was sure that he had rejected these same cans of milk at some time earlier in the day. He went out to investigate, and around the corner found a couple of truckers in business. They were carefully straining the milk that had been rejected and loading it onto a truck that still hadn't gone to the plant. The inspector, Pete Bogaerts, is reported to have said with his Dutch accent, "I shushpected something was wrong."

Because of such practices, a regulation was consequently passed requiring that all rejected milk be coloured. This action did stop dirty, rejected milk from being strained and returned, usually to the same plant that had rejected it.

In the meantime, surplus milk posed a continuing problem with the Toronto Milk Producers. Unlike the fairly orderly producer marketing conditions that had existed in the Hamilton and London markets, Toronto distributors had a tendency to take on too many producers, winding up with a resultant surplus. Surplus milk had been used by certain distributors for a number of years in the Toronto market to disrupt the orderly purchase of milk from the producers. Orville Sinclair, who was with the Ontario Milk Distributors' Association, was critical in later years of the practices of the Toronto distributors and suggested that they themselves were significantly responsible for the discord in that market. Sinclair was executive secretary of the Ontario Dairy Council in later years.

In the early 1950s, shutoff of producers by dairies in the Toronto market was relatively common. Surplus milk was increasing. The farmers didn't know what to do with it. The Toronto producers considered the attitude and actions of certain Toronto dairies "irresponsible."

It was decided to form a co-operative, and the idea was approved at the semi-annual meeting of the Toronto Milk Producers on May 21, 1953. At the first meeting of the co-op in Brampton more than 300 members were present and fund-raising commenced. The concentrated milk producers were concerned that there would be increased surplus fluid milk, adding to their surpluses. They were making statements such as, "If this kind of thing is going to happen, we'll feel free to invade the fluid milk market."

The new plant was built at Wilson Avenue and Highway 400 and was officially opened February 23, 1955, by the minister of agriculture, the Honourable Fletcher Thomas. Thomas, a graduate of Guelph and member from Elgin, was dedicated to making needed changes to Ontario agriculture. Unfortunately, he died from a sudden illness before he could introduce his plans, one of which was to move the Department of Agriculture to Guelph.

The Wilson Avenue plant was committed to handle only surplus milk from the Toronto market. From the start they lacked sufficient operating capital and uniform supplies of milk to operate the plant on an economically sound basis. They sought funds from the Toronto Milk

Producers' Association. This was not possible.

To ensure that the plant had a regular supply of milk, they took on a number of shippers who hadn't wanted to install bulk milk tanks.

There were many strained times between the Toronto association, the co-op and other processors. It was not really a happy situation, aside from the fact that many agreed the situation was a direct result of the ill-considered activities of certain milk distributors. There were producers, as well, who suggested it was also a shining example of why producers should stay out of milk processing and leave the risk taking to the side of the industry that understood the business.

By 1954, the industry was not ready for radical changes, but there appeared to be adequate support for the first move to coordinate the dairy administration and give some mild legislative encouragement to the four producer groups to begin attempts at working more closely together.

The Ontario minister, the Honourable Fletcher Thomas, had guided the passage of the Milk Industry Act of 1954. The new act brought together nine different pieces of legislation. It still provided for the Milk Control Board, which retained the responsibility for fluid milk. It created a new milk products board to deal with all aspects of nonfluid milk products. It provided for the appointment by cabinet of the Milk Producers' Co-ordinating Board, with the general responsibility to coordinate and improve the production and marketing of milk and milk products. The appointment by order-in-council was a subtle move. A selection of the senior people was made from each of the four producer groups to become members of this board.

The idea of a co-ordinating board had been conceived back in 1951 as a voluntary means of bringing the four producer organizations together to discuss matters of common interest and, in particular, milk marketing. Bob Jardine, the first secretary, continued under 1954 legislation until he joined the Ontario Department of Agriculture in 1958. He was succeeded by Cliff Weaver of Owen Sound, a former president of the Ontario Whole Milk Producers' League and a champion of organized milk marketing.

The co-ordinating board was intended to become the focal point for producers. The move had some degree of success. The board received no real marketing powers. All dairy administration was brought together under the supervision of the dairy commissioner, resulting in a unified administration for the first time.

Two members of the first co-ordinating board, Orm Coon and Harold Martin, went on to serve on the first Ontario Milk Marketing Board. Orm was a member and Harold Martin was the founding secretary. Roy Lick, the stalwart secretary-manager of the whole milk league and a strong leader for change, was also on this first co-ordinating board.

The medical officer of health in each municipality had the responsibility under the Public Health Act to inspect fluid milk-producing farms. Many municipalities didn't have any by-laws dealing with farm premises. Others, where they existed, were quite unrealistic, with requirements such as having a milk house several feet from the barn or stable and with no connecting entrance. This was considered a great idea for the snow belt areas. There was at least one by-law in existence that was concerned with how cows should be tied up in the stable so as to keep them out of the gutter. There was absolutely no coordination between the requirements of the various municipal by-laws brought in on the recommendation of the medical officer of health.

Any attempts to change the system were fought violently by certain medical officers of health, and in a more dignified way by the Sanitary Engineering Division of the Ontario Department of Health. It was an extremely sensitive issue. The new legislation took the first tentative step to bring some uniformity to production standards on farms. It required that all by-laws, before coming into effect in a municipality, had to be approved by the minister of agriculture.

The fluid milk pricing formula, which had been receiving attention for about three years, was finalized in 1954 and voluntarily adopted by most of the fluid milk markets. The new legislation provided for the use of the formula but didn't force it on the markets. The formula was quite effective in bringing harmony and understanding to those involved with price changes.

The first formula was calculated monthly and applied to the Toronto basic price of $4.13 per hundredweight. The price in every other market was expressed as a plus or minus differential in relation to that of Toronto. The formula was far from an exact instrument, but it was simple to understand and it was an indication of economic change affecting the milk producers. It had taken many calculations to determine the right base period, which resulted in a historical series of price changes that convinced the interested parties that the indices and weightings in the formula would result in future price change indications in line with the general economy.

The formula took much of the fight and front-page rhetoric out of the combatants involved in fluid milk pricing. A nineteen-cent increase per hundredweight to the farmer was soon translated into a one-cent increase per quart on the retail market.

Other industry initiatives were also getting started. The first Dairy Queen

Everett Biggs, as Ontario Deputy Minister of Agriculture, addresses the 1966 Dairy Princess competition in the Coliseum at the Canadian National Exhibition. From the early years of the OMMB, the annually chosen Dairy Princess served as an effective promotional representative of Ontario's milk industry.

competition was organized by the dairy branch in 1956 at the Canadian National Exhibition. Fifty young women competed in this first effort. The joint dairy breeds were co-sponsors the first year but were replaced by the co-ordinating board in 1957. The name, Dairy Queen, was changed in 1960 to Dairy Princess in order "to avoid any possibility of name conflict with an established commercial firm." The competition was originally conceived as an extension program to encourage high quality milk production.

Jim Baker of the dairy branch made contact with Valerie Boyd of the National Milk Publicity Council of England and Wales; and so the annual visits to Ontario of their Dairy Princess started in 1958, with Valerie as chaperone. The Ontario princess also began annual visits to England.

I'll never forget the first girl to come over from across the pond. She was a lovely young blonde Welsh girl with the beautiful name of Eirlys Morgan. It was decided that I should fly her and a CBC photographer the short distance from Brampton to London in a small, single-engine plane. We would visit a few farms, take a few pictures and fly back. The weather was supposed to be good. All in all, it promised to be a delightful little trip.

We were not far from Brampton when I started to pick up bad weather warnings on the radio for the Windsor area, with the advice that it was moving fairly rapidly eastward. I was wearing a headset, so the others couldn't hear the broadcast. They were blissfully admiring the scenery.

Some ten miles out of London the wind picked up, and heavy, dark clouds started to move in. We were being kicked around. The visibility dropped. There was only one radio in the aircraft, and when I switched to the ADF for navigational purposes I couldn't hear the London tower. When I switched to the tower we lost the navigational aid. We were getting close to the London airport and I was listening and talking to the London tower, and when I turned the ADF back on, the needle was pointing in the opposite direction. We had missed the airport! Heading back toward London at low level I spotted the Fanshawe Dam and knew where we were. We landed and were fortunate enough to beat the real storm by only ten minutes. The wind was so strong that we had to tie down the aircraft. Keith Riddell, the local agricultural representative, met us there. His son Jack was later to become the Ontario minister of agriculture and food.

We had a great visit in Middlesex County. But when it was all over, the CBC cameraman balked.

"There's no way I'm flying back to Brampton in that small plane!"

He took the bus back to Toronto.

Another three years elapsed. The producers were working a little more closely together. Within the Department of Agriculture the Dairy Administration was functioning as a unit. Bill Goodfellow was now minister of agriculture. He decided to introduce the Milk Industry Act of 1957. It replaced the existing 1954 statute. This new legislation took a few more steps. The Milk Industry Board was established, combining the functions of the Milk Control Board and the Milk Products Board. Legislation was provided for a milk marketing plan. The right to inspect producers' premises was completely removed from the municipalities and Department of Health and placed under the Department of Agriculture. From a provincial standpoint the production and marketing of milk in Ontario was now covered by a single statute.

The fluid milk market was still tied to home delivery. There were still approximately 500 regular distributors and a large number of distribution areas. If a distributor wished to expand into another market, he had to buy a dairy located within that market. The protection of dairies by the distribution area system condoned inefficiency and did not encourage marketing innovations. It also protected certain individual producers because a producer's welfare and income were tied directly to the dairy to which he shipped. Too much competition between the dairies didn't help either individual producers or the small dairies. Many producers tended to protect the inefficient system because of their vested interest.

The production picture was beginning to change. By the beginning of 1957 farm bulk milk tanks were in 14 markets involving 32 dairies, 63 transporters and 1,365 milk producers.

Pressures for changes in the retail selling of fluid milk were starting to mount. Jan Verdun of Aylmer was defying the Milk Control Board; he had introduced "cash and carry" jug milk to Aylmer in 1956. The Milk Control Board had tried to stop him.

Producers and established milk distributors were upset. Distributors had hallucinated regarding any situation that would give the chain stores a reason for demanding cheaper milk for sale at retail. Jugs were quickly moving to Guelph, Hamilton and other centres. There was great concern. Chain stores were now demanding cheaper milk from distributors.

Plans for the invasion of the Ontario retail milk market had already been made south of the border. Many had noted the story in *Readers' Digest* of the gallon jug milk being sold on a cash and carry basis from convenience stores in Akron, Ohio. Bruce Becker and Bob Lowe, who had been together in the American Air Force, applied in 1957 for a milk distributor's licence in Toronto. They were refused based on the statutory requirement to show "need for an additional distributor licence in a distribution area."

The two had the idea of opening a cash and carry jug milk store. Actually they were thinking of several jug milk stores. The established industry, including most producers, didn't want any part of them. The stores were viciously opposed by both producers and distributors.

Becker and Lowe had to find a milk supply. They also had to find a means of pasteurizing and bottling the milk for the proposed jug sales. Of course, none of the existing distributors in Toronto would help them. But they were able to find Frank Bazos, who owned Devon Ice Cream. Bazos agreed to pasteurize and bottle the milk for them. It was reported that he also provided significant funding. Becker and Lowe, however, still needed some milk to get started. They found it at the Toronto Milk Producers' surplus plant.

In 1957, at the annual meeting of the Toronto Milk Producers, addressing over 500 members, president Bill Hoiles of Nobleton said, "I have to report one of the gloomiest and blackest pictures of the dairy industry in Toronto. The American cheap jug milk people have managed to get in the back door of our industry, and they're using an ice cream plant to pasteurize their milk at night." At the time, Bill Hoiles was unaware that the Toronto Milk Producers' surplus plant was supplying milk to Becker's!

Becker's stores, as they came to be known, were corner convenience stores. At the beginning they featured bread as a big item, along with milk, of course. Other items were quickly added. The American gallon jug had been sold in the United States, but the imperial gallon was considered too large for a normal refrigerator. It was decided to sell milk in three-quart containers.

Three quarts of milk in a jug at the Becker's stores could be purchased at twenty cents less by the consumer than the home delivery price. Until this time the distributors had been able to resist any cheaper prices for store outlets, and milk in stores was maintained at a higher price than that of home delivery. The distributors certainly did not want to encourage store sales. Frantic attempts were made to preserve the home delivery of milk.

The volume of sales at a Becker's store allowed it to sell at a reduced price. As other products were added there was increased attraction and overall revenue. Becker's employed families to operate each store.

Becker's stores also were open seven days a week which, of course, was in contravention of existing Toronto by-laws. Summons were issued. At one time there were more than forty summons outstanding, as Becker's lawyers managed to have hearings postponed and then postponed again.

The stores had become a nuisance; they were regarded as an extreme threat to the status quo of the industry. They were a public embarrassment to both the provincial and municipal governments because consumers had decided they liked this way of buying milk. They were supported also by the media.

Because of the relative prices, the consumers liked the stores. In effect, Toronto council eventually gave up and changed the by-law. It was recognized, clearly, that they were convenience stores, which allowed them to operate on Sundays. The fact that the housewife wanted them was a message the municipal politicians understood!

There was great pressure upon the government of Ontario to outlaw the Becker merchandising methods and the Becker's stores. In face of consumer reaction, however, there was no choice of alternatives. Besides, Becker's stores virtually ignored most regulations and by-laws. The government eventually had to accept the inevitable.

This was the major turning point in the retail selling of milk and milk products. Until then the retail market had been a virtual closed shop in the retail trade, and little progress had been made in merchandising innovations. The milk control legislation, while right for its time, now was an impediment to progress.

Becker's did find a regular source of milk, and the company attracted large producers. It became a very lucrative market for these producers since they were paid on a 90/10 basis.

Russell Rowntree of Woodbridge, later of Brampton, was such a producer. The Rowntree family had started by shipping two eight-gallon cans of milk in 1938; this had increased to more than 4,000 pounds by the end of World War II. In 1957 Rowntree was already a very large producer. While not known well publicly, he purchased a bulk milk tanker and became engaged in an extensive milk trucking business with Bob Lowe of Becker's.

About this time, visits were made to the Fraser Valley Milk Producers Co-operative in British Columbia. While going through their laboratory I noticed an instrument.

"What's that?" I asked. "What's it used for?"

"Oh, we check samples of milk that comes in for water content," the Fraser Valley man replied.

Laughing, I said, "In Ontario, water in milk went out with the pump handle."

"Pump handles," said the chap wryly, "may be gone on most farms, but the odd farmer here still knows how to turn on the water tap."

The man had a point. After returning to Toronto, tests were initiated to determine if Ontario milk contained any added water. It was indeed found in several cases and, in a few, in substantial amounts. One test, for example, revealed additional water content as high as twenty-eight or thirty percent above normal. Applying the freezing point test for water content immediately became a routine practice.

The industry was beginning to move. Use of the three-quart container was pushing eastward to Peterborough. The paper container was replacing glass in retail stores. Two-percent milk had been on the market for some time. Formula pricing was widely adopted in most markets. The number of farm bulk tanks was growing. The dairy processors were joining their organizations to present a unified front as the Milk Producers' Co-ordinating Board and calling it the Ontario Dairy Processors' Council. A new regulation required all milk transport trucks to have insulated bodies by January 1st, 1960.

The tempo of the industry had picked up dramatically. The stage was set for change. People were talking about it. Ideas for change were being covered in the newspapers and on radio. No one realized it would be another eight years, however, before any really dramatic change would take place.

On the other hand, everyone believed something was about to happen. There was increased activity on the part of the Milk Producers' Co-ordinating Board. The processors were becoming apprehensive. The co-ordinating board was made up of the executives of the four producer groups. Provincial regulations were brought in covering the quality of all milk for fluid purposes and for industrial purposes. The dairy branch field staff were gradually taking over all farm inspection. It was proudly stated by the Department of Agriculture that, "The aim is to eventually have all milk for human consumption and processing to a common standard."

"Eventually" proved to be much longer than anticipated.

Renewed interest in a possible milk marketing plan resulted in the idea of the milk industry advisory committee's being revived. The 1957 act had made provision for such a committee.

Mike Simpson, of the Ontario Milk Distributors' Association, was adamant that "The communication between the Ontario Milk Producers' Co-ordinating Board and the processors is not at all satisfactory. The advisory committee, with equal membership from processors and producers, must play an essential role. Its membership is made up of key people from the industry."

These members included such people as Sam Ault of the processors and Glen Cole and Orm Coon of the producers. Jack Palmer, associate director of the dairy branch, was secretary.

The Milk Producers' Co-ordinating Board, with five members from each of the four groups, was flexing its muscles. Its mandate had now been stated in law: "It forms the official contact between the Milk Industry Board and the producers." This wording, coming from the Department of Agriculture, was a subtle encouragement to the producers to start working together.

The processors desired similar recognition for the Ontario Dairy Processors' Council. It was not granted. But they, in turn, were indicating that the council spoke for the whole processing industry and that it was the official processor contact for government. Even without legislation, the six processor organizations at provincial level had been forced to unite.

Increasing numbers of concentrated producers were eyeing the higher prices being received for fluid milk. Much of the thinking about the price situation was relatively simplistic, with "price blending" as the catch word. Considerations such as farm premises, milk quality and transportation were not given much thought. Equality of opportunity in the higher priced market was being demanded.

Producer representatives went to British Columbia, the United States, the U.K., Sweden and Denmark. The principles of a new milk marketing plan were discussed at producer meetings across the province. Arguments and discussions were hot and heavy. Various criteria for a possible marketing plan were drafted and debated by producer organizations. The whole matter received great media coverage.

Progress became frustrating within the Milk Producers' Co-ordinating Board, and so a team of economists - David McFarlane from McDonald College, Dr. Arthur Wood from the University of Manitoba, and Dr. John Carncross from Rutgers in New Jersey - were asked to study the milk situation. They brought in a report on February 27, 1960. The Milk Industry Act was strengthened to provide all necessary powers for producers to establish a unified milk marketing plan.

Bill Goodfellow, in a speech to the semi-annual meeting of the concentrated milk producers in 1961, attempted to bring some logic to the milk marketing situation. George Lowry, of Lanark County in eastern Ontario and a prominent concentrated milk leader, stated, "We are four different groups pulling in different directions." The Cheese Producers' Marketing Board had demanded and later repeated to the Hennessey Inquiry that "The provincial government should rescind the legislation protecting the whole milk shippers."

Bill Stewart was now minister of agriculture.

He had been determined to get something moving in the industry, and so he challenged the leaders of the four groups to do something about it. He appointed the provisional board in April, 1962 and attempted to extract some logic and reason from the uncoordinated ideas and passions that were swirling around the countryside. While the provisional board was attempting to fulfill the position of leadership that the minister had given to them, the summer of 1962 saw many resolutions coming from both eastern and western Ontario, some intended to be helpful, some others just adding to the dissension.

A resolution from the Mitchell local of the concentrated milk producers suggested, "Within two years after implementation of the plan and on completion of the farm inspection and grading by the dairy branch, all grade 'A' shippers share on a blended price basis in all fluid milk sales and not just on increased sales. Stabilization deductions for cheese export costs (should) be made gradually and then only on the condition that the federal government contribute a like amount into the fund each year, until such time as the milk producers in the province of Quebec contribute equally on

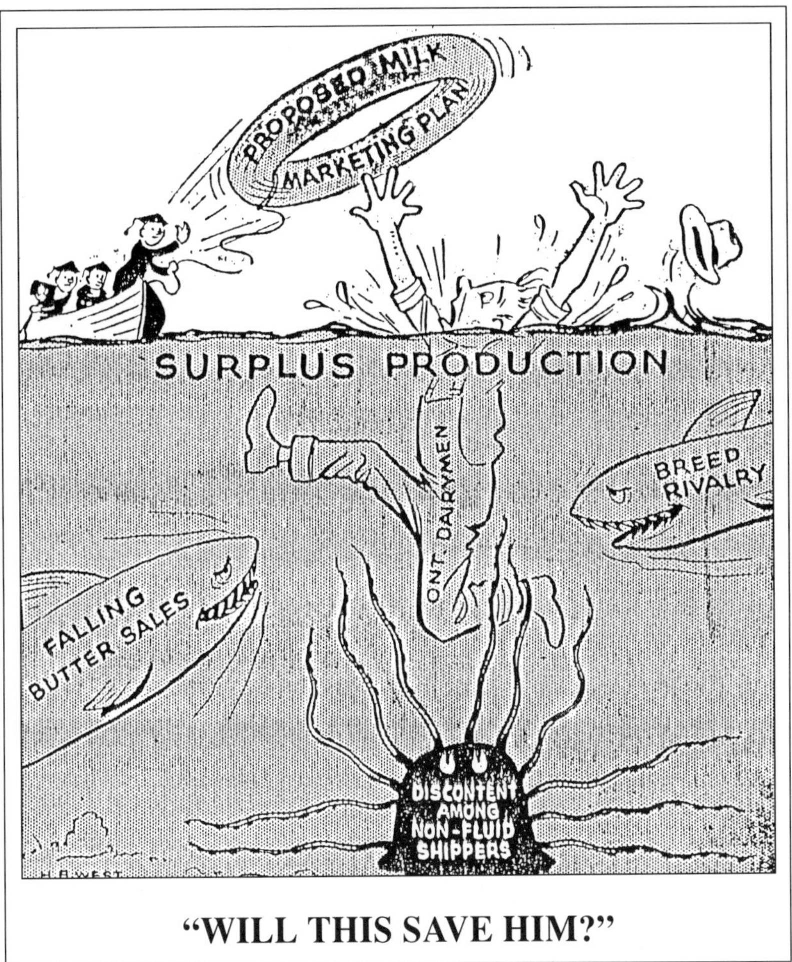

"WILL THIS SAVE HIM?"

This cartoon, appearing in The Farmers Advocate March 25, 1961, describes the plight of Ontario dairymen before the establishment of the OMMB. Bill Stewart, who became Minister of Agriculture later that year, inherited the problems of the dairy industry as his to solve.

a pro rata basis and the fund becomes national in aspect."

This particular resolution recognized that the cheese producers had been supporting the industry on the export market to the benefit of the whole industry, and that the support of exports was a responsibility of the whole industry and all milk-producing provinces.

The impatience of the concentrated producers was indicated in another resolution from the Mitchell local. The resolution, discussed but not approved, was "that the Ontario Concentrated Milk Producers' Marketing Board commence at once to draft a marketing plan and to seek agency powers and that it make known its intention to sell milk in any or all markets within the province on a quality basis and will carry this policy through to a decision in the courts if need be."

Fighting words!

Bill Stewart painted the picture:

"I don't believe, in my experience as a farmer or as one associated with government, that I've ever witnessed a situation so mixed with conflicting opinions, divergent efforts and misleading and misunderstood information. Possibly this bubbling dairy pot is being stirred with the spoon of disunity and discontent by some people who may have interests other than those of the well-being of the dairy industry.

"When the point of decision-making is reached, any attempts at consolidation of thought or policies are nullified by stumbling blocks of insular thinking, watered down by individual dairy commodity group interests."

The provisional board found the situation completely impossible to bring into focus so that any uniform or common vision could be seen by the milk producers in the province. They became frustrated and resigned. Fortunately, they resigned only as a provisional marketing board. There was extreme fear at the time that they would take that extra step and resign their positions in the four producer organizations.

When Jim Baker, George McCague and I discussed the situation on Thursday afternoon, November 2, 1963, there were great fears that this could very well happen.

"I'm sure the thought has crossed their minds," said Jim Baker. "They've all stuck their necks out on this thing, and all they can see out there is a state of utter confusion mixed with some downright antagonism between producers, and a lot of it directed towards them. They certainly have had all they can take. They're in a state of shock right now."

George McCague was worried: "There's sure one thing we don't need now, and that's some of these people resigning from the league or the concentrated board. It would be a real mess."

Jim Baker called Emerson Farnsworth to reassure him and impress on him how essential and important it was that the league and the concentrated board remain firm.

They had remained firm. The twenty-one month pause provided by the Hennessey Inquiry, leading to the introduction and passage of the Milk Act in the spring of 1965, had brought all segments of the industry together in a common expectancy of change, albeit with still very visible divisions. The focus was now much clearer. Bill Stewart had said that there would be a milk marketing plan for Ontario. He had appointed the province's first official milk marketing board, and he had scheduled their first meeting for Thursday, August 19, 1965.

CHAPTER TWO

Point of No Return

In which Bill Stewart

- Thinks about the 1965 milk situation
- Considers the Hennessey report
- Decides to disallow a vote on the milk plan
- Recalls Richard Trehane's interest in Ontario
- Appreciates Harry Hays' cooperation
- Remembers the support of the Ontario legislature
- Meets with the two Georges
- Meets with the new 14-person milk board

August 19, 1965. Bill Stewart was heading for the first, and fateful, meeting of the new board. But first, a bit of breakfast. Standing before the elevator, waiting for it to arrive, Stewart remembered a man from Northumberland. William A. Goodfellow had preceded him as minister of agriculture. Early in November 1961, after he had been sworn in as minister, Bill Goodfellow had warned Stewart, "I had hoped to have the milk marketing mess cleaned up. But I couldn't get the producers to agree to work together. I'm afraid you'll have to do it, and the sooner the better, or the problems will just get worse."

Stewart knew he was getting good advice, because behind Goodfellow's twinkling eyes and slight smile was an astute politician, one who understood the needs of Ontario agriculture and, in particular, the problems of milk producers in eastern Ontario.

Thus, Stewart used that advice. Some eight weeks later, on the evening of January 4, 1962, in the Royal York Hotel he addressed a joint banquet of

• *Emerson Farnsworth, who resigned September 1966, was not replaced.*

the Ontario Whole Milk Producers' League and the Ontario Cheese Producers' Marketing Board.

Recognizing the importance of cooperation between Ontario and Quebec - because together they were responsible for about two-thirds of the milk and cream production in Canada - Stewart remarked on the great significance of the presence of the parliamentary assistant to the Honourable Alcide Courcey, minister of agriculture for Quebec, and the deputy minister, Dr. Ernest Mercier.

He also bluntly stated, "The Ontario Whole Milk Producers' League, the cheese milk producers, the concentrated milk producers and the cream producers have been operating separately, though with some loose harmonization through the Milk Producers' Co-ordinating Board.

"Because of the four divisions in the dairy producer marketing structure," Stewart continued, "your executives have found themselves in an almost impossible position in attempting to develop realistic policies and actions. The necessity for interprovincial and even a common national dairy policy has been recognized. There are far too many weak links in the dairy chain. If our milk marketing problems are to be solved, the solutions must start at the level where the problems exist, and that's within the province.

"It's essential that a milk marketing plan be established in Ontario in 1962. Immediate steps should be taken by your leaders to finalize the details and ensure that they're understood by all dairy farmers in Ontario. Then initiate a vote! I'm therefore inviting the four dairy producer executives to meet with me in my office as early as possible this month to assess the current situation. I'll be pleased to meet with them the afternoon of Tuesday, January 9, five days from now."

"Before there can be a milk marketing plan," Stewart cautioned, "producers must show their approval - or disapproval - by secret ballot. No dairy producer will vote for a marketing plan that he thinks will be harmful to him or that won't benefit him at some time in the future. Our progress in milk marketing, therefore, may have to be quite evolutionary. A marketing plan must be developed that will not destroy or break down in any way a particular section of the industry; rather, it must strengthen and build up all sections.

"We must be realistic and maintain the present quota of the fluid milk shippers. This may be an unpopular statement with the concentrated milk shippers, but again, we've got to be realistic. Present fluid milk shippers would form the grade 'A' nucleus. Adjustments and changes would take place under a marketing plan to the point that all grade 'A' shippers would be incorporated within an orderly framework without disrupting the industry or any individual producer."

Stewart certainly hadn't been optimistic that there would be a marketing plan in place in 1962. The idea was to keep the pressure on and see what happened.

The January 9 meeting took place. All four groups had been eager. The concentrated producers and the whole milk league were all fired up to get something moving. The concentrated leaders were impatient. The fluid representatives, on the other hand, were more cautious: The cream producers had their own particular problems with farm-separated cream because of the type of enterprise involved. They were not as impatient as the concentrated people, but certainly among their leadership was a realization that some change was needed for the overall good of the industry.

It's quite clear that most of the cheese producer leaders were inward-looking, preoccupied with the responsibilities and problems of marketing cheese. Orm Coon, the former chairman of the cheese board, was an exception. A Guelph graduate, Coon was a good choice as one of the minister's selections for the new milk board. He had always been interested in marketing; in 1947 the then minister of agriculture had even sent him to the U.K. to study the British system.

Following Bill Stewart's meeting with the four groups on January 9, the groups held a series of meetings. After further discussions a press release went out from the minister in April 1962, announcing the creation of a Provisional Milk Marketing Board. The objectives were listed and the constituency of the board was outlined: There were to be three representatives from each of the four groups and one from the Channel Islands Breeds. Unfortunately, the very makeup of the board seemed to have doomed it to failure from the start. There was no way Hector Arnold of the cheese producers and Emerson Farnsworth of the fluid milk producers would ever agree. Arnold had tunnel vision for cheese marketing, and Farnsworth had a short fuse. Perhaps, however, the gods would be merciful. There were two chances of that - fat and slim. Time would tell.

Bill Stewart entered the elevator and pushed the button for the basement of the Royal York. As the elevator descended, he recalled another dominant group involving influential people in the livestock industry. The Channel Islands Milk Producers had been represented on the provisional board by John Bull, a large and successful Jersey cattle breeder from Brampton. Milk was a by-product of Bull's operation. The expansion of "All Jersey" milk sales had been recognized in the mid-'50s as a means of selling more Jersey cattle at better prices. He was giving aggressive marketing leadership, and he had developed an effective organization. He'd also given notice that he would support a marketing plan only if it didn't weaken the market for Jersey and Guernsey milk.

For some time John Bull had sensed a danger for the Jersey breed in the development of an overall milk marketing plan. He had been concerned enough to oppose my appointment as deputy minister of agriculture. The appointment seemed logical in the eyes of others, however, apparently because of my extreme interest in marketing at a time when concerns were shifting to the new challenges facing agriculture in the marketplace.

It was somewhat ironic that in late 1961, shortly after my appointment as deputy minister, a visitor came to my home to make an announcement in no uncertain terms. Jack Fraser of Streetsville, a prominent Holstein breeder and Becker shipper, strongly advised me, in a standup encounter in the living room, that I "should not allow my friendship with John Bull to result in preferred treatment for the Jersey breed or my future might be in jeopardy." Not terribly amused, I didn't tell the minister of this experience.

Bill Stewart didn't know John Bull very well, but he did know of Bull's favourite story. To wit: It seems that Bull had taken over the family Jersey empire, something more than 1,000 acres immediately south of Brampton. The family had played a very visible role in the history of Peel County and on the world Jersey scene as well.

The Bull farm sold sires and females and maintained a financial and breeding interest in some of them. Some of the sires happened to be located in the United States. On occasion John went across the border to take bull semen for use back home in the Brampton herd. He always carried the equipment in his golf bag. Apparently, one time, on the way back from the States, a suspicious customs inspector had asked Bull to open his bags for examination - including the golf bag, which quite obviously didn't hold any golf clubs. To the customs inspector this seemed unusual enough to warrant careful investigation.

The inspector reached into the bag, found a strange-looking, elongated object and peered at it quizzically. In all of his years as a customs official he had never seen anything quite like it.

"All right, what's that?" demanded the inspector, holding the object up in front of Bull.

"That? Oh, that's an artificial vagina."

When Bull passed through the customs station, the golf bag hanging from his shoulder, the official was still standing there stunned, his mouth hanging open.

John Bull had grown up with Jersey cattle. He was a good friend of mine, but that friendship didn't interfere with business or with his ambitions for the Jersey breed.

The elevator stopped at the basement level, and the minister got out. Entering the hotel cafeteria nearby, he picked up *The Globe and Mail*. The paper showed the date, Thursday, August 19, 1965. Stewart glanced at the front page. The prime minister, Lester B. Pearson, was opening the Canadian National Exhibition the next day. The year is passing so quickly, thought Stewart. So much has happened in such a short time. There's so much to do in a very short period of time.

His mind shifted back. The Hennessey report, officially entitled "Report of the Ontario Milk Industry Inquiry Committee," had been formally submitted to him on March 5, 1965, even though it was actually dated January 1965. Stewart had hoped for an earlier report so an immediate move could be made on the necessary legislation. But Hennessey, the chairman, had insisted on hearing everyone who had something to say. This insistence showed wisdom on his part, for doubtless that decision prevented criticism from those who may not have been heard otherwise. Other than allowing speakers to air their complaints - and thus providing food for thought in later decisions - the extra time spent hadn't really mattered much; most of the new legislation was already in draft form when the report was officially received.

A professor from the University of Toronto, Hennessey was a hard taskmaster. His able colleagues on the inquiry, Frank Wood, treasurer of Abitibi, and Jack McArthur of the Royal Bank, were appropriate foils for his impatience and stubbornness. It had been a good team. They had been ably assisted by St. Elmo Smith of Price Waterhouse, the prestigious accounting firm, and Tom Hicks of the Ontario Department of Agriculture. Tom had acted as secretary of the committee.

The inquiry committee had been appointed by order-in-council on May 30, 1963. At the time, the milk industry was seething with currents of protectionism and cross-currents of suspicion. The Channel Islands Breeds Milk Producers, for example, were fighting to preserve the marketing of their milk as a special product. They were happy to see the price of Jersey and Guernsey cows rise. The marketing of milk and the extreme rivalry of the purebred breeders were intertwined.

Individual fluid milk markets, with their separate marketing organizations, were very loosely coordinated by the whole milk league. The distributors and the processors were muddying the waters whenever and wherever possible. Milk transporters were not milk plan missionaries. The Becker shippers were downright nasty. Paradoxically, however, coming through it all was a strong, if not unified, message in support of change, in favour of needed improvements. There was confusion and a lot of misunderstanding, but the message was there loud and clear.

The Provisional Milk Marketing Board, appointed by Stewart in 1962 under the chairmanship of Emerson Farnsworth, and with the objective of developing a marketing plan, had battled long and vigorously both internally and externally. Farnsworth, an astute and capable leader from Huntsville, had talked with board members whom he knew supported a change in milk marketing methods and procedures. The problem was that the provisional board was split down the middle on their interests and the details of how to reach their goals. Declaring their frustration, they sought advicc from Jim Baker, the dairy commissioner for Ontario.

"The only approach you should consider is a public inquiry into the whole industry," concluded Baker.

They had agreed. On November 2, 1962, Harold Martin, secretary of the provisional board, had advised the minister by telephone that every member of the provisional board had resigned. The same information had been conveyed to the Milk Producers' Co-ordinating Board.

On November 5, Martin, on behalf of the then defunct provisional board, sent a letter (with a copy sent also to Jim Baker) asking "...the provincial minister of agriculture, the Honourable William A. Stewart, to request the federal minister of agriculture, the Honourable Alvin Hamilton, for a full scale royal commission on all phases of the dairy industry in Canada with the recommendation that this be implemented and a report submitted at the earliest possible date."

The letter also advised that a standing recorded vote on the resolution of the provisional board had resulted in six members voting in favour and five opposed to the motion requesting the royal commission - but only after Emerson Farnsworth, as chairman, had cast the critical deciding vote that broke a five-five tie, thus affirming the board's request for the commission. Two members were absent at the time of the vote; John Bull of Brampton and Ab Hicks of Kinburn, a cheese board director, had not appeared. There was no explanation for their absence. If Bull and Hicks had been present, the vote doubtless would have been lost, and then who knows what might have happened? Bill Stewart never learned why they were absent from the crucial meeting.

The letter created great consternation in the Ontario Department of Agriculture. There was no way anyone in the department wanted a royal commission carried out at the federal level. The problems were provincial and consequently had to be solved at that level. The national situation could be dealt with later.

Glen Cole was very upset at breakfast in the Royal York with Bill Stewart on November 3rd, the morning following the vote.

"Bill," said Cole, "something has to be done. Hector Arnold and

Farnsworth have been at each other's throats. We don't want a federal royal commission. Anything could happen. That's why I voted against the resolution when it came to the board."

A short time afterward Stewart telephoned Emerson Farnsworth at home and confirmed that matters were about to blow. Jim Baker had very quickly telephoned Harold Martin at the co-ordinating board and arranged that the request to the minister be changed to read: "a public inquiry to be carried out on all matters concerning the milk industry in Ontario."

It was never clear how the wording of that resolution could have been changed so quickly by a board that had resigned and been officially dismantled three days earlier!

The Ontario cabinet did not immediately approve their request, but Bill Stewart proceeded, in any case, with the internal organization for the inquiry. During the spring of 1963 the league and the concentrated producers were giving strong support to the minister for an official inquiry. Cabinet had given its official approval by an order-in-council dated May 30, 1963.

The Hennessey Inquiry had been a necessary strategic move. Very little that was new emerged in the final report. There were twenty principal recommendations. Stewart recalled going over them. He had seriously questioned eight, found five unacceptable and only seven with which he was comfortable.

The report did not recommend a milk marketing board with the broad powers as provided for in the new Milk Act of 1965. Hennessey's recommendations in this area likely would not have worked. The report had recommended a voluntary milk producers pool covering southern Ontario. It was to apply to Grade "A" milk only. Northern Ontario was to have been left out. And the northern producers didn't want to be left out.

The Grade "A" quota system would have been terminated and some other method devised. The inquiry had recommended that the holders of fluid milk quota be compensated at a possible rate of $5.00 per pound and at a total cost of approximately $20 million. This money was to come from the government of Ontario and perhaps some from the federal government.

The minister of agriculture had not accepted this recommendation. Aside from its establishing a precedent, he believed it was not right. Quotas were needed to control production in some way. How could quotas without a value be allocated to producers?

The inquiry had served an important purpose. The minister had been able to go ahead and recommend the necessary legislation to the Ontario cabinet. The report had provided an essential hiatus of twenty-one months, allowing the industry a period of self-examination and critical analysis. It had jelled the problems of the industry into a concise, understandable form. That a few of the ideas were not workable did not matter; it provided a launching pad for action. That's what Bill Stewart had wanted. The industry and everyone interested was expecting something to happen, and soon!

In the legislature, Bob Nixon, member from Brant, future Ontario treasurer and son of a former premier, while debating whether or not the government should pay fluid producers for their quotas, had tried to needle Stewart, remarking, "The provincial treasurer is reported to have said, 'There will be two moons in the sky before money from the treasurer would be used for this purpose.'" But Bob Nixon had said this with a twinkle in his eye; he was generally very supportive of the proposed legislation.

Bill Stewart was pleased with the great support he was receiving from the government caucus and the solidarity of the cabinet on the whole matter. He also knew that he had the support of the key members on the opposite side of the house, such as Bob Nixon and Murray Gaunt of the Liberals and Donald MacDonald of the NDP, irrespective of what they said in debate. Stewart was sure the Liberals were having real arguments in their caucus because some of their members were involved in milk processing and distribution, such as Ross Whicher, member for Bruce, and Stan Farquhar from Manitoulin. But both were fair-minded operators.

Stewart knew some of his colleagues were under great pressure. Opponents of the marketing plan were accusing cabinet ministers of refusing to meet with them. An unsigned document was being circulated among fluid producers stating, "Immediately upon inauguration of the marketing plan there will be 5,000 concentrated milk shippers ready to invade the fluid milk market and ruin the price."

Becker shippers, while enjoying 90 percent of their sales at top price, were playing hardball politics. They represented some large influential and vocal fluid shippers. They were pressuring provincial members in Peterborough and other areas, making accusations such as, "Bill Stewart is bringing in this milk board without a vote of producers. He knows there's not enough support for it. Bill Stewart is a beef producer. He lives in a beef-producing area in Middlesex County. His constituents don't care what happens to milk producers. Bill Stewart will be elected in the next election, but you won't. Your voters are milk producers!"

Stewart had to reassure some of these members from time to time but was gratified by their support and trust. He realized, of course, that the general lack of difficulty and obvious support the legislation had enjoyed during its debate and passage through the house had given much confidence to the members irrespective of their party. Most recognized the need for change and that the major opposition was coming from vested interests in both producer and processor sectors.

The minister had given much soul-searching thought to the question of having or disallowing a vote on the proposed marketing plan. He knew the support for a marketing plan was out there but that it was a confused support. He was also convinced that if a vote were to be called, an all-out war would result. This would tear the industry apart. The idea of organized milk marketing by producers would be set back by several years.

The opposition group within the industry had sufficient money and the ability to launch a vigorous and vicious campaign. They would be able to count on many distributors and processors, as well as truckers, to be their emissaries. The producers would become even more confused and the whole matter would become a political football.

A vote, therefore, was out of the question. Stewart knew he would receive strong criticism and questioning for this decision, even from a few of his supporters. But it was the proper decision, he realized, though a very dangerous one.

Bill Stewart was well aware of the existing lack of effective communication between the producer leaders and the rank and file of the producers. To ask the new milk marketing board to be immediately answerable to their producers, and at the same time to make objective decisions, would be virtually impossible and completely unfair.

A period of respite from producer accountability would allow the new board to organize its own communication system. They would be able to give a more positive type of consideration to the policies needed.

This had not been possible with the provisional board, and they had never been able to come up with a clear marketing proposal with the necessary detail that producers were looking for. Stewart also realized that during this period of non-accountability the board members would be accused of being tools of Ontario's government.

An election by producers of the members of the first board would likely also result in the election of opponents of the new milk marketing plan. This would create an unnecessary strain on board solidarity and dilute effective action. The first Ontario Milk Marketing Board had been personally selected by him and would be appointed by order-in-council.

Stewart recalled very vividly a meeting he and I had had with Premier John Robarts several months earlier. The premier, an action-oriented individual, had said, "My philosophy is very simple: Decide whether or not an idea is right. Make sure it has sufficient support, and then go ahead and do it."

Bill Stewart had considered Ottawa policies and the possible reaction from Quebec. There was an interprovincial movement of fluid milk in Montreal and Ottawa. He knew that I was a good friend of Ernest Mercier, the Quebec deputy minister, and that I had kept him informed, on a confidential basis, of all developments.

Stewart had talked to Harry Hays, the federal agriculture minister, before Christmas, and early in January he and I had gone to Ottawa for a meeting with Hays. Stewart had advised, "Harry, the milk inquiry report should be in soon. I plan to bring in legislation during the spring session providing for the establishment of a milk marketing board in Ontario. Before the inquiry started, the concentrated milk producers in Ontario were threatening to invade the fluid market. What can be done at federal level to keep things on an even keel?"

"I have a mess to clean up here too!" Hays had answered. "We have to separate dairy from the Agricultural Stabilization Administration, so I'm going to get legislation for a dairy commission. I've also been working on Treasury to see if we can get a little more money to support the manufactured milk producers."

The minister thought, "Harry had come through, and promptly too. On March 26, he announced a new dairy policy that was intended to provide a national average return to producers of $3.50 per hundredweight for domestically used manufacturing milk. He also disclosed plans that he had suggested were 'the result of working in cooperation with the provinces,' to establish a Canadian dairy commission." Bill Stewart's lines of communication with Harry Hays had always been excellent.

The minister finished his breakfast and folded *The Globe and Mail*. He'd brought his briefcase with him so it wasn't necessary to go back to his room. He picked it up and headed toward the east door of the Royal York, where he knew Nick, his driver, would be waiting. As they drove up University Avenue, Stewart noted it was almost 8:00 a.m. and the morning rush-hour traffic was already heavy. The day would certainly be warm, uncomfortably so.

Arriving at his office Stewart sat down and unlocked the desk. He took out a folder of correspondence that he had not had time to sign the evening before, and after carefully reading the letters, he signed them with the clear signature that was becoming so well known across Ontario and beyond. He had never tried to cultivate a signature, as did so many others, that was distinctive but completely illegible.

Stewart buzzed me on the intercom.

"Will you bring in the final draft of the press release on the milk board? I want to release it later this morning so we can catch George Atkins' noon CBC broadcast."

A complete text would go out on the CP wires and be made available to all media that day.

I went into his office, and after laying the proposed press release on his desk, sat down in the nearest chair. I looked at him without saying anything, rather surprised that he looked so fresh, considering the pressure he was under.

After glancing briefly at the proposed release to ensure that it was in the form he had approved the previous day, he quickly reviewed his earlier thoughts and plans for the meeting with the new board.

He then buzzed George McCague. McCague was the chairman of the milk industry board. He would be named chairman of the milk commission when the Milk Act of 1965 was proclaimed. McCague and Jim Baker had been close advisors to Frank Gallant, the senior department solicitor, during the drafting of the new legislation.

McCague came in and settled down beside me with his usual half-smile.

"Well, Mr. Minister, how do you feel this morning?"

Stewart smiled in return and handed a copy of the proposed press release to George.

"I feel good." He continued as if he were again reassuring us, and himself as well, that the right decisions had been made.

"This whole thing is too important to gamble on failure now," said the minister. "Everybody has given this a lot of thought. I've talked to many of my colleagues and I've talked to many dairy farmers. We're going to have a marketing plan and it's going to come in without a vote. There may be one sometime, but it won't be now. That would be absolute chaos. Everything that has been done by so many people would be down the drain. That just can't happen!"

George McCague was a natural worrier, but he agreed. He always gave a lot of thought to problems but usually came up with a workable answer. This whole matter had been debated many times and there was no doubt whatsoever in his mind.

However, he again cautioned the minister.

"You're appointing this fourteen-man milk board by order-in-council. You've stressed in the press release that these producers represent dairy farmers from all parts of the province. But they haven't been elected by the producers. Most producers don't know them personally. They may have heard of them. The very critical position of chairman is being filled by George McLaughlin. He's your choice, not the choice of the producers. Don't you think people will say that George McLaughlin is your puppet and this really is a government board, not a farmers' board?"

Stewart paused for a moment before replying. "We've gone over all of this many times in discussion and many times in our own minds. Sure, that's going to happen. But there's nothing we can do about it. They'll say it, if for no other reason than to get under George McLaughlin's skin and to try to weaken the board. They'll try to use it to get at me. That's the risk we have to run.

"We have to remember that these men have been carefully selected," he continued. "They're all experienced. They're committed and dedicated to developing a successful and practical milk marketing plan for Ontario. I've visited each one of them on their farms. I've talked to them and I've looked at their operations. I know they're good farmers.

"George McLaughlin has been in my office. He was here less than a week ago, and we've talked on the telephone at least three times since. We've talked at great length about where we have to go, and there's no doubt in my mind about his abilities. He's been to the U.K. a couple of times, once with Ev and Herb Arbuckle in 1960 when they looked at marketing in England and Europe, and another time for a Holstein meeting.

"McLaughlin has kept in touch with the English board and its chairman, Richard Trehane. Richard has been taking a lot of interest in Ontario milk marketing. He visited Bill Goodfellow in 1961. And Jim Baker, Ev and I had a good meeting with him last spring in the Royal York.

"Moreover, McLaughlin has studied the milk industry thoroughly. He's tough and aggressive. He can handle himself on the platform. That's the sort of thing that's needed.

"Furthermore, I don't think these fourteen men will be puppets to anyone. Any such accusations will likely make them more independent and determined. Confidentially, within this office, I think we could very well be faced at some time in the future with the problem of too much independent thinking, particularly on the part of George McLaughlin. If this happens the board will have to remember they've been delegated broad legislative powers, more than any other marketing board that I'm aware of.

"This will be one of the responsibilities of the commission, to see at all times that these powers aren't abused. These are powers that will give them virtually complete control over the destiny of the dairy industry in Ontario."

It was about 8:30 a.m. when Stewart finished reaffirming his decisions, and the minister's secretary buzzed to announce that George McLaughlin had arrived. He came into the office, and everyone chatted about such trivia as the weather and Toronto's horrendous traffic situation for a few minutes. Then the minister handed McLaughlin the press release.

During the general discussion that ensued, Stewart summarized, for McLaughlin's benefit, what had been decided:

"This will go out later this morning after I've met with the board. I know you have certain ideas as to how you intend to proceed. We were talking before you arrived about the board's being appointed by the government. There are those who'll say that you're really a government board that's not representing producers. There's nothing much we can do about that.

"We know you'll represent the producers. There will be some difficult days ahead. Many people have sweated a lot of blood over the past three or four years to reach what's going to happen today. As a government we have a vested interest in the whole matter. We're prepared to take some risk but we're not prepared to accept failure. We won't even think about it."

The minister smiled and went on, continuing to address his remarks to McLaughlin.

"Hennessey was convinced that the two Georges were the best people for the jobs at hand. George McCague will be chairman of the new milk commission. We're really pleased you've agreed to be chairman of the first board. You have a pretty good idea of what's ahead."

The meeting of the minister's selections for the first Ontario Milk Marketing Board was being held in the board room down the hall from his office. It was to start about 9:00 a.m., but already, at 8:45, the new board members were arriving. Some, such as Frank Todd and Maurice Beaty, had driven in that morning. Frank Todd was a Toronto milk producer and Maurice was a Channel Islands shipper. Emerson Farnsworth had managed an early start and driven in from Huntsville.

Orm Coon, as well, was one of the early arrivals. He told me later about the thoughts that flew through his mind while waiting for the meeting to start: There wasn't any coffee available, so he sat down, curiously regarding the display of pictures of ministers and deputy ministers of agriculture that graced the south wall of the board room. Coon noted idly that there were far more ministers than deputy ministers. Then his eyes stopped at the photo of Colonel Tom Kennedy. He noticed the rather obvious scarred mouth and jaw where a bullet had cruelly passed through and shattered the bones, a vivid reminder of Kennedy's participation in the European Theatre during World War I.

To himself Coon mused: "The Colonel really took the first big step in milk marketing in Ontario with the introduction of the Milk Control Act back in the 1930s. That was the fluid milk, of course, but the farmers had nothing then. Fluid milk producers in the Ottawa market were being told by the distributors they had to accept ninety cents per hundredweight. They had no bargaining power, but the Ottawa milk producers in those early days were a pretty tough organization."

In 1947 the Colonel had sent Coon to England to study the milk marketing system there. He remembered his report to the annual meeting of the cheese producers in 1947. He also recalled having discussions with the Colonel regarding the possibility of appointing a dairy commissioner to coordinate the administration and initiate changes that he hoped would eventually lead to an overall milk marketing plan in Ontario. The cheese producers had pressured the Colonel in 1949 for a commitment, which he had given.

Coon's reminiscences were interrupted by boisterous guffawing, as someone at the table apparently had shared a new joke.

The group was gathering very quickly, and by 8:50 all were there except George McLaughlin, who was still in the minister's office. There was an obvious atmosphere of tense excitement as the group sat around the board room table chatting about the weather and how the crops had been. They conspicuously avoided the subject of milk marketing.

Jim Jewson, who would serve as the secretary of the new milk commission, arrived and took a seat. Promptly at 9:00 a.m. the minister and the two Georges walked in. I made it a point not to attend, because we had agreed that it would be more appropriate for just the two dairy administrators to be present with the minister of agriculture.

Bill Stewart immediately noticed there was no coffee and somewhat irritably asked Jim Jewson to find some and arrange to have it delivered. After a few pleasantries the minister paused for a moment, looked searchingly around the table and spoke.

"A short time ago we were chatting in my office and I said that this is the point of no return. There's no turning back now. This press release will go out in an hour or so, and I'd like each of you to have a copy.

"The release states that a fourteen-man board is being appointed to handle milk marketing in Ontario. It says that the establishment of the Ontario Milk Marketing Board is a first step toward implementation of the Ontario Milk Act, passed during the last session of the provincial legislature. It also lists all of your names and indicates what you've done and where you've come from. It's the official announcement of your new appointments.

"Some may be concerned about where you're going, but I'm not. I've visited all of you on your farms. We've talked about milk marketing as it has been and where we want it to go."

Stewart swept a brief glance around the table at the faces before him.

"You've been selected for your experience and leadership abilities," he emphasized. "Since your appointment will be by order-in-council, you can devote all of your thoughts and energies to the development of a milk marketing plan and put the necessary administrative machinery in place.

"You will get abuse and criticism, but you won't be kicked out in the next election. On the other hand, I may be." He smiled and continued: "We've all agreed that to have a vote would be suicidal. There's a lot of confusion out there now. It would be undesirable if the opposition forces were provided a platform on which to work in an organized way."

The minister went on to discuss the generally strong support he had received for Bill 135, the Milk Act. He stated that this should be considered a real vote of confidence for the board.

"George McLaughlin tells me you'll be settling in and immediately getting down to work so that your official appointment under the legislation can take place as early as possible in the fall."

He paused for a moment, looking at them.

"Well, gentlemen," he said, "that's what it's all about. We've been moving pretty quickly. We officially received the Hennessey report on March 5, 1965. The legislation was introduced on May 7. There was a thorough debate in the house and at the committee stage, and the bill received royal assent on June 29. This indicates the kind of government support you have.

"The legislation was drafted in close consultation with the Quebec minister, the Honourable Alcide Courcy and the federal minister of agriculture, the Honourable Harry Hays. Our most recent joint meeting was in Ottawa on May 3rd last. We all must work together, not only in this, but in the development of long term dairy policies.

"George McLaughlin has agreed to be the first chairman of the board. George is a very special individual. He's the man for the job and that's a fact. I guess we're all going to have to pose for a picture later but I must get back to the office. I'm leaving George McCague to outline in more detail the new legislation and in particular the operation of the milk commission. We're lucky to have a person of George McCague's stature and experience to head this new body."

The minister smiled, nodded to the group and left the room.

George McCague then briefly outlined the responsibilities of the milk commission and the anticipated association with the milk marketing board. After Jim Jewson explained the reporting of expense accounts and other administrative matters to the board members, he and George McCague left the new board to itself.

It was a dramatic moment as George McLaughlin took the chairman's position at the head of the table and the new board met together for the first time.

Emerson Farnsworth, a former president of the Ontario Whole Milk Producers' League, past chairman of the Ontario Milk Producers' Co-ordinating Board, and chairman of the ill-fated Provisional Milk Marketing Board of 1962, extended the congratulations of the group to George McLaughlin.

"We want to start off as a cohesive group working together. For our first official act, I move that we endorse the minister's appointment of George McLaughlin as the first chairman of the Ontario Milk Marketing Board."

The motion was enthusiastically approved by the members.

With the same enthusiasm Orvil Guy was elected as the first vice-chairman. Harold Martin, who had been secretary of the co-ordinating board, was appointed the first secretary of the new board.

George McLaughlin looked down at the table for a moment, then looked up and spoke.

"Gentlemen, this is it. We've been given a major responsibility. We've been asking for it, so it's up to us to make it work. The road won't be smooth. There are a lot of rough players out there! It's going to take longer than we may think to develop a milk marketing plan the way we want it. To be rushed or bullied into hasty decisions or unwise action will have to be avoided.

On a hot August 19, 1965, the first appointed members of the Ontario Milk Marketing Board met for its initial official meeting with Bill Stewart. Seated from left to right, Alvin Stewart, Orvil Guy, vice-chairman, Bill Stewart, George McLaughlin, chairman, George McCague, chairman of the Milk Commission of Ontario, and Emerson Farnsworth, Standing, from left to right, Maurice Beaty, Benoît Duchesne, Glen Cole, Orm Coon, Laverne Dyment, Frank Todd, Ken McKinnon, Allen Ketcheson, Sid Pearson and Lucien Cazabon.

"You know that Harry Hays, the federal minister of agriculture, announced his new dairy policy on March 26 this year. And you know he promised to provide a national support price of $3.50 per hundredweight for domestically used manufactured milk. That has really relieved some of the potential pressure from the concentrated milk producers.

"His promise to appoint a Canadian dairy commission has also raised the hopes of the manufactured milk sector. It's had a good psychological effect on the industry."

McLaughlin looked seriously and intently at the new members and spoke more slowly.

"We must have solidarity within our board. Everything that's done and every decision that's made must be perceived to be the decision of the board and not that of any individual. In the past, milk producer organizations have been weak in the face of the strength of the processors and distributors. That must change, and it will change. We have to understand that our responsibility as a board is policy development and not the details of administration. There are staff who will come to us from existing milk groups, but we will add to these. We'll get the best people we can find. If necessary, we'll take them away from the processing side of the industry. We'll have a staff capable of carrying out the new policies that we're going to be developing.

"I have nothing to say about what's gone on in the past. That's past. We've all been thinking and even dreaming about the Hennessey report, the debates in the legislature and the coverage in the media. That, too, is behind us. It's now our turn to begin making history."

The meeting broke up into general discussion, with the members pointing out some of the reactions they were getting from their particular areas. Someone mentioned the rumors that were flying around the province regarding what might happen with a new board in operation, what the new board would be doing, and the downright opposition that existed in certain parts of the province and in certain groups, such as the Channel Islands Milk Producers and the Becker shippers in Toronto.

Emerson Farnsworth emphasized the mixed apprehensions of the northern producers and certain special conditions existing there. Then a member reminded them that the minister was expecting an official photograph to mark the occasion.

"Before we line up," he suggested, "let's take off our suit coats. We should be in our shirtsleeves. Let's make it look like we're ready for some hard work."

"Great idea," another replied. "Let's do it."

The suggestion met with general agreement - except with Orm Coon.

"Wait," Coon protested. "Is it entirely necessary for us to appear in shirtsleeves? I'm not sure I want to do that."

"Why?" asked one of the new members.

"Well, uh..." Coon paused. "Well, because I'm wearing suspenders, and I'll be embarrassed."

"Oh come on, Orm," replied another. "That's what farmers are supposed to wear, eh?"

Amid general laughter Coon stifled his embarrassment and acquiesced, and the picture was taken with all the men in their shirtsleeves.

Following the picture-taking session, general discussion continued for a while. Then George McLaughlin broke in.

"This is our first meeting. We'll have to spend quite a lot of time on the preparation of the necessary regulations to get the board under way. It's most important that as little time as possible elapse between this meeting and when the board assumes its full authority under the legislation. We can't waste any time making our presence felt.

"I'd like to suggest that we shoot for November 1st for the official inaugural meeting of the board with our full delegated authority under the Milk Act."

It was agreed.

After further discussion, the chairman was asked to interview the leaders of the existing dairy producer organizations regarding their adjustment to the board's operation, with a target date set of December 31, 1965.

Ken McKinnon of Port Elgin, the youngest member on the new board, and a man who had been a very active leader in the concentrated producers, suggested, "It's vital to keep the other organizations informed of what's happening so the board can use the established communications link, weak as it is. We must have their support during the transition period."

Orvil Guy, the new vice-chairman, had been a strong leader in the concentrated producers. He was a proven team player.

"We have to remember remember the Ontario farm organizations," said Guy. "They're getting very militant these days, so we should make sure they have a good understanding of what we want to do."

As a result of Guy's suggestion, someone suggested that the chairman meet with the leaders of the Ontario Federation of Agriculture and the Ontario Farmers' Union before the next meeting of the board and set up future meeting dates for consultative purposes.

It was also decided that during the organizational period the board would meet one day a week starting at 9:00 a.m. in the producer offices at 409 Huron Street, Toronto.

The meeting broke up. The members filed out, and judging from their faces, with a rarefied mixed feeling of challenge and responsibility. They had lunch in the cafeteria, after which they all started for home in a state of nervous anticipation and some real trepidation. Only George McLaughlin stayed behind for an hour's chat with George McCague.

It had been a very exciting day for everyone. They had met with the minister. The first meeting of the board was over, and their work was clearly cut out for them. They had their mandate. For all of the new board members there was much to accomplish in the weeks and months ahead.

Bill Stewart was anxious to learn how the rest of the meeting with the new board had gone. Immediately after lunch, therefore, he called George McCague and asked him to come around to his office. I was also there when McCague arrived. As soon as he was through the door the minister turned to him and asked impatiently, "Well, how did it go?"

McCague looked at him for a moment.

"There's one thing for certain," said McCague. "We got a head of steam going. I think everyone knows where we want to go. I'm just not too sure what the road is going to be like. George McLaughlin dropped in for about an hour after the meeting was over and he's all set to go."

"Good," replied the minister. "The press release got out on time. George Atkins carried it over his noon broadcast, and it was on the CP wires, so it's across Canada now. I've had a call from the London Free Press wanting to develop the story a little more. John Bradshaw wanted an interview for his Sunday morning show on CFRB. I just wasn't able to fit it in. Perhaps it's just as well. The press release said everything there is to say for the moment. The action is on the milk board's desk, at least for the moment."

Suddenly realizing that he hadn't allowed McCague to answer his question fully, Stewart turned again to him and added, "I'm sorry I interrupted. I'd asked how things went after I left the meeting."

Twisting his face slightly, McCague volunteered, "Well, I'm concerned. The new board is full of enthusiasm. George McLaughlin has left no doubt that he's going to run a tight ship, and I think he's already in high gear. Northern Ontario is restless. Kent and Essex have some producers who are more than a little unhappy. We'll see some rumblings come out of Middlesex too.

"I know you have the best man in George McLaughlin, but he has the bit in his teeth and he can be very determined. We've had some marketing problems with the other commodities from time to time, but they won't come anywhere near the pressures you and the rest of us are going to face from this one. It hits a lot of farmers and consumers, and the media are very conscious of milk and milk products."

I joined in: "There must be more than 60,000 milk and cream producers still in Ontario. Many are small producers, and many have serious financial problems. Most of the processors, particularly the cheese plants, are small. Rationalization will put a tremendous strain on the industry. The natural reaction will be to put the blame on the government."

Bill Stewart looked at his watch. "Well, it's 5:30 p.m. Thursday, August 19th, 1965. I hope what we've started will be around for a long time."

We took the hint and went back to our offices, pausing only for a minute to chat outside my office door before heading home.

CHAPTER THREE

The Die is Cast

In which the Ontario Milk Marketing Board

- Establishes the county and district milk committees
- Meets the Channel Islands Breeds Milk Producers
- Hires a general manager and director of finance
- Discusses quotas
- Establishes six basic objectives
- Receives their delegated marketing authority
- Joins the Dairy Farmers of Canada
- Establishes uniform prices for fluid milk
- Assumes marketing authority and assets of cheese producers
- Feels the authority of the milk commission
- Takes a look at transportation
- Has some rowdy meetings
- Establishes the northern pool

The meeting with the minister was over. The members met for the second time on August 26. They didn't have any legislative authority, but it was now less than ten weeks before the planned November 1 proclamation of the new Milk Act. About all the members had was a place to hang their hats at 409 Huron Street and a very temporary expense account from the Ontario Department of Agriculture. There was much to be done.

On the suggestion of the chairman, the first motion to be made was that the official title of the board be The Ontario Milk Marketing Board.

• *The Ontario Department of Agriculture was renamed the Department of Agriculture and Food in 1966. It became the Ontario Ministry of Agriculture and Food in 1971.*

The board didn't have that key person, a general manager, to place an early, firm hand on the administrative rudder. George McLaughlin was concerned.

"We have to get somebody to head up the administration, and we have to find him fast."

Orvil Guy, a former concentrated milk shipper from Winchester, had been elected vice-chairman. He had a lot of experience in farm organizations.

"We have to get the right person," said Guy. "We want someone who has the ability and believes in the same things we do. I don't even mind if he's a little smarter. It'll take some time to find the right person, but we shouldn't be in a hurry."

Emerson Farnsworth nodded. An old league man, he had an appreciation for good staff people. Roy Lick, a former secretary-manager of the league, was one of these.

"We can make all the policy we want to, and if we haven't got somebody here to make sure it's carried out, we'll be in real trouble," said Farnsworth. "That person has to be strong and know more than just the dairy industry. Any time spent in looking won't be wasted, because it'll likely go a long way in helping to make sure this board doesn't fall on its face."

The board members very quickly authorized the chairman to take the steps necessary to begin the search for the first general manager. Orvil Guy was asked to work with the chairman.

Alvin Stewart, an outstanding farmer and businessman from Richmond and a selected member of the first board, remembers, "Farnsworth was a very stubborn man. He'd taken a lot of flack before the board was formed and had quite a temper. During those first few months on the board, McLaughlin and Farnsworth were really at each other's throats, and Farnsworth even threatened to resign at one time. Apparently, before the board was formed, there had been meetings, with Emerson in attendance. George had been there, and he really hammered them, and this included Farnsworth. Some of the old wounds really hadn't healed, I guess. In any case, Emerson left the board after a short time because his farm had been sold."

George McLaughlin glanced at his agenda. He was moving quickly to place a firm hand on the chairman's gavel. "In a couple of months or so we'll be given our authority under the Milk Act. Edge Harris, our solicitor from St. Catharines, is drafting the necessary regulations and will be talking to us. In the meantime we can let people out there know we're here.

"We've had some work done on our logo and I'd like to pass it around. It's simple. The message is there. It says "milk" and that's what we're all about."

He handed the logo mock-up to Harold Martin, sitting on his left, who passed it on.

"We're going to have to build a system of communication with the producers," continued McLaughlin. "The old organizations, built around markets for fluid milk and around plants for concentrated milk, simply have to go. They can't be part of the new structure. They'd be divisive. But we must have contacts at local level who are selected at local level by the producers."

A member commented, "If these people are elected at local level we're going to end up with divided support out there."

"I don't know what you're thinking," replied McKinnon, "but having this board appointed by the government is going to be tough enough. We'll have a hard time living with that. I've worked a long time with farmers, and if we're going to make a success of this thing we're going to have to take the kicks. The important thing is to ensure that whatever comes from the country represents milk producer thinking. We don't need any 'yes men' out there or in here. If we don't have that, I can tell you now, we'll be in a lot of trouble."

Glen Cole, starting to become impatient, was squirming in his chair. On the board he represented the cream producers. Cole was known to be "a little short in the grain" at times.

"We have no choice," Cole said. "The farmers can't be put in a straitjacket as far as their opinions are concerned. The cream board for a long time has had locals that weren't tied to plants but acted on a county basis. I move that we establish county locals."

George McLaughlin had been listening to the discussion and watching the expressions on the faces of the board members.

"I've been giving this matter some thought and I've talked with some of you," he said. "What do you think about a name such as 'County and District Milk Committee.' It's new, and it slides off the tongue quite easily. As Glen says, the cream people have had county organization for some time. The English board apparently uses the name, 'county milk committees.' Crop improvement is organized on a county basis as well. If this is agreeable, it will take a little time, but we could have them in place by early spring."

Glen Cole quickly formalized a resolution to the effect that there be such committees formed and that they be in place by March 31, 1966.

Orvil Guy was looking a little worried. "We need some help here. If we try to organize a meeting on our own, we may create some trouble right off. We've got the two secretaries here. Jack Rouse has all the lists of the fluid milk producers and Charlie Milton has the concentrated producers. We may not be able to get the cheese list, but we can always advertise the meetings. You know, any time we have a difficult meeting in our county it's always the agricultural representative who acts as chairman."

"That's it!" said Orm Coon. "The agricultural representatives are used to running these sorts of meetings. Nobody will question their integrity. Let's get on with it, and I move that Jack and Charlie contact the ag reps and make all the arrangements."

There was enthusiastic approval. Everyone had been concerned about local organization, and they could see this approach working.

Jack Rouse and Charlie Milton had consulted with Edge Harris, the board's legal eagle, and under the general guidance of George McLaughlin, they moved aggressively to form the county and district milk committees.

The first committee was organized in Northumberland County on October 5, 1965, in the Warkworth Town Hall. It was a productive meeting. Some 175 producers were present, and they elected nine committee members.

By March 31, 1966, there were 54 county and district milk committees totaling 660 members. Regional meetings of the committees were arranged for April, with a provincial meeting of the executives scheduled for October. Producer organization at local level had moved quickly.

The Channel Islands Breeds Milk Producers' Association, representing the Jersey and Guernsey breeds, was of concern to George McLaughlin. He was a standard milk shipper and a Holstein breeder. The cholesterol scare had arrived in the 1950s, and the high test breeds in Ontario had moved aggressively to market their two-percent "All Jersey" and "Guernsey Gold" trademark milk.

Colonel Kennedy had approved a regulation in 1952 allowing partly skimmed, or two-percent milk, in order to soften the public reaction to a fluid milk price increase in Ontario.

Sales of high test milk and Jersey and Guernsey cattle had been dwindling. The Channel Islands advertising and marketing program had been pursued vigorously with the dairies, and it had met with significant success. Sales of Channel Islands milk had increased, and the price of Jersey and Guernsey cattle had risen. Channel Islands producers were receiving the top price for their milk. Their breed journals featured progress reports on milk marketing on a regular basis. The CI producers were not particularly enthusiastic about the new milk marketing plan. They feared it would dominate the milk marketing scene and that they would lose control of their CI marketing program. Maurice Beaty was a member of the board who represented the Channel Islands producers. He was regarded as a very fine person by the members of the board and wished to make a presentation to the board on behalf of the Channel Islands producers.

Alvin Stewart, another member, recalls asking Beaty before his talk to the board, "Are you ready to make your presentation, Maurice?"

"I ought to be," replied Beaty, "Last night I went over it at least a dozen times in my sleep!"

Beaty made his presentation, describing the CI program accurately and sincerely. The problem was that while the board recognized the marketing efforts of the CI producers, they were not particularly receptive to requests that they feared could divide and weaken their first efforts to start building a strong producer marketing structure.

Beaty had spoken earnestly: "Gentlemen, we were losing sales of Jersey and Guernsey milk and cattle. We decided we have a product that's different and we should try to sell it. There's been good marketing sense displayed and we've been able to gain acceptance of the idea that Channel Islands milk is higher in milk solids and more nutritious. We'd been getting a lot of surplus milk. By 1957, instead of having 40 percent surplus price, we had almost 100 percent at top price. A lot of our milk producers are breeders who depend on selling cattle for a significant part of their revenue.

"As a board we can expect some pretty tough reactions if we attempt to destroy what's taken about ten years to build up," Beaty continued. "With all due respect, I'm saying that while the standard milk producers were scrapping among themselves to see who was going to get the higher priced market, the Channel Islands people settled in and successfully established a market for themselves.

"I'm saying this because we have to meet with this group on September 29."

Alvin Stewart challenged Maurice.

"Hennessey listened to the Jersey and Guernsey people. He concluded that there isn't much difference in milk produced by the Channel Islands cattle and the Holstein and Ayrshire breeds. We have to admit your program has had some success. This board's been given the power to market all milk. I don't think we know exactly what form this is going to take, but aside from anything else, Bill Stewart expects it. I've got a little newspaper clipping here in which he says, 'The OMMB will act on behalf of all milk producers regardless of the final destination of the milk. When in full operation, the board will in effect buy milk from producers, sell it for the best price and remit the proceeds to the individual producer concerned.'"

He put down the clipping.

"We may have our work cut out for us," Stewart concluded, "but that looks like the way it has to be."

Beaty hesitated. "I'm not questioning the legislation or anything Bill Stewart has said. The Milk Act will be law and Bill Stewart's the minister. But I hope the board will recognize that we're dealing with a group of sincere and earnest people. I think they're entitled to every consideration the board can give them, and we should try to fit that into any marketing structure that may be devised."

Alvin Stewart retorted, "You may have built up a successful program, but we've practically had a breed war on our hands, and it certainly hasn't disappeared yet. I ran into a report the other day that said that in a relatively short time dairy cattle in Ontario will be predominantly Jersey and Guernsey. Now you and I know that's a bunch of nonsense, but there are a lot of farmers out there who are getting paid for a lot of surplus milk who may believe it."

George McLaughlin stepped in.

"Well, we don't want any wars here. Maurice, I think every board member understands your position and appreciates what the Channel Islands producers have accomplished. I think most of your people, while they may not like it, accept the fact that there is a Milk Act. We'll have to hear them out but at the same time reach conclusions based on what, in our opinion, is the best for all milk producers in the province."

The delegation representing the Channel Islands Milk Producers appeared before the board on September 29, 1965. They took a firm stand, stating, "All Jersey and Guernsey producers involved in the special milk promotion are contributing voluntarily ten cents per hundredweight on all fluid milk sales. Cooperating distributors contribute a like amount. We want the board to deduct the ten cents and submit it to the Channel Islands promotion committee. We also want to be able to continue the sales of our specialty two-percent milk. The program has been a success and is selling more milk. This means the milk will have to be kept separate from standard milk in transportation."

Ken McKinnon had reservations: "We want to sell more milk, and every effort helps. You say your sales are increasing, but isn't this at the expense of other milk sales? Distributors are getting nervous and are beginning to question the whole program since the minister announced the formation of the milk board. Mr. Chairman, we've got our responsibility in this thing and I think we need a lot more information than we can get from the out-of-date government statistics. We should get something from the dairies.

"I can't see much of a problem collecting the ten cents, providing the program is sound. I think we have to survey the dairies and try to find out their needs for this high test milk, and the Channel Islands association should be prepared to stand or fall on what the market indicates, regardless of the marketing structure that may evolve."

McKinnon took the floor again.

"The Channel Islands people believe they have a special product that requires special treatment. We're going to be pooling prices in Ontario, and that's the whole crux of the matter. When this happens we'll be asked to establish a separate pool for Channel Islands milk. I don't have the answer now, but there are a lot of questions that we have to look at."

George McLaughlin closed off the discussion, addressing his comments to the Channel Islands producers.

"We're all concerned about this matter. We have to admire the aggressive program you've followed for the last ten or eleven years with some obvious success. If you hadn't been gaining in market share, I don't imagine the standard milk producers would be complaining. We're taking this matter very seriously, but in fairness to you and everybody else we should make a formal survey of the distributors to determine the demand, and the potential demand, for Jersey and Guernsey milk. We'll certainly be giving early attention to this matter, particularly your ten-cent promotion levy."

The delegation left obviously dissatisfied with the results of their presentation. They were heard to comment to the effect that, "We really hadn't expected anything different from a board dominated by standard milk shippers."

The board realized immediately that it would be handling a great deal of money. Members were not only concerned about the absence of a full-time general manager, but as well, the absence of a director of finance. For the latter position, they were fortunate to find Bill MacPherson in Vancouver, who started with the board February 1, 1966. MacPherson had been working with the review section of corporate assessments in the Department of National Revenue. He was rather pleased to come to

Ontario, as his wife was a native of Lanark County.

No initiative was required by the board to find a suitable bank. Invitations for meetings and luncheon get-togethers began almost immediately. The banks realized very quickly that the milk board account would be a very lucrative one.

The board wanted a bank sympathetic to agriculture and its needs. There were many considerations, however. After several discussions and much thought the board selected the Royal Bank of Canada. The Royal had shown initiative and leadership in recognizing the specialized needs and nature of the agricultural community. It was perhaps most fitting that the Royal was selected. Jack McArthur had not only given leadership on agricultural matters within the Royal, but as well played an influential role on the Hennessey Inquiry.

The Milk Act made provisions for advisory committees. These committees were to be chaired by George McCague, the chairman of the milk commission. It was a wise and necessary move because a legislated common meeting ground for the parties involved was essential. The board was invited to name members to the first committee, which would deal with marketing matters concerning milk. There were to be eight producers and eight processors under the chairmanship of McCague.

The role of this committee was to prove very critical in the development of the milk marketing structure in Ontario, and it was credited later with avoiding many potential pitfalls. The advisory committee on milk was appointed on November 1, 1965, on the same day the milk board was delegated its powers under the legislation.

Quotas had been the basis of sales for fluid milk producers for many years. They represented possibly one of the more diverse patterns of various abuses in milk marketing.

The welfare of individual producers was tied to the strength or weakness of a particular dairy. Many producers had large quantities of surplus milk. Others, because of the success of their dairy or because of their own personal circumstances, had been able to sell a lot of their milk at top price. These were the so-called preferred shippers.

Some producers, as was the case with Walnut Dairy in Toronto, were forced to give significant kickbacks under the table to the dairy in order to maintain their permission to ship to that particular dairy. There were many forms of quota abuses in the fluid market that had existed before the milk board was authorized, and which existed afterwards for a while.

One very successful milk producer who milks well over 100 cows, and who wishes not to be named, recalled his first year as a shipper to the local market before the board was formed.

"I had quota, and half of it started to be returned coloured, indicating unacceptable quality. There was no way. It was all the same milk. The dairy was just colouring milk they didn't need and rejecting it. They were buying nonquota milk from around (the town) at about half the agreement price. They were sending the quota milk they should have paid for back to the farmers. I watched them doing it one morning, and I told them too!"

Generally speaking, quotas were under the control of dairies and truckers. Truckers, perhaps acting as agents of a dairy, or in their own interest, arranged for producers to get quota or to get on a trucking route.

Alan Ross of Harriston, a board member in the late '70s and early '80s and, at the time of writing, a member of the Farm Products Appeal Tribunal, recalls, "Up in this area, to be a fluid milk producer you had to be on a county road or on the highway. Trucks had to be sure of getting into your place because it's a snow belt here. Truckers were pretty selective too, but I think the dairies made the final decision."

The Ontario Whole Milk Producers' League had tried hard to deal with quota abuses and had even met with some success. The major problem was the multitude of markets with different prices and different agreements. The agreements were complicated and had been designed and administered at local level with a great lack of uniformity, both in detail and enforcement.

In discussing quotas at an early meeting of the board, George McLaughlin said, "This is our basic major problem: If we're going to build on the grade 'A' fluid milk structure, then we have to straighten out this quota and pricing mess. There's just no foundation here that will stand up under anything."

Emerson Farnsworth, who was still on the board at that time, quickly suggested he could make a contribution in the matter of quota policy. "We'll have to form a quota committee, and I'll be glad to act as chairman."

McLaughlin recalls, "Frank Todd and Orvil Guy were on the committee and I forget who else. We thought we'd be getting options to discuss. But two meetings later Emerson Farnsworth came back with a quota policy!"

Farnsworth still had his fluid milk loyalties; his suggested policy stated, "Any fluid milk consumption increases would be shared equally between fluid and industrial milk producers."

Farnsworth didn't want fluid to give up anything. There were two or three board members in favour, but all the rest were opposed. Ken McKinnon exploded.

"There's no way that will fly! Let's treat this matter seriously."

Farnsworth, with his quick temper, blamed McLaughlin for the failure of the policy, claiming he had poured cold water on the proposal before the vote was taken. Farnsworth stormed out of the room in a tantrum but, apparently having given the matter of his absence some quick thought, decided to come back. "You have to be careful how fluid milk quotas are going to be shared," he said, trying to be conciliatory. "I'd be glad to work on this. There's a lot of information on file in the League office. Let's get something moving."

George McLaughlin, aware of Farnsworth's line of thinking, had to carefully encourage him by saying, "Great, that's a good idea. Orvil Guy and Ken McKinnon will be pleased to work with you. We'll shoot for a report to come to the board by the end of October."

Ken McKinnon ended up being the chairman of the quota committee.

The big day, November 1, 1965, was fast approaching. Edge Harris, in consultation with Frank Gallant, the senior solicitor from the Department of Agriculture, had the regulations all in place. It was agreed that the board would meet November 1 at 409 Huron Street and then go on to the Parliament buildings for the 11:00 a.m. meeting with the milk commission.

George McLaughlin cautioned, "Since our August meeting the media have been relatively quiet. But once we get our marketing authority they'll be on us like a bunch of locusts. We'll all be asked questions. Our outlook and responses should be as uniform as possible. Ken McKinnon, Harold Martin and I have prepared a few objectives for your consideration.

"This is October 26th," McLaughlin went on. "If we can agree on something, we can take a draft of the new objectives home and then finalize them on November 1. These are general enough that we can build on them as we develop our policies into actions."

"Someone asked, "Will these be given to the press or published in *The Milk Producer*?"

"Primarily they're intended as a guide to all of us in our thinking and making public comments," said McLaughlin. "There's no doubt that when we're comfortable with the wording they will be published. These points are important. We're saying the milk producers in Ontario are going to get a stronger collective countervailing power in the marketplace. We're going to get improved prices for milk.

"Milk will move into those products that bring the highest return," continued McLaughlin. "The board is going to straighten out this nonsense that's developed with the criss-crossing of transport routes, and there's going to be rationalization of transportation.

"We believe that with a properly conducted dairy product advertising and promotion program we can sell more milk and milk products. We want a marketing system that will eliminate abuses and discrimination and provide fair and equitable treatment to producers. Special deals between dairies and individual producers will be eliminated.

"This board is determined to remove the fear that producers have had about losing their market if they don't knuckle under to the wishes of certain transporters and dairy operators. Our objective is ultimately to have all producers of milk of the same quality receiving a comparable price."

Smiling wryly, Orm Coon said, "I guess that just about covers it."

November 1st arrived. The board had convened its eleventh meeting at 409 Huron Street and recessed to reconvene at 11:00 a.m. with the milk commission at Queen's Park. The board received the delegated marketing authority from the commission under Regulation 295-65. The members realized that from now on, when they spoke or acted it would be with the whole weight and authority of an act and regulations of the government of Ontario.

George McCague had cautioned, "The extent of your authority is greater than that of any other marketing board. The government is entrusting you with it. But you know, the public interest must be protected. The legislation gives that responsibility to the milk commission. You know, men, we've got to work together. There's real concern out there. No doubt, as time passes many people will need a lot or reassurance."

After more discussion, George McCague and the other OMAF staff left the meeting.

Emerson Farnsworth, the old campaigner, said, "Well, we've been asking for this for a long time. I'm selling the farm and will be leaving the board shortly. No one has any idea what it means to me to experience the sensation of this moment."

Orm Coon, in his rather gruff voice and with some emotion, said, "When Colonel Tom Kennedy sent me to visit the English board in 1947, I didn't know it would take so long, but it's great to be here!"

It was necessary for the board to put its official stamp on a couple of matters. The appointment of the Royal Bank of Canada as the board's bank was approved. The fiscal year of the board was set at twelve months ending October 31 of each year. A committee on quality was formed. The board had previously decided to give leadership in milk and milk product research, and so a research committee was approved. The six objectives of the board, as previously outlined by the chairman, were adopted. The board, with its new mantle of responsibility and authority, now had to meet its constituents. It had been a heady day.

It had been previously decided that the chairman would meet with the Ontario Federation of Agriculture and the Ontario Farmers' Union. This had taken place, and George McLaughlin had been satisfied that both organizations understood and were supporting the objectives of the board.

McLaughlin, however, had just received a copy of the OFA's annual brief to the Ontario cabinet. The brief attempted to address the concerns of all of the farmers in Ontario, but had shown a distinct lack of understanding of some of the situations facing the board. It was fully appreciated that many farmers were upset about the milk situation, and no doubt the OFA was reflecting this.

But board members were critical of the OFA.

"If this group can't speak about milk marketing problems with some understanding and support, then they'd better keep quiet. There's a lot of misunderstanding out there still, and it certainly won't help us find a solution by repeating these things to cabinet.

"How are we going to build up a strong organization and do an effective job if we have an organization like the OFA, which lacks both financial and human resources and doesn't seem to understand the problems, creating interference?"

To some degree board members were divided in their attitudes toward the OFA. Some had worked closely with the OFA in the past and others had not.

Orvil Guy, who quite often in the future was to act as a foil during some of the board's difficult situations and through some of George McLaughlin's outbursts, said at the time, "I guess that's been one of the problems; the OFA never had enough money to adequately represent the farmers. They try hard and they still have a lot of support at county level. We really need them, and I'd suggest that we form a joint board/OFA committee to have a regular exchange of ideas. Let's see if we can harness them in some way that will help us. We're going to need all the support we can get."

The members agreed to this suggestion.

Recognizing that one of the limitations of the board's authority was that products could move interprovincially and into export beyond the jurisdiction of the board, it was decided that a strong voice was needed at the national level. They were aware of the discussions that had gone on among Bill Stewart and his officials with Quebec, as well as meetings between Stewart and Harry Hays regarding the formation of the Canadian Dairy Commission. Stewart had been careful to have assurance that there would be a new national dairy policy before he introduced the Ontario Milk Act. He also had discussed the principles of the proposed bill with Hays before it had been introduced.

George McLaughlin became president of the Dairy Farmers of Canada in 1966, and Glen Cole was a vice-president at the time. Cole was also on the milk board representing the cream producers. Ontario had always played a major and significant role in the Dairy Farmers of Canada, and the board recognized that this was the vehicle that would play the major role in future national dairy policy.

Cole had said, "Look, we have to be part of this as a board. The future of the industrial milk producers is very much a part of our responsibilities. Our hands will be tied if we can't really speak for these people, who are well represented out there on the county milk committees and so dependent on national policies. As a board we've got to become a member of the Dairy Farmers."

Allen Ketcheson had commented, "The cheese producers have always been concerned with national policy because we've been so dependent on the export market. We certainly need a national voice and more support at the Ottawa level. We just have to be part of those things that affect Ontario industrial milk producers."

The members present at the meeting had agreed that the board should join the Dairy Farmers of Canada effective January 20, 1966, the date of the Dairy Farmers' annual meeting.

The price and market clutter among the fluid milk producers were regarded as a priority. George McLaughlin said, "We have to clean up this mess before we do anything else, because if we don't clean it up we won't be able to do anything else."

There were continuing discussions at meetings of the milk advisory committee under the chairmanship of George McCague. Substantial agreement had been reached on the board's proposal for a uniform price for fluid milk requirements. The board kept up the pressure on the fluid milk distributors.

In 1965 there were 179 separate market agreements regarding price and conditions of sale for fluid milk. These agreements provided for 83 different prices ranging from $4.19 per hundredweight in southern Ontario to $6.50 in one northern Ontario market.

The board moved decisively. In nine months, by August 1, 1966, it succeeded in establishing a single price of $5.75 for all fresh fluid milk in southern Ontario and $6.32 for similar milk in northern Ontario.

At the same time the 54 county and district milk committees had replaced nearly all of the fluid milk producer associations across the province as well as the concentrated plant locals.

The 1965 meeting of cheese producers had been restless. A resolution, retroactive to 1962, had been approved to change the by-laws to limit the tenure of the chair holder to three years.

Hector Arnold presided at the 33rd annual meeting of the cheese producers in the Chateau Laurier, Ottawa, in January 1966. For years the cheese producers traditionally had met in the Royal York Hotel, Toronto. They had suddenly switched, in 1964, to the Chateau Laurier - as far away from Queen's Park as they could get, it seemed. It was Arnold's tenth year as chairman of the board. He had been a member of the board for a total of twenty-one years. He did not stand for re-election, but in his address advised the meeting, "The government's decision, as stated to the county presidents yesterday, will mean that the powers required for the marketing of cheese will be exercised by the milk board of Ontario through the Ontario Cheese Producers Co-operative Limited."

George McCague, chairman of the milk commission, addressed the meeting at length.

"There is very sound and solid enthusiasm on the dairy marketing scene. The new Milk Act is clearing a way for dairy policy in Ontario, which will reflect itself at national level in providing a permanent, continuing and progressive national dairy policy for which we have been searching for years. The milk marketing plan provides a single, unified approach to marketing.

"It was the view of the Ontario Milk Commission and The Ontario Milk Marketing Board, the Ontario Cheese Producers' Marketing Board and even the Ontario Department of Agriculture that the Ontario Cheese Producers' Marketing Board would continue on its own.

"However, it has become increasingly evident in the last two or three months that the participation of cheese producers in the overall plan was not only desirable to producer interests but that isolation would be difficult and could result in losing ground and losing out on the success and values secured by the Cheese Producers' Marketing Board during its long history. This has been discussed at county milk meetings and at county cheese producer meetings. The export levy on cheese which has been borne by the cheese industry will be spread over all milk.

"The Cheese Producers' Marketing Board, following the winding up of the cheese producers' marketing plan, could very well become an advisory body to the Ontario Milk Marketing Board because of their experience and knowledge of the cheese marketing world."

The milk board actually asked Hector Arnold to act in an advisory capacity to them, which he did for a short period.

Charles Huffman, president of the Ontario Federation of Agriculture, spoke of the valuable service that the cheese board had rendered to the industry.

"Its program, despite difficulties and criticism, has worked. Now it must go even further and face new and heavier responsibilities, some of which may be unpalatable."

The delegates at the annual meeting, by resolution, congratulated Bill Stewart for the new Milk Act and for the formation of the new milk marketing board. And by resolution they agreed to "the total absorption of the Ontario Cheese Producers' Marketing Board and the Ontario Cheese Producers' Co-operative Limited and the Ontario Cheese Producers' Association by the Ontario Milk Marketing Board."

On February 17, 1966, therefore, the Ontario Cheese Producers' Marketing Board was dissolved and all assets were transferred to and vested in the Ontario Milk Marketing Board.

A special meeting was held in Belleville, on February 17, of the milk commission, the Cheese Producers' Marketing Board and the OMMB. It had been a very ticklish situation. Hector Arnold had appeared convinced that the preservation of the cheese board was in the best interests of the cheese industry. With such persons as Orm Coon and Allen Ketcheson on the milk board, however, producers had some confidence in the change. The 33rd annual meeting had seen its members speak, but some tensions were still high. George McCague deliberately stayed away from the meeting.

All legal matters that allowed the assumption of the powers of the cheese board by the milk board and the transfer of assets were handled at this meeting. The milk board now had the responsibility for marketing all milk produced in Ontario.

This was quite a change. Milk processors and distributors were fearful for the future with such broad marketing powers in the hands of the producers, who for many years had virtually lived within the dictates of pressures beyond their control. Sam Ault, who had grown up in the family processing business in Winchester, later summed it up: "We were downright frightened."

Fluid milk distributors were forced into a more competitive market. Many welcomed it, but others were fearful of store sales and higher quality skim milk powder. The early spring of 1966 saw distributors maintaining that the reconstitution of milk was a natural outcome of the competition facing them from instant skim milk powder and concentrated liquid milk. They wanted to "reconstitute skim and sell it, and if this wasn't to be, the government must regulate skim powder and concentrated liquid milk."

They wanted the competition regulated because they saw no flexibility in the price they had to pay for the raw product. The milk board was sympathetic, but producers were beginning to feel a sense of freedom, because of their emerging market strength.

But this was a difficult period. The regulatory lines were being cast out by the board, but they were slack in many areas. In the north, markets were requesting price increases. There were problems with reconstituted milk, concentrated liquid milk and imports of fresh fluid milk from southern Ontario.

Lucien Cazabon, from Sturgeon Falls, was the first representative from the north and, as many affirmed, "a good man to have around." At the time of his appointment to the board he had been the chairman of the Sudbury Milk Producers' Association. He was understood and respected by the producers in the area. But he was frustrated.

"Things are untidy in the north. Dairies move milk wherever they want to, and they're charging the farmers for the trucking. The farther they have to truck it, the more money they're paid. We have to decide where the north begins."

An early decision placed the boundary of north and south at the French and Mattawa Rivers.

Cazabon had other frustrations.

"For one thing, I had great difficulty convincing Toronto of the need for the 57-cent price differential between the north and the south. Markets were requesting price increases. There were problems associated with reconstituted milk, concentrated milk (multi-milk) and imports of cheap fluid milk from southern Ontario, which certain dairies were reportedly selling at a profit.

Lucien Cazabon had difficult times. Timmins producers were complaining that a dairy was requesting milk to be delivered at 9:00 a.m., and when the drivers got there, no one was there to receive it until noon, requiring that they had to wait the three hours - outside, in minus forty degree cold!

Some producers just couldn't grasp the plans of the milk board. In Hearst, Cazabon had attempted to explain it to them:

"We will supply all the dairies with their milk. All of the money will be put into one box. And then producers will be paid the same price all around."

There were a couple of farmers on the other side of Hearst who understood, but for the others, the ideas were so different from what they had been used to, they just didn't understand, Cazabon reported. Later, however, he said, "By 1968 they all seemed to be very pleased."

Multi-milk was being promoted by Canada Dairies in Burgessville. Sterilized milk had been on the market for a long time in the U.K. and was a commonly accepted product there because of the lack of refrigeration in the homes. Canada Dairies maintained that there were extra costs involved and they wanted the raw product at a cheaper price. The board and other distributors were concerned because of the promotions that claimed this milk could have broad use in tourist and other areas where there wasn't a regular delivery of fresh milk. Canada Dairies protested that the regular price of $5.29 per hundredweight would put them out of business; the highest price they could pay was about $4.15.

The board met with the milk commission.

George McCague reminded the board representatives, "This multi-milk is a new product. It's quite possible that more milk can be sold in total if we allow some of these new products onto the market. We hope the board won't be too inflexible in this matter."

The board's reply was: "If it does everything they say it will, it's going to cut into the sales of fresh fluid milk, which is the highest priced product for the farmers. It'll also cut into skim milk powder sales. We're not satisfied that it's a good thing for the industry, but we have promised Canada Dairies that we would reconsider the whole matter."

The board did seriously reconsider the matter. Opinions were divided.

"Look," suggested Orm Coon, "the cheese industry has been married to cheddar cheese since the beginning. Some of us can see benefits in gross sales by moving toward more processed cheese and specialty cheeses. With all this talk about butterfat, maybe we shouldn't close the door on a new product that might sell."

Laverne Dyment, a long-time fluid leader in the Hamilton market, in the league and a founding member of the milk board, was a genial but very stubborn man.

"I've watched grocery products in the chain stores," said Dyment. "They promise great things with a lot of advertising, but all it does is replace some other product and add to the cost of marketing to the consumer. I'm not against new products; I just have a feeling this one is not going to do much for us or for the distributors."

There was heated discussion.

George McLaughlin looked around.

"I was hoping it was going to be an easy decision," he said. "It looks as if the board is badly split. I think we should have a vote by ballot."

The majority agreed that the board should maintain its position that milk be paid for at $5.29 per hundredweight, the regular fluid milk price. This was one of the few times a board vote was taken by ballot and so recorded in the minutes.

Canada Dairies appealed to the milk commission.

The milk commission reduced the $5.29 price to $4.85 per hundredweight and gave the board the choice either to file a regulation reducing its price or the commission would make an order requiring the board to do so. The commission believed that this would allow a fair competitive price between the sterilized product and the fresh milk. The board was annoyed, but it agreed to file the necessary regulation. This was the first of several instances of strained relations between the Milk Commission of Ontario and the milk board.

Board decisions were routinely being appealed to the milk commission, and in a number of cases the board was being overruled. The board was not happy.

Glen Cole exploded at one meeting with the commission and stormed out of the room.

"I'd thought we were set up by the minister to market the farmers' milk," he complained. "We might as well quit if the commission keeps cutting us down!"

Someone who had left the meeting for a moment returned to find Cole missing. "Where's Glen Cole?" he asked.

"If he kept up the speed he left here with," Ken McKinnon replied, "he should be home by now."

The board was upset with the commission. At a later meeting, while recognizing the responsibility of the commission, the board decided to give the appeal question more attention and at the same time create greater visibility for itself. They requested the commission to "notify the board of all appeals, give the board ten days clear notice of appeals, and advise on the nature of all appeals."

Lorne Hurd assumed the post of the Board's General Manager on March 1, 1966.

"We will have representation at all appeal hearings, if necessary with legal council, and if necessary participate in as many appeals as we have to. We'll let everyone see we mean business."

Lorne Hurd of Saskatchewan joined the board as its general manager March 1, 1966. He had been carefully selected after several possible candidates were considered. Hurd attended his first board meeting on March 10. George McLaughlin was obviously satisfied. Although Hurd had previously met with all board members, the chairman formally introduced him.

"You've all met Lorne Hurd by this time. He's been around here for a few days, but this is his first board meeting. I'd like to formally install the first general manager of the Ontario Milk Marketing Board.

"We've been looking for more than four months. There were a number of possibilities. We interviewed some of them, and you as a board have talked to Lorne and given your stamp of approval. He's young and he's got the experience we want. He has a couple of degrees, one of them in agriculture. Despite his young age he's had senior administrative positions with the Agricultural Institute of Canada, the National Dairy Council and the Canadian Federation of Agriculture. He's also been senior editor of *The Country Guide*.

"I think we're all convinced that Lorne is a person who sees the dairy industry as it should be seen and that he'll be dedicated to helping ensure that this industry is around and viable for a long time."

Everyone enthusiastically rose to shake Hurd's hand and to officially welcome him.

Board inquiries had revealed that Hurd was a perfectionist. He gave the impression of being in control of himself at all times. Serious, considered conversation appeared to come more easily than joviality and smiles.

"I'm pleased to be here," said Hurd. "Not everyone gets the opportunity to start at the birth of an organization and, hopefully, grow with it. Everybody has been watching what has been happening in the dairy industry in Ontario and I'm happy to be part of it.

"I'm impressed with the sincerity I see around this table," he continued. "I think I understand what you want and I'll do my best. That's about all I have to say."

George McLaughlin recalls one of the reasons for Hurd's being hired.

"I was heading west and we stopped at Winnipeg. Lorne came on board and sat in the empty seat beside me. He was doing some sort of a survey for the Canadian Federation of Agriculture and was on his way to Vancouver. He asked a lot of questions about milk marketing and about my marketing philosophy and all that sort of stuff. We talked about Quebec and some of the other provinces, and I always remember his saying, 'You know, some of the things you want to do won't be able to be done because they'll have to be done nationally. The other provinces will take advantage of you.'

"Anyway, I contacted Dave Kirk of the CFA and asked him if I could approach Lorne for the general manager's job. And I asked if he had any objections. He did. In any case, we got Lorne down to Toronto, and Orvil Guy and I talked to him first, and we hired him."

Transporters had traditionally been very independent souls. They tended to develop their own routes and act from time to time as unofficial agents of processors and distributors, and they had created a disorderly map of milk transportation based upon their own individual activities.

A significant number of producers hauled their own milk. Interest was being shown in cooperative trucking. Some processors had their own trucks. Over the years the individual trucker had been closer to his producers than any other person or organization. Most of them didn't hesitate to pass on opinions to their shippers. They loved their relative freedom of action, and with the maze of truckers out there it was difficult for the board to know where to start in the rationalization process.

There was a tremendous variation in rates, particularly with industrial milk between regions and between routes, and in many cases between individual shippers on the same route.

Competitive subsidies to attract milk were being paid by manufacturing plants to processors.

The board had strongly supported McLaughlin in his insistence that the rationalization of trucking receive top priority: "The control of trucking is vital to orderly marketing. We have to move on it. Getting some order into the route mess will result in savings of several hundred thousand dollars!"

A uniform maximum trucking rate was discussed. It could mean that some transporters would be paid more than they were asking or that they actually required. The board decided that they would have to attack the problem through consultation with the individual truckers and shippers on the various routes.

Ken McKinnon said, "Look, we've got a lot of truckers out there, and there are a lot of routes. Talking to them all will certainly be part of the final solution, but our first move has to be something that's sound enough to apply to all the industrial milk truckers as well as being something they all can see. They must understand we mean business!"

After more heated discussion, the board decided they should set a rate for handling industrial milk in cans and that any transporter who thought he needed more could make application to the board for a transportation rate adjustment.

Orvil Guy argued, "You know, this is like waving a red flag in front of certain truckers. We should develop a policy position and take it to the transportation advisory committee, and we could call it an interim policy."

Most agreed that this seemed like a good idea.

Meanwhile, the milk commission was meeting with transporters, and McCague was leaning on them.

"Look men, we have to get some reason into these transportation rates. We have to have a system and there isn't one now. If there isn't a voluntary settling of this whole thing, then we'll draft a regulation giving the milk board power to negotiate rates with you. If you can't agree, a settlement will be arbitrated."

Similar advice was passed on to the milk board. Orvil Guy advised the commission, "The board will consider the matter and let you know its decision."

Meanwhile, meetings had taken place between certain processor representatives and officials of the United Dairy and Poultry Co-op (UDPC) regarding transportation rates. The milk board had requested Jack Rouse, the board's secretary, to advise the parties that rates could be changed only through negotiation procedures laid down under the legislation.

George McLaughlin was receiving telephone calls at his home and at the office from some county milk committee chairmen. McLaughlin advised the board, "We've talked about the involvement of local producers in the transportation question. I think we should move formally before there's any misunderstanding. I'd suggest that the local negotiation committees for transportation rates should have two members named by the chairman of each county committee and a third by this board."

The members, while agreeing to this suggestion, added a proviso that it be clearly understood - and advised to the county committees by letter - that the board's choice for the third member would be the chairman of each county milk committee.

Ken McKinnon suggested, "The board must have a presence at all of these meetings. I think at the beginning our transportation supervisor should be in attendance at as many of the early meetings as possible and after that the field staff can carry on. We must have somebody there at all meetings."

This was agreed.

The NFU was being very militant. McLaughlin and Guy had attended a meeting in the fairgrounds building in Mitchell. Harold Scott from Stratford, chairman of the milk committee, was with them. This was where the concentrated local had generated such militancy prior to and during the Hennessey Inquiry. They had threatened to invade the fluid milk market.

George McLaughlin gave a report: "It was scary. They were almost hanging from the rafters, and as happens in crowds like this, there were some pretty wild statements, and speakers from the floor were egged on by at least a few people who came there just to be entertained. We had difficulty making ourselves heard. They want the top price and they want it now, and they don't think the board is doing very much about it."

At the board meeting of June 14, members were advised there had been another meeting sponsored by the NFU at Formosa with about 1,000 people present. This had taken place June 9. The majority of people there were apparently industrial shippers. They were very critical of the increased trucking rates for producers and expressed concerns about their net receipts.

McLaughlin advised, "I understand there are two more meetings to be held in Peterborough and Richmond on June 23rd and 24th. I'm busy, but I think Orvil should go, and certainly Alvin Stewart."

This also was agreed.

Orvil Guy reported later, particularly on the Richmond meeting, "The meetings were something else. The farmers were nasty, and they just wouldn't listen to us. I expect there were some reasonable people there, but I didn't see them."

Elphege Lefebvre, from St. Eugene, smiled and said, "I talked to some of the producers after the Richmond meeting. We did have some friends there. They told me that the OFU was having these meetings to gain members and that the leaders weren't too interested in the price of milk. I think we should let the farmers' union people answer all the questions at future meetings. It can't do us any more harm."

The members generally agreed that the board should not be party to any future meetings designed by the OFU to generate membership. Discussion indicated that the board members believed they had better things to do than to present themselves as punching bags at meetings of prearranged, loaded questions and the propaganda-based outbursts by members of the audience.

The year 1966 was one of near violence with the OFU. The big tractor parade at Queen's Park gained headlines in July 20 editions put out by the Toronto press. Protests went beyond the matter of milk marketing and included other commodities.

Accepting the distractions, the board was aggressively moving ahead. It wanted to implement a grade "A" pool as soon as possible. Consideration was given to an area in the province that might be set up as a pilot project to develop administrative procedures. Lorne Hurd suggested that the board might wish to look at northeastern Ontario.

"It doesn't involve many producers," he explained. "There's some buffering from outside influences on all sides. A pool up there right now could be of benefit and straighten out some of the existing problems with certain of the distributors in that area. It is a wise move from a marketing standpoint."

George McLaughlin, the OMMB's first chairman, addresses producer delegates assembled at an early annual meeting at Toronto's Royal York Hotel.

Hurd also recalls the meeting in the north in the Sturgeon Falls firehall.

"Mr. McLaughlin had spelled out the board's plans for the pilot pool. A major distributor got to his feet and complained, 'George, you have got to be kidding.'

"McLaughlin replied, 'We're not kidding, and we're going to do it!'"

The board agreed to have the necessary regulations prepared for a price pool to cover the districts of Nipissing, Sudbury and Manitoulin. It was to be regarded as a pilot project. The board was anxious to get moving.

Questions were raised about additional requirements for Channel Islands milk within the pilot pool when it got under way.

There were five Channel Islands milk producers who were being left out of the northern pool at the beginning and allowed to carry on their normal shipments of milk. It was emphasized that this was not to be construed as a precedent. Whatever the policy might eventually be, these five producers would be required to conform to it.

On October 1, 1966, a regional office was established at North Bay, and the board inaugurated a pilot price pool for Manitoulin, Nipissing and Sudbury.

Sarsfield O'Connor, a recent addition to the board staff from the Nestle company at Chesterville, was sent to the North Bay office to be there during the period of the development of the pool.

"The northern experience very quickly showed the need to have adequate credit arrangements for the processors," recalls Bill MacPherson. "This, of course, was before the creation of the fund for milk and cream producers which came into effect in 1967. We had one processor that we had to place on the basis of cash on delivery. This really meant cash in advance for a week. If we didn't get this, we wouldn't agree to deliver milk for the subsequent week. The money was paid directly into the office in North Bay.

"One evening when I was up there arranging for the delivery of the payments in advance, the plant's truck driver came knocking on the building door and we had to let him in. He'd gone around to all the retail establishments and the dairy's customers and had picked up cash. He stood there bringing cash out of every pocket of everything that he was wearing, and then he piled it on the desk. There were cheques, social assistance cheques, cash, but no IOUs. We had to insist that he stay while we counted the cash so we'd agree on the amount. With this experience we decided we would have to have a better payment system!

"We adopted a system that we called the voluntary plant pooling system," MacPherson continued. "Everything was manual and we wouldn't bring all of the producers and all of the processors into the pool at the same time. The arrangement was to bill each dairy and pay each producer to the dairy in a way that they had been accustomed to, and as the dairy had paid them. We did this to get the trust of the dairies and showed them that we could pay their producers as well as they could. Then we started paying the producers directly."

McLaughlin commented, "This pilot project should prove invaluable as a stepping stone to operating a province-wide milk marketing system."

Within days, nineteen producers were protesting the amount of quota allocated to them within the pilot pool. Frank Todd, a board member from Churchill and a former Toronto milk shipper, wondered, "If we've got nineteen appeals from just this small pool, what's going to happen when we start the big pool for the rest of the province?"

Everyone shook their heads, trying not to envision that scenario.

As had been emphasized earlier by George McLaughlin, quota was a difficult question on everyone's mind, but one that had to be dealt with. He had been thinking about it since he had been appointed chairman. He'd recently had several discussions with Lorne Hurd. Emerson Farnsworth had by then left the board.

The chairman emphasized to Hurd, "Look, we have to get some answers and we need professional help on some of these things. I think we can get professor Bob Marshall from the OAC economics department for a few months to assist in developing the board's permanent quota policy. But we have to look at industrial milk."

Hurd volunteered, "I think professor Ralph Campbell, who's now at the University of Toronto, is prepared to take twenty or twenty-five days between now and February to study the selling of industrial milk."

The matter was taken to the board, and everyone agreed that the board should retain both Campbell and Marshall.

October was drawing to a close. The first annual report of the board was being written. In the first year the board had taken steps to clearly indicate a new sense of direction was coming to the industry. The board was launched. The die was cast.

CHAPTER FOUR

A Presence Felt

In which the board

- Recognizes the need for French in communications
- Welcomes Algoma to the northern pool
- Makes decisions on Channel Islands milk
- Considers transportation rationalization and the role of co-operative transport
- Hears from northern Ontario
- Listens to cheese concerns
- Establishes the graduated entry program
- Hears that it is playing "Robin Hood"
- Is challenged by the Becker shippers
- Begins the southern Ontario group one pool
- Supports the commission's move to reduce distribution areas
- Considers the marketing of industrial milk

A full-scale marketing program for milk producers was taking longer to get into operation than anticipated. The magnitude and complexity of the task had been underestimated. Legal challenges to the board's authority were causing spreading concern. The members were examining the board's effectiveness in communicating with the milk producers.

It was November 1, 1966. The board had been in position for one year. Ken McKinnon had commented, "Regarding communications, thank goodness for the county and district milk committees. I don't know what we would do without them in maintaining producer contact."

Lucien Cazabon of Sturgeon Falls and a former member of the Sudbury milk producers agreed. "But," he said, "we must think about communicating also with the French-speaking producers, especially in the north and east. Most of them speak only French in the house, the barn and with their neighbours."

Elphege Lefebvre of St. Eugene supported Cazabon's suggestion, adding, "French should be in *The Milk Producer* magazine too. We should also think about the annual report."

There was general agreement that the use of French would strengthen communication with producers and that Lefebvre's request was reasonable. The general belief was that this suggestion should become policy and that any correspondence received in French should be answered in that language.

Later, George McLaughlin asked Cazabon whether or not the translations were helping.

Cazabon was disgusted.

"If that's the way you're going to translate it, forget about it," he replied. "The English is being translated word for word, and that just doesn't make sense in French. I'm having real problems in getting some of my producers to understand what the board is trying to do. Maybe some correct French would help."

McLaughlin moved quickly on Cazabon's criticism to settle the language problem. "Afterwards," recalls Cazabon, "the translation in the magazine was very well done."

The board's general manager, Lorne Hurd, had been on staff for less than a year, but his presence was being strongly felt within the administration and in the industry generally. From the beginning there seemed to be clear understanding between him and George McLaughlin regarding the division between policy making and the administration of policy. From the outset this had resulted in an understanding of staff reporting procedures. In an early speech in April 1967, Hurd stated, "The board has established clear objectives and is organized to accomplish these objectives. There are two quite distinct functional arms for this purpose - a policy arm and an operating arm.

"There are thirteen appointed milk producer members of the board who make policy. They make the policy decisions in keeping with the powers delegated by the milk commission. The milk commission is concerned with policy development and has the right to intervene in policy matters if it's deemed necessary in the interests of the dairy industry as a whole. If the board is to be successful, it must reflect the wishes of at least a majority of the producers it's been set up to serve. County and district milk committees influence and assist the board members in reaching policy decisions.

"The operating arm is headed by the board's general manager," continued Hurd. "There are five separate operating divisions consisting of finance, cheese, marketing, production, and public relations. These divisions are charged with the responsibility of developing and administering the programs required to put the board's policy decisions into practice. The general manager is responsible for all of this through the chairman of the board."

Meanwhile, policy decisions were being made by the board and implemented by staff.

The northern pool was progressing very well. Producers were paid twice a month and there was good cooperation from the dairies. There were some credit problems before the fund for milk and cream was established to protect producers from plants with financial difficulties.

During the spring of 1967 there was some discussion regarding possible expansion of the northern pool. There had been suggestions that Algoma be considered for inclusion in the northern pool, but it was reported that some of the producers were opposed.

"What's wrong with those guys up there?" a board member wondered. "It wasn't so long ago that they were fighting with the distributors and trying to get into the distribution business with the North Shore Co-operative. The distributors gave them a good deal on price before the board got started trying to persuade them they didn't need a marketing plan. Now it seems they're still not sure!"

"Algoma would give us some experience in administering a pool located over a wide area," suggested Hurd. "There would also be some psychological value in examining the northern pool before everything is set up under data processing. We've actually been advised that the Algoma producers now have no objection to becoming part of the pool. Sure, there's going to be more work in preparing 100 or more producer statements by hand, and this could delay the settlement date by maybe a day."

George McLaughlin thought it desirable to move ahead so that the board could get experience and also give the public some indication that pooling was making progress. It was agreed that Algoma be included in the northern pool, with the target date of June 1, 1967.

Staff reported there were still pressures from the northern pool regarding Channel Islands milk. The chairman was irritated.

"We'll have to make a difficult decision one of these days. We've listened to the Channel Islands people and we've made it clear to them that the five shippers in the northern pool are not to be regarded as setting a precedent for special treatment. Staff say that Silverwoods is asking for more Channel Islands milk. That's a prize one! I don't know what sort of games they're trying to play. Silverwoods is saying they're 40 percent short of Jersey milk in relation to present sales. The figures indicate that the present sales of Jersey milk are considerably lower now than they were last year. Staff will have to take a good look at this one."

The board decided that in light of plans for the southern Ontario pool, decisions had to be made regarding Channel Islands milk. At 7:00 p.m. on July 11, 1967, a delegation appeared before the board requesting a separate pool for Channel Islands milk: "If that isn't possible we want special quotas allotted to Channel Islands producers in direct relation to the requirements for Channel Islands milk. We're agreeable to a payout of 90/10.

"The quota policy must provide for entry into the group one pool of new Channel Islands producers. As well, the butterfat differential for fluid milk should be kept to a point no higher than the price a distributor can recover on the open market for churning cream, in order that there be no economic advantage to either high test producers or standard producers. We wish to continue our own advertising program."

The requests resulted in an open and sometimes heated two-hour discussion among the members. George McLaughlin finally said, "It's getting late. Everyone's tired, but we should settle this. We know as much about the problem as we'll ever know."

Maurice Beaty was concerned. "I know these men and they won't give up," he said. "You know they'll take the board to the Supreme Court of Canada if the chips are down."

Glen Cole had driven in from Bewdley that morning and was feeling it.

"Look," he said. "In less than a year we're bringing in the group one pool. We have to start shoving back at some of these groups or they're going to step all over us. Let them challenge us, but I think all milk producers should be treated the same."

Some wondered whether or not they should sleep on it, considering that they were meeting the next day. Ken McKinnon, who had seriously considered at one stage switching to Jerseys at the suggestion of Ron Guest, his trucker, stepped in.

"We'll sleep better tonight if we settle it now. I suggest that the Channel Islands producers be included in each pool on the same basis as other producers, but that their quotas be allotted on the same base period, July 1,

1966 to March 31, 1967, a year later than has been set for the other producers. Any new producers should come into the pools the same as everybody else. Quota adjustments should be the same. I make that a motion."

"They'll fight it," suggested Orvil Guy, "but I'll second it with an amendment that the staff work out some method whereby the board can make deductions for their advertising program."

Maurice Beaty was reported to have been extremely uncomfortable, but that his great honesty of thought came to the fore and that he had suggested, "I may get shot for what we're doing tonight, but I must admit I'm convinced it's the only workable course to follow."

There was general approval of the policy decision, and the meeting broke up at about 10:30 p.m. after an exhausting evening.

The Ontario Farmers' Union was continuing its militant activities. The year 1966 had seen the rowdy meetings, tractor marches on Queen's Park, headlines in the Toronto press and noisy farmers around Bill Stewart's farm at Denfield. Now in 1967 the OFU was threatening a strike if its members didn't like the new federal dairy policy.

A board member stated, "Look, we're a responsible group, and there's no way we can be seen in the same bed with that outfit, let alone in the same house."

The board made a public statement which said, "The board does not support milk strike action because it doesn't believe such action to be in the best interests of the producers or that it will work. The main losers will be the producers whose milk doesn't go to market. The board is concerned that such action will result in imports of dairy products. The board doesn't object to individual farmers deciding to withhold milk from the market, but it does object if any such action adversely affects the marketing of milk offered for sale by other producers."

There were also real concerns for quota matters in the country, and even some in the Ontario legislature. County annual meetings were indicating that quota was a major issue, even more than price.

In the Ontario legislature during the debate on the Department of Agriculture and Food's 1967 estimates, questions were asked of Bill Stewart implying that board members, or persons close to them, had benefited from quota transfers.

Donald MacDonald had made the statement: "Some of us have given the minister considerable support in the passage of the Milk Act. The least we can expect is that he make sure his personal appointments on the milk board are not taking advantage of their positions. I understand that some of them and some of their friends have made special deals on milk quota. Has the minister looked into this obvious conflict of interest?"

At that point one government member interjected, "Oh, you've been talking to your friends in the farmers' union again."

Bill Stewart glanced across the floor. He had been getting a lot of pressure on milk - letters and telephone calls.

"The member from York South," replied Stewart, "is speaking in unfounded generalities again."

MacDonald, in his usual forceful way, responded, "The minister knows I want to see the milk plan work as much as he does, and I'm serious. Accusations are being made in the country that during the period March 22 to May 18, 1966, certain members of the milk board and their friends were involved in quota transfers which were beneficial to them. Will the minister treat the matter with the seriousness it deserves?"

Stewart answered sharply, "I will look into it and advise the house."

The minister of agriculture and food therefore requested a full explanation from the board and a list of all persons involved in quota transfers during the period under question. The board provided him with the list. Everyone was satisfied, as it turned out, and the whole matter ended up as just another example of some personal attacks that were being made without good reason on board members simply in an effort to weaken the board's effectiveness.

The board had enough difficulties to worry about without having people fabricate them. Transportation, for example, continued to be a nagging problem. A great many transporters, it seemed, were "free-wheeling souls." Some truckers were finding difficulty in understanding the new regulations.

The board had proposed to cancel the licence of a particular milk transporter, and so he indicated that he wished to appear before the board. He didn't show up at the appointed time, nor had he advised anyone of his plans beforehand. Thus, the board promptly canceled the order appointing him as an agent of the board. This meant his producers would be transferred or assigned to another transporter. The transporter in question then said that he had sold his business to another company and requested that the board assign the producers to that company. The board did this.

At about the same time, staff had received verbal information from a third party that he had purchased the business of the first transporter and wanted the producers assigned to him. The situation was that the original transporter's licence had been canceled by the board. His producers had been assigned to the second transporter. The original trucker had apparently sold his business to two different transporters.

After giving the sticky matter thought, the board's legal advisor expressed the opinion, "In this unorthodox situation the board has transferred the producers to trucker number two so they do have transportation for their milk. All other matters should be settled among the three parties involved, hopefully with the assistance of their lawyers."

The continuing subsidization of transportation by some processing plants was still a concern. Generally, transportation subsidies were used to maintain or increase a plant's supply of milk.

Grant Cameron, an eastern Ontario board field man and later a board member, stated, "We had a big subsidy program available either in the form of bonuses or subsidized transportation. What you saw in prices wasn't the real price. The Ontario processors were competing with Quebec. At that time, Ontario quality standards were higher than in Quebec, and this created some problems because if some milk was rejected in Ontario, there were plants in Quebec who would accept it. There was a lot of friction as a result."

Commenting in April 1990 on the same subject, Cameron emphasized, "That generation has changed, and now we have a very impressive young group of farmers along the border in Prescott and Glengarry counties. They're very successful and they can't be bothered with interprovincial matters. They are business oriented and they're doing a very good job."

A start was being made on the rationalization of transportation routes. The board had agreed not to oppose the use of compensation payments made by a receiving transporter to one that was losing shippers to him, providing this was solely a business arrangement between the transporters involved and that such compensation payments did not enter into the setting of remuneration for its transporter agents. The advisory committee on transportation, under the chairmanship of George McCague, was taking on new importance.

The Ottawa Transport Association was complaining about the formation of a co-operative trucking organization in that market. They wanted to appear before the board. Alvin Stewart, the board member from Richmond, advised, "We'll have to be careful because I think they're trying to get us to say whether or not we support co-op trucking. We're having discussions with the transportation committee."

Bill Schouten, who would later become a board member, had come to

Canada from Holland in 1952 and was in the process of building up an impressive dairy operation. He thought the producers were being overcharged for transportation. He decided to fight.

"Why the hell don't we start transporting our own milk?" Schouten asked.

Some of the producers had gone through an unfortunate experience with a feed co-op that had gone bankrupt. Their first reaction was, "It will be a flop."

"By golly, it can't flop," Schouten responded. "We are not buying and selling stuff; we are transporting it. You have to milk your cows. The milk has to be transported, and it can't flop!"

Existing transporters in the area dropped their charges by four cents. Schouten recalls, "It backfired. There were a lot of hard feelings. We got seventy-eight members and started to pick up milk in 1968."

Lorne Hurd reported that the Ottawa Valley Milk Transport Association wanted the board to take over the Ottawa market as a pilot project in connection with the proposed southern pool.

"I would recommend against this," he said, "and it's really only coming because of the anticipated activities of the new Carleton Co-operative Milk Transport."

The board decided that this was not a matter that could be dealt with at that time.

In northwestern Ontario, traditional feelings of isolation were continuing. Over the years many had said that the people of this region felt closer to Manitoba and Winnipeg than they did to eastern Ontario. This was understandable. The milk producers weren't any different from anyone else in that regard. They felt isolated, especially since they considered that they lacked representation on the milk board. Moreover, they believed their conditions were different from those of the rest of the province. They didn't think their problems were being adequately considered or even understood, particularly, they felt, without having a representative on the board.

Kenora and Fort Frances districts were requesting the formation of a new Region 13 for northwestern Ontario, to include Fort William, Port Arthur, Dryden, Kenora and Fort Frances. Distances in that neck of the woods were a problem, and it was a long way from Rainy River to Toronto.

"These producer leaders are very vocal," said Ken McKinnon, "and there's a great potential for more milk production, particularly in the Rainy

River area. They think they're not being heard down here. I was recently at a meeting of the Fort Frances producers. Milk sales are at a record high there, and they want to become part the northern Ontario pool. They report milk coming in from Manitoba, particularly through the Safeway stores, and this is creating excess milk for the producers in Dryden, Kenora and Fort Frances. They're not very happy."

Bernie Gallagher of Powassan, who joined the board in 1969 as a producer-elected member from northern Ontario, explained the situation in the region.

"I sense that it's sometimes very difficult to envision the expanse of the north. My responsibility as a board member stretches from the Quebec border on the east to the Manitoba border on the west. We also border on Michigan and Minnesota. A person traveling from Windsor to Montreal wouldn't cover the distance I have to cover. There are confined areas up there, and people are more conscious of what's happening within their community than perhaps in other areas. For example, several producers in the Fort Frances area transport their own milk. Since the board has come along, they're concerned, and this is being felt by the other producers, particularly since transportation has been a continuing problem in northwestern Ontario."

Lorne Hurd responded, "I think the board should be aware of everything that's happening in the north. Staff will be making a study of the whole system and the situation in northwestern Ontario almost immediately and will be reporting back to you."

Some of the smaller cheese factories in eastern Ontario were having difficulty paying the minimum regulated price for milk. They had grown up with a system wherein they contracted with a cheesemaker to make the cheese, sold the cheese on the cheese exchange, and after paying the cheesemaker, divided up what was left among the patrons of the factory. Far too often little or nothing was spent on the upkeep of the factory. Leland Wannamaker of Napanee used to say, "The plant's location depended upon how far a team of horses could carry the milk, and this meant they weren't too far apart. These small plants were a community unto themselves, and producers felt an allegiance to them. Their thoughts generally concerned the price of cheese on the exchange rather than the price of milk."

George McCague had met with the board. "Some of these cheese plants could have their licences revoked," he said, "because they're not financially capable of paying for the milk. There's really no way of knowing until the end of the season whether the gross money received by the patrons will be equal to or less than the minimum milk price. We'll certainly do everything possible to ensure that all cheese factories pay at least the minimum regulated price. But this problem may go away anyway, because a lot of these plants are fast disappearing. Aside from the demands of the changed marketing system, many can't meet the expenditures for improved sanitation."

"There are a lot of problems with the factories," Elphege Lefebvre admitted. "There's too much second grade cheese and we're getting more winter cheese all the time. These small factories can't get rid of the whey and waste. Some of the whey was in the ditches last summer and it stunk worse than any pigpen."

Glen Cole became annoyed: "The board has been trying to divert milk away from cheese factories and it hasn't been successful, and it has cost money. We asked the government to help finance the program and the answer was, 'Lower the price of cheese on the exchanges.' No hope for financial help was offered by government.

"I guess we have no choice, but I don't think the board should be taking the whole rap on cheese. We inherited a bad situation, and it just wasn't the whey in the ditches. The cheese industry has been mixed up with politics most of its existence. If the government can't help with the cheese milk diversion program, the least they can do is to carry out a study to see how improvements can be made. We should ask for this."

The board thought it was a good idea and asked staff to prepare possible terms of reference for a study so that it could be discussed with Bill Stewart.

Lorne Hurd advised, "The devaluation of the British pound and other U.K. market conditions are making it virtually impossible to sell any winter cheese in the U.K. market. If the milk diversion program isn't a success, there may be a real problem in selling the winter cheese produced. But there's still a decent demand in the U.K. for good cheddar and specialty products such as Black Diamond."

"Speaking of Black Diamond," interrupted Orvil Guy, "that reminds me of a story." Orvil was from Winchester, and his Irish background usually provided a story when the situation needed an amusing anecdote.

"Three years ago at the Ottawa Exhibition I was watching Mayor Charlotte Whitton visit the Ontario Department of Agriculture's exhibit of old cheese equipment, which was complete with an old wooden vat that was half full of curd.

"Ev Biggs was manning the exhibit because of the mayor's visit. She arrived and started telling everyone about her grandparents coming to Northumberland County in 1840. According to her, a cheese factory was put up in 1874 at Wellman's Corners in Hastings County. The plant was

Ev Biggs looks on as Charlotte Whitton, mayor of Ottawa, accidently samples a piece of cheese curd preserved with formaldehyde at the Department of Agriculture cheese exhibit at the Ottawa Centennial celebrations in 1964.

later renamed the Plum Grove factory, with her grandfather as manager. It went on to become the Black Diamond company of today.

"Anyway, at the exhibit Charlotte continued talking, and as she did, she grabbed a handful of curd from the vat and stuffed it in her mouth. She ate some but soon decided it didn't taste very good and spit it out. *The Ottawa Citizen* caught a good picture of it. Ev at last got the message through to her that the curd had been treated with formaldehyde to keep it from spoiling. The mayor, while still spitting out the curd, choked, "What? Are you trying to embalm me?"

The cheese milk diversion program and other matters related to cheese had been debated in the legislature during consideration of the estimates of the Department of Agriculture and Food on May 9, 1968. Murray Gaunt had posed a question for Bill Stewart: "There was a policy on the part of the board that they should divert milk in the winter to other plants. They could sell grass cheese, but not fodder cheese. This involved payments - I think they were called diversion payments. Were these payments taken from funds taken over from the cheese board? Were these funds actually used as diversion payments?"

The minister rose. "Diversion payments came out of collections made on all milk sold in Ontario," he replied. "The old cheese board bought cheese off the market and effectively established the cheese price for Canada. The price of the milk that went into that cheese was determined by what was left over after the cost of making the cheese was taken out. The milk board now establishes minimum prices for milk.

"The cheese manufacturer is caught in between. He doesn't have any room to play in, as he had before, and this is where the squeeze comes in."

With reference to producer ties to cheese plants, the minister glanced around at the members and said, "Now I ask you, which hat do you wear - as a cheese manufacturer or as a farmer owning a cheese factory through a joint stock company, and being a milk producer at the same time? Is it the hat of the cheese manufacturer caught in the admitted squeeze, or is it the hat of the farmer who is determined to have a minimum price for milk across the board everywhere in Ontario?"

The debate on the estimates continued, and it was rather hot in spots. Eddie Sargent accused the minister of losing the U.K. cheese market. Stewart had replied, "My honourable friend from Grey-Bruce doesn't know what he is talking about. Last year we shipped some 26 million pounds of cheese over there. Mr. McLaughlin is in England right now."

There were additional questions from others, including Bob Nixon. The minister advised that the milk board chairman would be appearing before the committee on agriculture June 18, but members continued their attempts to needle him about various matters, including possible close ties between the milk board and the government.

In a speech in Ottawa to the Ontario Dairy Processors' Council on January 30, 1968, Lorne Hurd explained the environment of the time.

"Everyone connected with the dairy industry is caught up in the challenge of change. We hope to have the group one pools fully operational by March 1. If pooling is going to work to the satisfaction of the majority of producers, it means the introduction of some fairly radical changes in respect to quotas. Quota has been set aside to raise the quotas of those producers with a minimum of 400 pounds a day. A free graduated entry program will start on September 1, 1968. Under the new policy, quotas will be freely negotiable between producers, subject to certain stipulated conditions. The policy is designed to allow all grade 'A' producers over time to share in the top price market on an equitable basis. Once pooling begins everyone will be treated exactly the same for payment purposes."

Lorne was speaking as the chief administrator given the task of implementing policy decided by his board. But there was still a great deal of restlessness in the country, some of it downright vicious antagonism.

Concerned noises were coming from certain milk committees. Not everyone wanted quota set aside to allow for the graduated entry program for new qualified producers. Significant numbers of fluid milk shippers were still objecting to giving up part of their market. Not everyone wanted the board to interfere with the level of quota. There was significant resentment by a number of producers about what many regarded as the very cavalier style of the milk board and certain of the staff.

In 1968 the media wrote, "The milk marketing board sticks to its Robin Hood role despite the producers' anger."

In a peri-urban area near Toronto that in a very few years would be overwhelmed by houses and streets, protests came from the Agincourt Milk Producers' Association. Kent producers were still demanding that they be left out of the group one pool. The Channel Islands producers had taken the board to the courts to challenge compulsory milk pooling; decisions were pending. The common denominator in all of these protests was the feeling that, "If certain producers were left alone and didn't have to be concerned with other producers, they would get a higher price for their milk."

Before the board's formation, a hobby farmer outside of Toronto sold all his milk at top price to a dairy that happened to have exclusive rights to sell milk in an apartment block the producer owned in the city. That neighbours could sell only part of their milk at top price didn't matter to him.

Bill MacPherson, director of finance for the board, was being quoted as saying, "The goal of the milk marketing board is to take away the preferred position the fluid producer has had for many years. There is no question that we are taking from the rich and giving to the poor. That's what we're here for."

The Agincourt milk producers didn't want any part of the milk pool. One of their leaders, Elliott Harrington, was quoted as saying it was "...nothing more than a socialist grab of the money paid to some producers so that other producers can get paid more for their milk. It is unbelievable in this day and age that a government would attempt to solve the problem of dairy farmers by arbitrarily taking money from the top group and giving it to the other farmers."

In eastern Ontario some writers referred to George McLaughlin, in reporting some of his free-swinging encounters, as "that banty rooster from Toronto." Others talked about the chairman and his "ruthless, statistics-loaded logic." McLaughlin could indeed be rough at meetings, and he usually gave back more than he was given! He and his board had emerged as a real presence on the milk scene.

The board members were conscious that they were walking a very slender tightrope separating needed market solutions and the several thousand milk producers clamoring for a place in the milk marketing sun. Bill Stewart was getting letters from irate producers. Pressures were being put on other cabinet ministers. The opponents of the milk marketing plan were recognizing that the board was gaining strength and that new policies were being planned and implemented. Opposition in the Toronto area was attempting to recruit support in other parts of the province.

The Agincourt milk producers met at the Bolton Golf Club on Monday, July 29, 1968. Alan Leishman, head of the group, was there along with the secretary, Elliott Harrington. Harrington reported that they now had 158 paid memberships. Ironically, they had been asking the milk board to deduct three cents per hundredweight to finance their organization. They were talking in terms of an overall membership of a possible 450.

R.J. Stewart of Bolton, and a Becker shipper, reported, "Our organization is having success in Essex and Kent counties, and I've recently received inquiries from interested producers in Ottawa, Bruce, Glengarry and Fort William. A branch has actually been formed in Essex and Kent."

R.J. Stewart was personally bitterly opposed to the milk marketing board, but was a topnotch milk producer and Holstein breeder. He had an unusual talent for spotting top cattle.

A Kent County spokesman reported on the discontent of their producers, claiming, "Quotas have been cut to allow industrial producers to come into the pool."

Robert Lowe, then president of the Becker Milk Company, was there. He was supporting the association and taking exception to the board's policies and marketing legislation of the government. He agreed fluid and industrial producers should not be merged.

The Honourable Matthew Dymond, Ontario minister of health, was also present. He bluntly stated, "The Milk Act was introduced by the Robarts government in the interests of all milk producers in the province. Present and past problems have resulted from inequality of treatment given milk producers. The government decided this had gone on long enough. Bill Stewart, as the responsible minister, took action. He has the complete backing of the government."

Dymond continued his tough stance.

"I won't accept Mr. Lowe's statements regarding the Ontario legislation," he said. "I question his motives. This is not the time or the place, but if Mr. Lowe wants a debate on some of his uninformed and biased opinions, I'll be only too glad to oblige him at any time he suggests. In the meantime, there might be merit, in my opinion, if he allowed Ontario milk producers to decide what is best for them, given our Ontario situation and marketing conditions."

This meeting and the events and activities that took place around this time were possibly the greatest test of the board's mettle and perseverance that it had experienced since its formation. The opposition was coming from several of the well established and successful milk producers. Although they were speaking with a logic that some considered selfish, it was based on the financial well-being of their own farm enterprises and from this perspective could be understood.

The Agincourt milk producers had earlier made a submission to the milk commission, maintaining, "It is to the advantage of producers everywhere in Ontario to organize outside of the framework of the milk committees, and we should receive the cooperation of the board with such organization. Anything else would be an infringement on rights and privileges of people."

In their submission to the milk commission they took exception to the quota policies: "The present approach has a punitive effect upon the largest, fastest growing and best equipped producers. Ambitious and progressive shippers are discouraged and frustrated by the loss of business."

Ken McKinnon had been at the Bolton meeting. He defended the board's policies but found no support from his listeners.

"The intent of the Milk Act," McKinnon explained, "is to provide fair and equitable treatment for all milk producers in Ontario. This means that the industrial milk producers must be allowed to participate in the graduated entry program. When this program is completed there will be a stronger and healthier marketing organization. These changes must take place. Meetings like this one have been going on for years with accusations and tempers flaring. Unless some order is introduced, there's going to be breakdown and chaos in the whole marketing structure. We can only ask for your understanding and at the same time express extreme concerns as to what will happen if producers remain pitted against each other with no flexibility of thought."

McKinnon sat down to unfriendly stares and an almost complete absence of applause.

He wasn't happy; in fact, he was downright worried. The organization of the group one pool was well under way, and any backing up or a successful road block could result in a complete disaster. As he was getting into his car, Matt Dymond came over to say something.

"Ken, this is a very political situation. I've been around politics for quite a while, and I can tell you that the opposition squeals the loudest when they think they're losing. You're winning, and the Ontario government is backing you right to the hilt."

Needless to say, McKinnon started to feel better.

The Agincourt organization was moving frantically to build opposition against the board. The active nucleus was mainly among the Becker shippers. In remembering his first year on the board, Grant Smith recalls that following the Bolton meeting there was another meeting at Wellandport, "...to raise hell with the milk board. They were criticizing Bill Stewart unmercifully. George McLaughlin kept taking notes and was getting primed to get up and really take a strip off everybody. The Honourable Bob Welch was on the platform. He got up at last and spoke very effectively, outlining the government's policy as far as milk marketing was concerned.

"Welch also quite bluntly stated that there was no way that he would accept anyone's criticizing his colleague, Bill Stewart, when he wasn't there to defend himself. That effectively ended the meeting. Welch really cooled down the meeting fast. George never did get on his feet. The crowd went home a whole lot quieter than when they had started out."

The year 1967 had seen the creation of thirteen regions, each of which would elect a member to the board. The elections at this time were based upon the electoral-college system, wherein a specific number of producers have the right to elect a member to an election committee, which in turn would select a board member. The 1967 board elections had brought in Grant Smith of Burgessville, Ray McDougall of Glanworth, and Harold Scott of Stratford. The 1968 elections brought in Ellard Powers of Beachburg and Francis Redelmeier of Maple. Bernie Gallagher from Powassan joined the board with the 1969 elections as the north's representative.

George McLaughlin liked the election system that involved a small group of elected people either selecting or electing the new board members. When it was later changed by OMAF it resulted in a very serious difference of opinion between Bill Stewart and McLaughlin. There was great political sensitivity at the time to ensure that board members truly represented producers, because the minister had selected the first board.

McLaughlin recalls, "We favoured the election committee system wherein producers elected a committee in each region. They, in turn, selected a member to represent the region on the board. I insisted that this was a democratic process, but Bill Stewart insisted on everyone in the region having the right to vote using a mail ballot. We had quite an argument."

On March 11, 1968, Frank Stenger of Enniskillen, president of the Channel Islands Milk Producers and a Jersey breeder, reported, "This has been a crucial year for our existence. We have continually asked for a separate pool. There had been voluntary deductions of more than a million dollars spent on developing markets and trademark products. The milk board has turned it all down."

They again appealed to the board, and when they were turned down, they appealed to the milk commission. No one, it seemed, sympathized with them. Their case was dismissed even by the Supreme Court of Ontario. They were frustrated by the Appeal Court, and on May 2, 1969, were advised their application to the Supreme Court of Canada had been denied.

Now they were furious. George McLaughlin had alleged, before the Standing Committee on Agriculture and Food of the Ontario legislature, that certain distributors were guilty of irregularities and improper practices in the sale of Channel Islands milk and in the payment of Channel Islands producers. They were appealing to the minister. They asked to meet the provincial Tory caucus.

Harold Crang, owner of Glenville Farms and Glenville Dairy in Newmarket, was a very successful Bay Street stockbroker and a Guernsey breeder. He complained, "I approached the minister, the deputy minister, and the chairman of the milk commission. They made agreeable noises, but they've taken no action."

The Channel Islands executive debated whether or not to make another approach to Bill Stewart, but decided it would be a waste of time and they had better bypass the minister and contact Premier Robarts directly. Alan Eagleson, of future hockey fame, helped them contact the premier. While sympathetic, Robarts chose not to interfere in Bill Stewart's administration.

George McLaughlin had made a presentation on February 11, 1969, to the Standing Committee on Agriculture and Food. His patience was at an end. His presentation regarding the sale of Channel Islands milk by distributors was ruthless and presented in a positive and conclusive way.

"Our records establish that the total volume of milk sold by dairies under the Channel Islands labels has exceeded the volume of Channel Islands milk delivered to such dairies. There just isn't sufficient Channel Islands milk to satisfy the volume being sold by dairies under Channel Islands labels. Payments to Channel Islands producers by some processors have no relationship to the utilization of Channel Islands milk by that processor.

"Records indicate instances where Channel Islands producers receive special prices from some plants where their milk was mixed in the same tank truck as milk from neighbours who produced standard milk. The records in our files were not set up specifically to reflect these conditions. They came to light as incidental parts of information gathered to establish the group one pool. A separate pool for Channel Islands milk would not simply be a matter of carrying into such a pool the discriminatory practices that accompanied Channel Islands milk marketing prior to March 1, 1968, but also producers would be required to maintain only pure Channel Islands herds.

"Sampling, handling and testing would have to be separate. Transporters would be required to maintain separate compartments on their trucks. Plants would be required to set aside separate storage facilities. Accounting would have to be set up on a basis that could be audited to satisfy the board as to the milk utilization. All extra costs, such as transportation, sampling, testing and accounting, and inspections created by the operation of a separate Channel Islands pool would have to be billed against the Channel Islands pool. Anything else would be unfair.

"Our studies, such as that done by Hennessey on Channel Islands milk, indicate that major consumer demand for two-percent milk is not associated with a particular breed of cow. There may be a hardship on some breeders of Channel Islands cattle, as well as producers who have enjoyed highly favourable individual market circumstances, but there is no justification for the segregation of milk from such cattle."

The Channel Islands producers had been frustrated at every turn. They'd taken their problems to the highest court in the land. They had met with the premier of Ontario. There was no support for what they considered were their rights in an attempt to market their specialty milks. They were losing their enthusiasm.

The northern Ontario pilot pool had been based on voluntary agreements between the board and distributors and between the board and transporters. This approach had worked well in the north, and it had been hoped that similar agreements could be arranged for the entire province. This was not to be.

There had been numerous meetings of the board with transporters, distributors and processors. At last George McLaughlin advised the board at a meeting in October, 1967, "There just isn't a hope of these things coming together voluntarily. Our target date for the inauguration of the southern group one pool is less than six months away. March 1 is sliding around pretty fast. We've no choice but to set it up by regulation, and maybe that'll be the best in the long run. We can spell out exactly what we want."

Lorne Hurd reported, "Bill MacPherson tells us that there are two large holdouts for a voluntary system. One is Dominion Dairies, and the other is Becker's. Apparently lawyers are advising them against accepting a voluntary payment program, and they don't want to conform until regulations are actually passed."

"What about the producers?" asked Orvil Guy. "I hear they're not all registered yet."

Lorne Hurd advised, "As of October 6 there were 193 fluid producers who had not yet made application for the licence to produce milk. They've all been notified in writing, and none have indicated they haven't signed because of religious beliefs. We've been keeping on top of it."

Grant Smith from Burgessville, who was just completing his first year on the board, was already showing indications that he liked to keep things moving.

"The board has been able to keep the pressure on, and I think that's essential," he said. "If we slacken or show any indecision, we'll be in trouble. The pressure on the Ontario politicians has been pretty rough, and the whole situation makes me a little nervous. Let's clean up these producers who aren't registered as quickly and as fairly as possible. Above all, let's be positive. They should all be advised by registered mail that no quota will be issued to an unlicensed producer, and no producer who has not been allotted a quota by the board will be permitted to enter the group one pool. All milk not sold through the group one pool will be paid for at the industrial milk price."

The board agreed and staff were asked to move immediately to send out the registered letters.

The target date of March 1, 1968, for the start of the group one pool, was fast approaching. It would be a historic event. There were still worries that pooling would result in quota reductions.

Haldimand County milk committee requested the board to: "...amend its proposed Group I policy so that no reduction of the quota allotment should be made to provide quota entry of new producers."

They were advised that the matter had been carefully and thoroughly studied and that there must be provision for the entry of qualified industrial producers into the group one pool.

Much planning had gone into the preparations for the group one pool. It had been discussed at the January 1967 annual meeting as well as at the Geneva Park conference in October of that year.

The board had started to take fluid milk producers into the central payment system on October 1, 1967, and when the pool was implemented on March 1, 1968, more than seventy-five percent of the parties involved were on the system. The board was selling milk to some 230 fluid processors and had arranged with 290 transporters for the transportation. As of the same date, the transporters of grade "A" milk were appointed agents of the board.

The pool quota order was published in *The Ontario Milk Producer* in March 1968; it detailed the individual quotas of more than 8,000 grade "A" producers along with the personal licence number of each producer. Subject to certain conditions, the quotas were completely negotiable.

Quotas were based on a nine-month period during 1965-66, indicating the producers' historical production. Everyone within the pool was to be treated exactly the same for payment purposes.

It was not an easy task for the board and its staff. The allocations initially made resulted in about 1,750 appeals. This was about twenty-two percent of the total allotted. The average group one quota was less than 600 pounds, but there were three producers with quotas well over 6,000 pounds a day. Producers were listed under the southern pool, the northern pool, Muskoka-Parry Sound, Thunder Bay, and Kenora-Rainy River.

The March 1968 issue of *The Ontario Milk Producer* indicated producer prices for fluid milk were $6.15 per hundredweight in the south and $6.72 in the north, with secondary milk at $3.54 in both areas. The total deductible licence fees from the fluid milk cheques for all producers amounted to 8-3/4 cents per hundredweight.

An interesting advertisement appeared in the March 1968 issue of *The Milk Producer* under the name of Allen Clark of R.R. 3, Kingsville, advertising 1,520 pounds of group one quota for sale at $5.00 per pound.

A major milestone had been reached. By March 1, 1968, all grade "A" milk purchased by the distributors in Ontario was purchased from the board under the board's direction. The transporters were now the agents of the board and under rationalization scrutiny. Group one milk was being cooled in bulk tanks, and producers were giving consideration to expansion or leaving the industry.

The pressure of change was also being felt by milk distributors. The milk commission wiped out the boundaries of the 170-plus distribution areas in the province and created ten new ones.

Distributors were cringing under merchandising and volume pressures. They were forced to consider franchising, selling out, or expansion. The milk distribution industry in Ontario was becoming very dynamic for the first time in its history.

The milk board's declared policy was designed to allow all grade "A" milk producers over time to share in the top price market on an equitable basis. This meant the development and start of the graduated entry program.

George McLaughlin has since said, "We needed a wedge, and graduated entry was the wedge that separated out the real threat of unmanageable disorder and created one the board could handle administratively. It was like a 'cattle squeeze.' Producers could enter only with the right quality of milk and with the right farm premises. The amount of new milk coming into the pool was under relative control. The number of producers who could come in at any time was also controlled.

The board had agreed that the evolution of the group one pool had to be an orderly process.

But Ken McKinnon said, "I can't forget the many meetings I've had in Mitchell and in other places. I know just how impatient these people are. We must also remember the influence of the Becker shippers and their 90/10. It's going to be a delicate balance. We have to keep the producers coming in, and we can't let the percentage at top price get too low either."

During that period McKinnon and Orvil Guy played a very effective and essential role in helping to curb the impatience of some of the concentrated milk producers.

Harold Scott, the board member from the Stratford area, suggested, "We can't forget all those fluid milk shippers who got a lot of surplus over the years. I think the majority of people out there will give us their support as long as they see that we're moving in the right direction."

The graduated entry program went into effect September 1, 1968, and 472 new producers entered the southern pool. Lorne Hurd recalls, "We had to take the proposed graduated entry plan across the province three times for discussion at committee level."

George McLaughlin emphasizes, "It was a key to a lot of things, and I give staff the credit for coming up with the basic idea. We'd said, 'Why don't you sit down and work things out and see what you can come up with, and let us have a look at it.'

"They came back to the board and said, 'There should be some sort of graduated way to bring the industrial people in.'

"They weren't very specific," McLaughlin recalls, "but there was a germ of an idea, and after discussion between the board and staff, the graduated entry program was developed. The board believed that if we had it over a period of five years, or four years plus one day, we could give the new entrants one-fifth of the basic production each year.

"The producer could go out and buy other quota if he wished. It was decided that the graduated entry program would be open to new entrants on September 1 each year."

Co-operatives quickly emerged as a challenge. It was difficult to deal with because it involved a philosophy and certain principles that had been embraced by many people for many years in several jurisdictions. With some, it was almost a religion.

There were some co-ops in the processed milk industry. This included the United Dairy and Poultry Co-operative, the New Dundee Co-operative and Villa Nova. Their patrons were very loyal and proud of their successes. But some were also feeling significant financial pressures.

There was increasing interest in the co-operative transportation of farmers' milk. Brampton area farmers had formed the Dairyland Co-op. John A. MacLeod of Owen Sound remembers the North Grey Milk Transport Co-operative.

"I became manager in June 1963 and continued until they finally disbanded in 1975," said MacLeod. "We were really more than a transport co-op, and in 1962 we became a marketing agency for Crystal Dairy Shippers, and in 1963 for the Wiarton Dairy Shippers. We were very successful in selling the surplus summer milk to the resort area dairies and also helped in times of fall milk shortages."

Fortunately for the board, the dairy processing co-ops in Ontario had not gained the strength enjoyed by the movement in Quebec.

The Department of Agriculture and Food had changed its name in 1966 to recognize food as an important responsibility of the ministry and, as well, had formed a co-operatives branch under the directorship of Ed O'Meara. O'Meara was steeped in co-op philosophy. His early training had been under Father Cody at St. Francis Xavier University, regarded by many as the father of the co-operative movement, particularly in eastern Canada. Department officials had been encouraging the development of co-operative trucking.

In the meantime, the board was busy giving attention to the rationalization of transportation, and they intended to direct milk to the markets bringing the best price. Farmers involved in the co-op movement were asking, "How will we receive our patronage dividends if our milk is directed to another plant or we ship it with another trucker?"

In a speech in the Hanover Coliseum on January 10, 1969, Lorne Hurd summed up the situation facing the board: "The board is participating in discussions as members of a committee set up by the Dairy Farmers of Canada to study the whole question. There is no way co-operatives can operate in the traditional sense when the board uses its powers to direct milk to plants, assigns producers to particular transporters, and all, in a way, designed to maximize producer returns. The board in fact places itself between the co-ops and at least some of its farmer members, thus interfering with the ability of the co-op to share its income equitably among its members on a patronage dividend basis.

"The board does not have as an objective the elimination of producer-owned facilities," continued Hurd. "It really becomes a matter of change in the manner of ownership. The board is willing to assist in this transition and will cooperate with producers owning such facilities."

Transport co-ops were becoming very concerned about their future. At the Geneva Park conference in 1968, David Armstrong of Brampton had made what he considered a compromise proposal. He argued, "The OMMB should always recognize the right of individual shippers within a rationalized route to handle their own milk co-operatively. I suggest when at least seventy-five percent of the shippers on a rationalized route have tried to haul their milk co-operatively, they should be allowed to do so. Where an organized co-op offers to buy the business and equipment of a private trucker that's for sale, and the co-op offers a reasonable price, the OMMB should appoint the co-op as the agent to haul milk on that route."

The board had agreed to consider the proposal, but some thought it was too arbitrary and likely fell beyond the powers of the board.

In the meantime, the rationalization of transportation had resulted in seventeen producers being assigned away from the Carleton Co-op Transport. An equal number, with approximately the same volume, had been transferred to them. This meant the co-op was being asked to transport milk produced by non-members and to cease transporting production of seventeen of its own members. The co-op was protesting and appealing the decision to the board.

The board pointed out, "We have the responsibility to all producers in Ontario to rationalize transportation in order to have the most efficient transportation possible. We're not saying producers can't be members of a co-op; we're saying how milk is to be transported."

The board dismissed the appeal.

While the creation of the group one pools was a priority and received a great deal of the board's attention, the marketing of industrial milk was also given early thought as far back as the fall of 1966. The Geneva Park conference of 1967 and the 1968 annual meeting of the board discussed the possibility of industrial milk being sold by auction. This had been one of professor Ralph Campbell's recommendations. There wasn't much enthusiasm for the auction sale of milk, but there was widespread support for the board's takeover of the marketing of industrial milk. An alternative proposal of a plant supply quota policy was accepted. It involved each plant's being assigned a quota based on available supplies and the plant's historical utilization of industrial milk.

The board had determined as an early objective that milk would be sold, to the greatest degree possible, for utilization that would bring the greatest financial return to the farmers. This wasn't easy because every plant, including the cheddar cheese plants, wanted what they considered to be adequate supplies of milk for their individual purposes.

The majority of board members were adamant: "That's our objective, and we have to stick to it," was the consensus.

Allen Ketcheson argued, "I come from Central Ontario. Agriculture there has been built on the cheese industry. Over the years we've taken a lot of milk from the fluid milk industry. As we've said before, every cheese factory is its own rural community. This isn't going to change too quickly. We'd better make sure we give serious thought to what happens to some of these small cheese plants, or I can tell you we'll be in trouble."

Under the proposed policy, plant quotas were to be transferrable in whole or in part between plants within specified geographic regions. They would be negotiable. This would permit adjustments and rationalization in the processing sector.

Certain processors were expressing concerns that the board would experience difficulty in achieving a fair distribution of available milk. Grumblings were starting. Cheddar cheese plants were contacting their local members of the Ontario legislature. Some cheese plants had difficulty paying the regulated price to their patrons. They could see some of their milk supply disappearing. There were storm clouds ahead on the horizon.

Harry Parker arrived at the board in June 1969 and later became secretary. He had been on the staff of the English board for eleven years. Parker remembers, "I had prepared some material for our guests from Ontario that initially piqued my interest in what was taking place in Ontario. It struck me that it would be a nice challenge to get in at the ground floor.

"Unlike some organizations, the secretary of the OMMB reports through the chairman to the board. Coming from the English board, I sensed that everybody seemed to be in a big hurry here. It often concerned me they would overlook some important factor and make a big mistake. I don't think that type of error actually happened."

Harry Parker looks and acts like the secretary of a board. He doesn't waste words, and they come clearly and deliberately. He gives the impression he is always very much aware that the position could be sensitive in between the administrative organization and the board. The secretary reports to the board.

"In terms of advantages, I think the board can be assured as far as possible that they have an independent person sitting as secretary, one who reports honestly and accurately on their decisions and records them as such in the minutes."

The third annual meeting of the Ontario Milk Producers' Marketing Board had as its theme, "The Challenge of Change." Change was coming, and coming about rapidly. The group one pool had started on March 1, 1968, and by September 1, 1969, there had been a decrease of 1,116 of the original producers in the pool.

There was almost an equal number of graduated entry producers.

The average size of quota was increasing, and by September 1969 it was 842 pounds for the non-graduated entry producers.

Quebec was aggressively modernizing its industrial milk industry, and now more than half of the industrial milk producers had bulk tank installations compared with one-quarter in Ontario. Quebec was now the nation's number one producer of dairy products. There had been significant financial assistance by the Quebec government to producers and the dairy processing co-ops.

The board was ending its year of "Challenge of Change" with a relatively firm policy on group one price pools involving some 8,000 producers, 270 processors, 350 transporters and an area 1,200 miles wide and 600 miles deep, serving a population of over seven million. The board had hoped to be as close as possible to a 90 percent top price payment in the group one pools. They had achieved a fraction of a point shy of 87 percent, which was a tremendous accomplishment.

The graduated entry program had provided the key by which all qualified industrial producers could enter the group one pool. Negotiable fluid quotas allowed producers to plan their operation. Classified pricing allowed milk to go to those products that generally brought higher returns.

The Challenge of Achievement

Administrative procedures and the marketing methods now allowed the board to have a firm data base for improved marketing, research and the development of policies. The direction of milk supplies by the board had saved the producers virtually hundreds of thousands of dollars. The rationalization of transportation was already creating visible efficiencies. Producers were no longer dependent on processors for their future or for their livelihood. The protection fund for milk and cream producers, under provincial legislation, protected all producers against plant failures.

The board was now elected by producers and was answerable to them. The perceived stigma of government appointment was no longer present. The establishment of the group one pool was history. The start of the group two pool was on the immediate horizon. A capable staff, under an unusually competent general manager, was in place.

On the threshold of the 1970s, everyone was anticipating with enthusiasm and determination the challenges that lay ahead. The dairy industry realized that the board was now established, and its presence was indeed making an impact.

CHAPTER FIVE

Authority Tested

In which the board

- Introduces MSQ in Ontario
- Brings in the group two pool
- Imposes the plant supply quota policy
- Faces a potential vote of producers
- Deals with undesirable quota sales
- Consider a study they label "a witch hunt"
- Withstands the test of the courts
- Weathers OFU picketing at Ingleside
- Considers northwestern Ontario restlessness
- Deals with water shenanigans
- Remains inflexible in application of policies

The start of the group two pool on April 1, 1970, was most significant. The board had become the sole buyer of all milk marketed in Ontario and the only source of supply for Ontario processors. At the same time, milk transporters became board agents, and transportation of all milk from farms to plants came under board control. More of the board's attention was now directed to the national and international milk marketing situations.

It had been a little more than five years since the board's inception, and much had been accomplished in that short time. A competent staff had been put in place under general manager Lorne Hurd. Under the chairmanship of George McLaughlin the board had been decisively aggressive in making its presence felt since that landmark meeting on November 1, 1965. They were now planning for the 1970s and moving resolutely forward.

The national dairy policy had been announced for the 1970-71 dairy year. The board was disappointed. It had moved quickly to convey its concerns to the federal government through the Dairy Farmers of Canada and directly to the federal minister of agriculture and the chairman of the Canadian Dairy Commission.

They were upset because there was no announcement regarding the start of a market sharing quota system. This had been a major issue at the annual meeting of the Dairy Farmers of Canada in January 1970. Quebec shared Ontario's support for the proposed program. Other provinces had thought that they needed more time to study the implications of the proposal.

The board was dedicated to the philosophy of supply management. They had carried their arguments and logic to the annual meeting of the Dairy Farmers of Canada in Vancouver in January 1970. Glen Cole had presented some of the arguments with such vigor and enthusiasm that his singleness of purpose almost got him into trouble. Grant Smith reported later, "Glen Cole was so taken up with the importance of the issue that he threatened to take anyone on who didn't agree with the principle of supply management."

The OMMB recognized that a market sharing quota system for industrial milk would be the integral and critical foundation of milk marketing in Ontario and in Canada as a whole.

Convinced of the importance of the policy, the board was not prepared to wait. They immediately proceeded to develop a system of market share quotas (MSQ) for Ontario. This was carried out in cooperation with the Canadian Dairy Commission and producer leaders from Quebec. The board was convinced that it was urgent to start such a program, because it had become very clear that the government of Canada did not propose to increase producers' returns for industrial milk until producers themselves initiated a program to curtail the overall surplus of milk in Canada.

Fluid milk producers had lived with a quota system and a form of supply management for many years, albeit haphazardly in some cases. Industrial producers had not experienced that system. Traditionally there had been uncoordinated processor demands encouraging industrial milk production and the resultant unmanageable surpluses of milk products. These had been a continuing problem not only for producer prices but also for the federal government, which had attempted to store the surplus products and dispose of them at significant losses on the international markets. In some cases, they gave them away.

To suggest that milk production should be cut back to the extent that it would avoid surpluses was a dollar and cents issue with the processors. Producers had concerns as well. They had been used to producing milk, without any control, for industrial purposes. Year after year, they had listened to Don Goodwillie of the dairy administration in Ottawa, who was a regular speaker at their annual meetings, give the usually bad news about skim milk powder and butter surpluses, and they had gone home thinking that this was a situation beyond their control, which it was. But now, in 1970, there was a new and determined player on the stage - the Ontario Milk Marketing Board.

The initial objectives of the Ontario program were to gradually bring the production of industrial milk into line with the domestic market demand and allow adjustments by producers in a fair and equitable manner. Producers who were creating a surplus would either curtail their production or bear the cost of disposing of it.

After much discussion and negotiation with the CDC and a developed understanding with the county and district milk committees, MSQ was to be introduced in both Ontario and Quebec on December 1, 1970.

There was an almost unanimous conclusion that without a means of tailoring milk supplies to the requirements of the domestic market, the possibilities of obtaining adequate producer prices for industrial milk were virtually nonexistent. MSQ meant that individual producers would share equitably in the available market for industrial milk.

In Ontario, subject to OMMB approval this quota would be freely negotiable. At this time there were approximately 14,000 industrial milk producers in the province.

The board had pursued the implementation of the MSQ policy without wavering. They had worked closely with the Canadian Dairy Commission. There were concerns in OMAF, however, that the policy would come into effect and levies would be imposed on Ontario producers before the policy's being put in place in Quebec.

The milk commission had resisted approving the extension of powers under the federal marketing legislation. This extension of powers was necessary for the board's implementation of MSQ. As well, there was some reaction to the pressures coming from others relative to the activities of the milk board, which appeared to concern the commission.

The commission had worked with the board in the establishment of six classes of milk for the purposes for sale to distributors and processors. This didn't make every plant happy from the standpoint of available milk supplies, but the board was adamant in supplying milk to those classes that brought the highest return to producers.

Matters were getting testy. The commission met with the board and expressed deep concern over reports that some plants in Ontario were close to having their maximum quota allotment within the first four months of the dairy year. The commission wanted information. The commission demanded a complete up-to-date list of all plants in Ontario and their quota and the percentage of milk received against the quota allocated. At the same time, George McLaughlin had been advised, "The commission is reserving its decision on the board's request for an extension of powers for the marketing of industrial milk under the proposed MSQ."

After discussion within the board, the chairman agreed to write to the milk commission, stating in urgent terms the problems that would exist if the extension of powers were not granted.

In a meeting between the commission and the board it emerged that the commission was most reluctant to have the board move into a system of MSQ with producer levies prior to a similar program's being effective in Quebec. There seemed to be a sincere fear on the part of the milk commission that the dairy industry in Ontario would be jeopardized unless Ontario and Quebec acted in concert in initiating the proposed MSQ program.

The board restated its established position that no levies would be imposed on Ontario producers unless they were also imposed on Quebec producers. The board was most anxious that the situation be clarified immediately, regardless of when the levies would be made, so that Ontario producers would be able to make the production management adjustments necessary to allow for a smooth transition into the program.

The board emphasized, "The program has been widely publicized. Producers are expecting to start December 1. They are anxiously waiting."

Eventually agreement was reached between the two bodies that the board would issue a levy order effective December 1, 1970, and that if Quebec did not make similar levies on the industrial producers in Quebec, the board would withdraw the order.

The board had started to plan for an industrial milk pool in 1968. They were faced with real problems, particularly in eastern Ontario. There were a large number of small community cheese factories. There were many thousands of producers who didn't really have much knowledge of the overall dairy industry situation and what was happening. There was little knowledge of prices and pricing systems. Thousands of producers were still shipping milk in cans. A large proportion of industrial milk shippers were on so-called mixed farms and generally producing anything that would sell. Many of the producers were living close to what could be considered by some standards as the poverty line.

In eastern Ontario the expression "poor but proud" was not an uncommon description of one's particular state.

Industrial milk marketing, especially in eastern Ontario, in many ways presented a confused picture. There were all sorts of deals and practices floating around. Some cheese plants had difficulty making payments to their producers. Another plant, having problems with an inadequate milk supply, was providing free transportation.

Sarsfield O'Connor, a long-term employee of the board, with most of his time spent in eastern Ontario, recalls, "And there were a lot of shenanigans with the big operators wheeling and dealing in subsidies on transportation. Some plants were even paying twenty cents a hundredweight for bulk milk on top of the subsidized transportation. There sure were a lot of shenanigans by the plants, such as frigging around with the butterfat tests."

In the development of the proposed industrial milk pool the board had held many discussions with the processors and with the milk commission. Contact had been maintained with Quebec and with the Canadian Dairy Commission. There were real concerns on the part of the processors that the board would not be able to manage milk supplies in a fair and equitable manner. Each plant had to look to its own balance sheet and had very personal concerns.

The board had hoped to bring in the group two pool by agreement. This was not possible, however, and because of the pressure of time, and recognizing that there would likely never be an agreement, the pool was brought in by regulation on April 1, 1970.

One month later, the plant supply quota policy came into effect. Every plant processing industrial milk into cheddar cheese, butter and powder and condensed milks was allotted a plant supply quota based on the amount of milk handled in the year-long period between the first of March 1968 and the end of February 1969.

The program got off to a bad start. Milk production was down and a lot of plants were making specialty cheese. Cheddar cheese plants, short of milk, were complaining bitterly to the provincial politicians. The board had benefited from the experience from the group one pools. But even with that basic knowledge the group two pool was a tremendous undertaking.

There were half again as many producers as in the group one pool. All of these had to be accurately recorded. All of the plants and all of the transporters had to be intricately fed into the system. Many plants were rebellious. Producers were upset. The transportation subsidies that many had received to encourage milk shipment to a particular plant suddenly disappeared. Plants were pleading, "Give us the milk we're entitled to, and forget about the subsidies. We're not paying them anymore."

Many transporters had difficulty understanding the system. Reports required of transporters had to be uncomplicated. All the milk collection reports were prepared in Toronto with the names of the milk shippers and other information required printed on them. After they had been completed by the trucker, they were collected and sent back to Toronto and fed into the computers. The whole exercise, of course, would have been impossible done on a manual basis.

The economic importance of the dairy industry to Quebec had been readily recognized by the government of that province. With generous subsidies they encouraged plant modernization, particularly with the Granby Co-operative. Grants were made to Quebec farmers to improve their dairy herds. They came to Ontario and not only bought cows but also industrial quota. There were decreases in the milk supply available to Ontario plants and this created problems for the plant supply quota system.

One of the basic objectives of the board was to increase the financial returns to milk producers. This also had an impact on certain processing plants. It involved two key elements of the industrial milk marketing plan - classified pricing and plant supply quotas. The board did recognize, however, that it had a moral and legal obligation to supply processing plants, if at all possible, with the milk they required. This, of course, had to be done within the available supplies and on a classified pricing basis.

This system gave priority to milk going into products that realized the highest return in the marketplace. The milk remaining was allocated to plants under the plant supply quota policy. This meant that plants such as cheddar cheese factories were not receiving the quantity of milk that some of them wanted. They were not happy.

The MSQ was designed with the basic purpose of satisfying Canada's needs for butterfat. The Canadian Dairy Commission carried the responsibility of disposing of any surpluses, primarily that of skim powder.

The Canadian Dairy Commission established two levies on industrial milk production. The basic or within-quota levy was paid by producers to carry the cost of exports resulting from the processing of quota milk. Milk produced over the quota was charged at a significantly higher levy, or an over-quota levy, which was intended to discourage surplus milk production as well as pay for the cost of selling whole milk products on the export market. At the beginning of the MSQ program these levies were established at twenty-six cents for within-quota, and $2.40 per hundredweight for over-quota. The Canadian Dairy Commission, of course, had established support prices by means of an offer-to-purchase program for milk products which enabled the board to establish prices for the various classes of milk purchased by processors.

The other provinces had given much study to the MSQ program;

Alberta, Saskatchewan and Manitoba joined with Quebec, Ontario and Prince Edward Island to become what was now looked upon as a "national milk marketing plan." It was a novel and workable undertaking. It was proclaimed "the first of its kind in the world."

But there were still many critics in the industry. The program was being regarded suspiciously and with concern by certain people in government and by some economists. Pressures increased on Bill Stewart, as minister of agriculture and food, to organize a vote of the producers on the Ontario milk marketing plan. Stewart, however, had never said that there would not be a vote at some time. His earlier attitudes had been based on the fact that the confused state of the industry would not allow informed conclusions to be made by milk producers.

Tory members were saying, "Let's have a vote and we'll take the pressure off the government. Let the producers make the decision."

But Stewart resisted once again and put his trust in the common-sense leadership of the OMMB. He had recognized, from a very practical standpoint, that any weakness of purpose shown in the early 1970s in Ontario would have resulted in situations hard to envisage and, because of the importance of the province and the seriousness of the entire milk picture, would likely have had impact on Quebec and other provinces.

Bill Stewart was far from happy, however. Some of his early concerns about the anticipated resolute and unbending leadership of George McLaughlin had now materialized on his desk. This was not going to be easy.

The deputy minister of agriculture at the time, Gord Bennett, recalled with a grin, "We were kept busy drafting replies to letters from people who wanted to get McLaughlin fired."

The OFU was calling for Bill Stewart's and my resignation too, as was clearly illustrated in a cartoon displayed in the *Ontario Union Farmer* of July 1969, showing Stewart and me being tossed overboard from "the Good Ship OFU."

A former board member recalls: "George was very adamant in his views at meetings. Sometimes a producer would ask a question and the answer come from George so quickly, the producer would be embarrassed and wonder, 'Why did I ask such a silly question?' They respected George for his abilities, but some thought he was too fast with his answers." (McLaughlin's apparently well-known retort often was, "You may be right, but I don't agree with you.")

Bernie Gallagher, however, was perceptive enough to have another perspective: "George could be flexible. He was firm in his position, and usually he was right."

On July 8, 1971, Orvil Guy, acting as chairman, reported to the board that a small committee of four had met with the minister on June 18, and they were convinced the minister was considering changes to the milk plan. One had said, "The minister advised us that he had received many letters critical of the milk board. He sure didn't waste any words, and he didn't do any smiling.

"The minister said that the board was getting out of touch with producers at large. He didn't like how we were handling the cheese situation, and he was unhappy with the MSQ and milk supplies for plants in Ontario."

Someone commented, "That doesn't leave very much on the plus side."

But the board still knew that the minister was backing them. He had brought in the milk plan, appointed the first board and was, in a real sense, as much a part of it as they were, perhaps more so. Most members, though not all, appreciated his difficult position.

George McLaughlin recalls, "We were certainly aware of the pressure on the minister to have a vote. We did a survey of the milk committees in 1971 and ninety percent came back with the question, 'What do you want to vote for?' Actually, I think most of the board members were in favour of having a vote. I think OMAF canvassed some of the ag reps too."

Lorne Hurd summed up the situation much later: "We all knew the pressures and the tenseness of the time. I guess we had a lot of faith in Mr. Stewart."

The board was facing continued demands for more industrial milk. It remained inflexible in its policy to give preference to those products that would realize the highest return for producers.

There were disturbing reports regarding the sale of MSQ. Undesirable activities reported involved auctioneers, cattle drovers and producers themselves in efforts intended to inflate the value of quotas or bring profits to a third party. Some auctioneers would not auction a producer's herd unless they were given the right to auction the quota as well. Quebec producers, subsidized by their government, were acquiring Ontario industrial milk quota.

Alex Bell of Smiths Falls became a member of the board in 1970. He advised the board, "Some of our milk committee tried to tell the auctioneer that the quota didn't have to move with the cattle, but we didn't have any luck. The auctioneers are doing very well out of selling quota. Quota quite often never gets where the cattle are going, but the auctioneer is making a good thing out of it. Sometimes the quota doesn't move with the cattle but is disposed of by the auctioneer by private tender.

"We try to persuade the farmer to sell through the board, but most of the time we've had little luck," Bell stated. "This system has to be changed. I don't know why they insist on selling it through the auction and through the drover. I guess that's money in hand, like the drover looking at some cattle in the field with a big wad of bills in his hip pocket."

Selling MSQ through the board at that time merely meant that the board acted as the middle man. They were made aware of where the quota was available, and if they received a call looking for quota, they put the two people together. The board, of course, kept records.

Effective April 1, 1971, the board suspended all auctioning of quota. It was decided that strong disciplinary action would be taken when any auctioneer or middle man was found to be involved in the transfer of quota. It was decided that the board field men would become more involved in quota transfers between producers. Milk producers were not entirely happy with the board's new policy.

The York County milk committee asked the board to "...reinstate the auctioning of quota until it comes up with a better alternative plan." Simcoe County milk committee also supported the sale of quota at auctions.

The board decided not to reinstate permission to auction quota, however, until a study was carried out and discussed at the Geneva Park conference in the fall of 1971. Third party participation in MSQ contravened the established rules of both the Canadian Dairy Commission and the board. The board was convinced that unless some workable solution were found, the entire MSQ program could be jeopardized.

Processors were upset. Lorne Hurd, the general manager, in a speech in the Royal York Hotel to the Concentrated Milk Manufacturers' Association, November 19, 1970, stated, "Concern has been expressed by some processors that the board may experience difficulty in achieving a reasonable distribution of the available milk supply among plants. Since the base setting period of 1968-69, many plants have closed - producers have changed their status from industrial to grade 'A' milk shippers.

"It's evident that existing levels of milk supply to industrial milk plants would be out of balance with quota levels established from a base period nearly two years old."

Hurd went on to explain that particularly in eastern Ontario there had been an increase in the demand for milk for specialty cheese production.

This tended to reduce the supplies of milk to plants normally receiving the milk, and further depleted the supply that would otherwise be available for quota plants. He admitted it was having an adverse effect on the plant's supply quota policy and that the commission and the board were giving the matter serious thought in hope of finding a way to overcome the obvious weakness. During this period there were serious and loud protests from the processors to the board and to the minister and to anyone who would listen.

It was clear that the board regarded obtaining the best returns for all milk producers as a major responsibility, but this resulted in a shortage of milk in certain eastern Ontario cheese factories. It was also clear that this objective could not be achieved while keeping every small cheese plant in business. The reaction of some board members was, "It should not be expected that milk producers throughout the province subsidize these situations so that they can continue operations."

There were cheese champions on the board, however. Some had grown up in the cheese plant culture of central and eastern Ontario. Allen Ketcheson, who had been appointed to the board by Bill Stewart in 1965, was to remain there until 1979. He was one such cheese champion. Addressing the board, he said, "There were about sixteen factories in my county when the board got under way. George, you remember when you came to speak at Stirling. The theatre was packed and you had said, 'You fellows get off your butts and sell your own cheese! I really think that you and some of the staff don't understand the cheese industry.'"

On September 24, 1971, the milk commission sent the board a copy of "an outline of a proposed study of the marketing of industrial milk in Ontario." The board concluded that the wording used in the outline indicated some preconceived opinions by the proponents and that the "study" was in reality a witch hunt.

The study was completed by a private consultant, Kates, Peat, Marwick and Company, after which the board met with the milk commission in August 1972. The board was not happy and conveyed this rather bluntly through their chairman, George McLaughlin:

"The report reads like the comments of a city man who considers farmers to be second-rate citizens and subject to manipulation by others. The recommendations are designed to give adequate returns to processors, and producer returns are made to look relatively unimportant. The suggestion that there be forced production of industrial milk by group one pool producers indicates a complete lack of understanding of the industry. The degree of direct control recommended for the milk commission, if implemented, would make the Ontario dairy industry into a public utility in a short time. Our understanding was that the marketing method for industrial milk was to be studied. This has not been done."

The Kates, Peat, Marwick study in question was conceived in a period of unrest in the industry, and amid adverse reactions from processors and others, and suggestions that the milk marketing board had taken over the complete development and administration of milk policy in Ontario. A major recommendation of the report was that "...the Milk Commission of Ontario undertake an expanded role emphasizing policy planning and development including negotiations, policy administration and the maintenance of the system itself." This suggested that the commission should be making decisions on Ontario's share of the total dairy industry and the future of the small cheese manufacturers, as well as the distribution priorities of available milk in relation to price, industry stability and industry rationalization. What form would future markets for milk and milk products take?

The study also recommended that the commission administer the policies and take a more active role in the negotiations with the Canadian Dairy Commission and the federal government. Furthermore, the commission should monitor the effects of policies and regulations "as its most important task." The board was not in a mood for this type of a report and made its feelings clearly known. A board member was quoted later as saying, "The private consultant's report quickly found its way to a well-earned position on some out-of-the-way shelf in OMAF where it very quickly began to gather less than its deserved share of dust." The board continued to persevere.

When the milk board was established in 1965 there were several producer distributors. They had cows and retailed their milk and, of course, realized a good price. They were not at all pleased with the board's policy that on one hand they had to sell their milk to the board and, on the other, purchase all of their needed supplies from the board.

Some resorted to action in the courts to obtain relief from those sections of the Milk Act that required them to market their raw milk through the board. The case had been argued in the Supreme Court of Ontario and dismissed. It was also dismissed by the Appeal Court; and the so-called Brant Dairy case went before the Supreme Court of Canada in March 1972. The decision resulting was most critical to the operations of the OMMB. It stated, among other things, "With respect to the constitutional question raised by the appellants, all members of the court agree that it fails."

The Milk Act and all of its regulations were upheld by the courts. The board's solicitor, Edge Harris of St. Catharines, stated, "The legality of the Ontario Milk Marketing Board has now been settled beyond question and given the extra strength of its authority, powers and functions."

Meanwhile, the board was being tested outside of the courts. On September 4, 1971, a *Toronto Star* editorial was headed, "Farmers Cheesed

Off." The editorial went on to state, "Canadian taxpayers are subsidizing the American companies that are forcing Canadian dairies to close down and put people out of work. Something has gone very wrong with the Ontario Milk Marketing Board."

In response, George McLaughlin wrote an appropriate letter to the editor intended to enlighten his or her (the editorial, naturally, was unsigned) apparent lack of knowledge of the milk marketing situation.

The Star's comments were a result of the continued sniping of the Ontario Farmers' Union. While still opposed to the board's policies, they were maintaining that their opposition and criticism were continuing because they considered the board to be under the control of the Ontario government and, of course, primarily Bill Stewart.

At 9:05 a.m. on July 28, 1971, the Winchester office of the OMMB received a telephone call from a transporter advising the board that OFU pickets were attempting to prevent milk trucks from entering the Kraft plant at Ingleside. Five minutes later, another transporter called in. The board's head office in Toronto then came on the line, advising of still other similar calls. All attempts to reach the Kraft plant by telephone failed because the lines were busy.

A memo dated June 30, 1971, to Bill MacPherson, director of the board's finance division, from Sarsfield O'Connor, regional marketing officer in Winchester, described the situation: "At 10:40 I arrived at the Kraft Ingleside plant. I noticed some three bulk tank and five can milk trucks across the road from Kraft in a large vacant lot. There were two groups of some fifteen picketers, each bearing flat cards and blocking the two entrances to the plant. The picketers were comprised of men, women and teenagers. Other OFU members whom I know personally were standing around in little groups talking to the truck drivers.

"Three Ontario Provincial Police constables advised that they were under orders to stand back about half a mile and survey at a distance. When we talked on the telephone you (MacPherson) expressed concern about the presence of the OPP, even at a distance. As you advised, I crossed the picket lines at about 11:15 a.m. to the vacant lot across the road from the plant and instructed the drivers to start up their motors and gently roll their trucks through the picket lines. Unfortunately, most of the drivers were hired help and stated they would not budge until their bosses arrived.

"Some of the OFU boys were happy witnesses to the scene, and they served free milk and sandwiches to the drivers.

"Two eastern Ontario directors of the OFU advised me that their fight was with the Kraft company, whom they wanted to pay higher prices for their milk, and not with the OMMB. They also advised that Walter Miller had been at the milk commission office in Toronto, advising them of the strike. The OFU people said that their pickets would stop the milk trucks from entering Kraft.

"The OFU directors made some negative comments about the election procedures for our board members. They also claimed the board should consider itself lucky that the proposed plebiscite had been temporarily postponed."

Continuing in his report, O'Connor stated, "At about 12:25 p.m. I made a second effort. There were about twelve trucks present. The OFU boys who were not on picket were milling around in an unhappy manner, and inch by inch a trucker named LaPorte got his big bulk truck through the well-rehearsed picket line. The young lad who was next behind, in his canned milk truck, got halfway through the picket line, but he froze in his tracks because of fright. I told him to move, but he seemed to get more scared. There was a lot of shouting going on now. The highway was hopelessly blocked, with trucks lining up.

"Halfway through the picket line, a young man picketer had taken a swing at a driver through an open truck window. There was a flurry of flying fists for a few moments. No telling blows were landed. Then a trucker lost control of his truck, and it took two great leaps forward. The picketers were not hurt, but they scattered quickly. The TV camera and reporters were active, but I evaded them.

"Because of concerns for the quality of the milk being held up, the canned milk trucks were then redirected to Aults in Winchester and Carnation at Alexandria. The big men from the OFU - Miller, Sanford, and Gudmundson - arrived from Toronto and the local directors were relegated to 'joe boy' status. The chairman and two members of the Dundas milk committee arrived, giving some moral support."

According to the files, O'Connor spotted a transporter named Murdock coming off of Highway 401. Apparently Murdock had had some experience in rolling his truck through picket lines, and so it was arranged that the truckers would start their engines and slowly roll through.

O'Connor continued: "Mr. Miller spouted off in his usual, characteristic style about agribusiness, corporate conglomerates, the squeeze on the little fellow, finally telling the drivers they were stooges if they crossed the picket lines.

"Tension again swept everybody, but mainly the OFU people. TV cameras took up positions. The first five trucks went through the well-trained picket lines in a slow and tedious manner. There was much hollering and cursing from the picketers. Miller and Sanford, demoralized by this time, swore that we would lose our jobs over this. Many of the drivers were threatened with violence and damage to their equipment. Grant Cameron, our area field man, phoned at about 10:30 p.m., and it was reassuring to hear from him."

Records of Thursday, July 29, indicate that the scene was quieter but that there was drenching rain, which probably dampened the spirits of the picketers as well as their persons. The trucks were moving through.

"Three carloads of board support arrived in the form of more Dundas milk committee members," reported O'Connor. "To avoid confrontation I asked them to observe from their cars. Fortunately, the news of a price increase of $1.15 per hundredweight for cheese milk was learned about noon on that day. The pickets withdrew.

"There was a meeting the following morning convened by the OFU, with 1,000 people in attendance from all over eastern Ontario. Kraft expressed annoyance because the meeting was held in a embarrassing location - in a large field facing the Kraft entrance. The National Farmers' Union was rumoured to be threatening a national boycott of Kraft's products, but they and their Ontario counterparts, the OFU, were satisfied with the milk price increase."

The Ingleside experience was very significant because it represented the particular problems facing the board because of the extreme importance of industrial milk to eastern Ontario. The situation was not the same in other parts of the province. The start of the group two pool had added to the tensions. That the board had survived was indicative of its determination and singleness of purpose. However, the significant degree of inflexiblity in the administration of policies and the refusal to waver from the decided direction did add to the early aggravation of the board's administration. It is likely, on the other hand, that if the members had wavered, they would have failed. Fortunately, they were able to maintain the momentum.

The eastern Ontario situation of the 1960s and the early 1970s is best summed up by Sarsfield O'Connor. Try to hear his colourful Irish brogue: "The marketing of industrial milk in eastern Ontario had always been governed by a law unto itself. Plants, transporters and producers had always been part of the funny goings-on that were often characterized by cutthroat aggressiveness, competition, political shenanigans, secret deals and squabbles. Most seemed to thrive on that sort of atmosphere. The several producer trust accounts at some of the small cheese factories were all part of the game. They had to be watched or they simply would not pay the farmer.

"Many of the producers and plants thought they were being smothered in red tape, policies and regulations of the board. They were completely lost, as far as comprehension was concerned, regarding the functions of the Canadian Dairy Commission, the milk commission and the milk board. And they were quick to listen to the smooth-talking propaganda of the OFU."

The OFU was not lying down. The election year of 1971 in Ontario had increased their vitality. They had proposed new legislation. Bill Stewart provided a copy of the OFU proposal to the board and asked for a reaction. He surely must have had his tongue in his cheek.

The OFU proposal strongly recommended that the milk board be restricted to an administrative responsibility only. There would be a government-appointed body that would negotiate the price of milk and the terms and conditions of its sale with the OFU. This government body and the board, to a significant degree, would be able to act only with the approval of the farmers' union. As well, only producers of milk who were members of the OFU would be allowed to vote on the ratification of a price agreement, and upon the initiation of any "withholding" action. The union was proposing that it should be established as the sole bargaining agent for producers - without any prior vote or approval of these producers.

The board reacted in almost complete disbelief to the OFU proposal: "After complaining for many years about government control and interference in producers' affairs, the OFU now proposes that a government-appointed 'marketing' agency buy and sell agricultural products in each province, while in fact that agency would be able to buy and sell only at the dictates of the OFU."

Another reaction at the time, attributed to a senior civil servant in OMAF, was less kind: "The OFU proposal is the obvious result of frantic brainstorming in the environment of an intelligence vacuum."

In any case, the OFU was getting considerable support from farmers. Agriculture had been passing through a difficult time of adjustment in the late '60s and early '70s. Many were prepared to blame the government and big business and were ready at least to listen, and quite often, accept the illogical gyrations of thought that were coming from the more radical elements of the farm sector. If nothing else, the OFU offered a hope of something better than the conditions that many of them were having to endure.

To add to the difficulties, there was growing restlessness in northern Ontario. In July 1971, Mike Zimmerman, chairman of the Kenora-Fort Frances milk committee, sent a letter to the Canadian Dairy Commission requesting exemption from any deduction under the MSQ program. The board advised him that the entire MSQ program, as it applied to northern Ontario, was currently under review by the board and the CDC.

The Challenge of Achievement

During the 1972 season, the Kenora-Fort Frances area had experienced only one-half of the usual rainfall, and as a result there were severe drought conditions and production problems.

There were also undesirable situations in the Thunder Bay area regarding transportation. The board had reduced the transportation rate paid to Palm Dairies in accordance with the factors in the transport rate formula that had been approved by the board and the transporter representatives. Palm Dairies wanted the rates restored to the old level that had existed before August 1, 1971. Similar arguments had been put up by Klomp and Wakefield Dairies. Klomp's letter to the board stated, "I propose to make some regulation of my own by which I will deduct the money considered due to me for the transport of milk purchased from the board."

He didn't, of course. Reportedly he said, "I felt better after writing it." Tempers were frayed.

The Dryden milk committee also wrote to the board, stating, "Since the formation of the milk marketing board a yearly income of $40,000 has been taken away from the seventeen producers left in our area. The Dryden area milk committee believes very strongly that the OMMB is trying to dispose of the Dryden area producers."

The board took the letter seriously and decided that the claims contained in the letter should be thoroughly investigated and a reply sent to the Dryden milk committee and to each producer in the area, as well as a copy to the minister of agriculture and food.

A secretary of the Dryden milk committee for more than twenty years, Gertrude Russell recalled in 1989, "Dryden producers missed the open quota of the summer months. In the early '70s we had a few hot sessions with the board."

Russell's husband, Lawrence, added, "We've been fighting with the board ever since they came in!"

Gertrude tried to placate the situation: "Let's say we had our differences. There's a lot of difference between eastern Ontario and our region."

Irvin Skeen, a former producer whose father had moved to the Dryden area in the 1920s, recalls, "Milk was brought in to take care of the general shortage during the tourist season in the summer. It came from Thunder Bay or through the Modern Dairy in Winnipeg. Safeway (Lucerne Dairies) milk from Manitoba was coming in as well."

Gordon Hatch, who had been the local Groveside Dairy distributor, suggested, "There were problems in the winter. The producers wouldn't level their production. With the board's arrival, dairying became more of a full-time production." (As of June 1989 only seven producers were left in the Dryden area.)

Northwestern Ontario from time to time had expressed concerns that because of the wide geographical area in the north they were not adequately represented on the board. During the fall 1971 election swing through northwestern Ontario, it was reported that Bill Stewart had been requested to have an additional member on the board to represent northwestern Ontario. Members of the board had made unanimous and emphatic objection to the possibility. They were still extremely sensitive to the statement, particularly coming from the OFU, that they were merely appointees and pawns of the minister. That the matter of representation had even been raised, however, served to emphasize the particular and delicate problems facing the board in supervising the marketing of milk in such a large geographical area, albeit with a relatively small number of producers compared to the rest of the province.

Bernie Gallagher of Powassan had joined the board in 1969. He came from a farm that had been established by his grandfather in 1894; he was a third generation farmer of the north. Gallagher recalls, "Several producers in Dryden were very concerned about the board. They even made representations to Bill Stewart, on one occasion asking to be let out of the program entirely. Stewart told them to go back to Dryden and call a meeting, and if it was the wish of the producers, they could get out. They could be on their own if they wanted to. So they had a local meeting, and as it turned out, the majority of producers decided to stay under the board's system. This was in the early 1970s, and I don't think there's a record of it."

Lucien Cazabon, one of the first appointed members of the board, recalls, "The biggest trouble area was in Sault Ste. Marie. Certain shippers were sending their surplus milk to Elliot Lake to a small dairy. It was all under the table."

"We couldn't handle surplus milk in the north. I remember in Sudbury we were selling surplus milk at $1.00 to $1.25 for an eight-gallon can. The plant was charging thirty cents to separate it, and we were paying thirty cents transportation. There wasn't much left."

Mike Zimmerman of Emo, near Fort Frances in the northwest, admired Cazabon and sympathized with his perspective. He understood Cazabon's views perfectly. Zimmerman was president of the Kenora-Rainy River Milk Producers in 1959 and in later terms. In 1990 he was still secretary of the area district committee. He has always been very conscious of the importance of communications for the industry, having made several broadcasts over the CBC in Thunder Bay over the years.

He recalls, "When the board came in there was uneasiness, lack of trust and continuing problems with education. There was a lot of friction." Though Toronto is a long way away from his region, according to Zimmerman, and though there is some concern about U.S. milk crossing the border, he also senses that "the board is now behind us."

"The meeting in May 1989," he continued optimistically, "indicated we would be getting a cheese plant in 1990 and given annual allotments of MSQ. We would at least realize a northwestern Ontario pool. The fifty-percent transfer assessment to be levied on any group one pool quota transferred out of northwestern Ontario will protect the future of the milk producers."

On the other hand, Mike Zimmerman and his committee were extremely annoyed with the sale of Manitoba milk in northwestern Ontario in the 1970s and the unfair competition that was being given by this lower priced milk. They were emphasizing the long-standing conviction of milk producers in northwestern Ontario, that milk sold by Safeway stores was being purchased from Manitoba farmers at prices lower than in the regular market.

The situation was frustrating because at the time OMAF had attempted without success to get pricing details from the Manitoba Department of Agriculture. The unofficial (and unconfirmed) explanation of the problem given at the time was that Modern Dairies of Winnipeg was able to exert great influence on the milk board in that province.

Bernie Gallagher reported to the board on March 9, 1972, that at the February 28 meeting at Bruce Station in Algoma, "The producers are somewhat rebellious and demanding their own pool because, they are saying, the farmers on the milk board are only bureaucrats who have forgotten why they're there and also who's paying them."

Bernie noted further, "...that producers apparently don't expect a reply from the board concerning establishment of a separate pool."

Time, fortunately, is a great healer. When I visited Algoma in 1988 and talked to several of the local retired farmers and dairymen, there seemed to be no recollection of the problems of those earlier days and the many headlines in the local press dealing with milk marketing problems, producer prices and the excitement of the North Shore Co-operative.

In the early 1970s, while the board was a ready and available target for arrows shot from many different directions, it was also prepared to give more that it received. A federal task force on agriculture had just completed a report that was somewhat critical of what they thought they saw in the dairy industry.

In the summer of 1970, speaking at a workshop at the University of Guelph, Lorne Hurd, while accepting certain of the recommendations concerning dairy policy, sizzled a response to others in very clear, precise terms:

"The dairy chapter in the report contains incorrect, misleading and superficial statements. The task force has underestimated the economic and policy forces that work to bring more viability to the dairy sector, and as a consequence it has misrepresented the state of the industry and misjudged its capabilities. In Ontario alone the number of milk and cream producers has dropped by nearly 30 percent in the past four years while maintaining the same level of milk output.

"The task force implies that world prices for dairy products are based wholly on comparative advantage and are truly competitive prices. This is nonsense. With the exception of New Zealand and Australia, world prices are highly subsidized, and in many European countries the domestic retail prices for dairy products are much higher than they are in Canada."

Shenanigans in the dairy industry were by no means restricted to eastern Ontario. Nor were they restricted to processors or transporters. In 1971, Dominion Dairies in Ottawa complained about a tankload of milk that tested only three percent butterfat and appeared to be watered down. Subsequent investigation indicated 10 percent added water. As a result, all producers on the load were sampled and tested. One farm sample indicated 39 percent added water, and another check test carried out two days later also indicated 39 percent added water. A check of the butterfat test of this particular shipper for the previous eleven months indicated a tested range from 2.5 to 3.6 percent.

It was calculated that according to the tests taken and the shipment record, 8,745 pounds of water had been added to the milk during the month of November 1971 alone. The board decided that the producer's quota would be reduced by 8,745 pounds and payments of milk adjusted accordingly, with repayment by the offending producer made to Dominion Dairies.

While continually accused of being somewhat inflexible in the administration of policies, the board was in fact very decisive. The staff and the board members were convinced that any inconsistency or weakness in the administration and application of policies would have very quickly resulted in unmanageable disrespect and an erosion of their authority. The tests and challenges to this authority in the early '70s had convinced them of this. They apparently didn't intend to change.

CHAPTER SIX

Settling In

In which the board

- Withstands high inflation
- Experiences an Ottawa excursion into fluid milk
- Moves on milk quality
- Begins to regulate can conversion
- Diverts milk from cheese
- Deals with a post office strike
- Worries about cheese imports
- Becomes involved in interprovincial movement of MSQ
- Struggles under milk surpluses
- Reacts to the national dairy policy
- Becomes incensed with Ottawa
- Considers quota policy
- Endures tensions with the milk commission
- Begins the ODFAP program
- Sees McLaughlin prepare to leave

The board was now well into the 1970s. When it reached its tenth anniversary on November 1, 1975, George McLaughlin made the statement, "The pressing problems of a decade ago caused the board to come of age and mature in a very short space of time. Immense progress has been made in many areas. A more equitable sharing among the producers of the industry's benefits and responsibilities has been provided. Better prices relative to costs have been obtained for producers. A greater bargaining strength regarding the terms and conditions of sale has been obtained. The efficiency of transportation has been increased. The authority granted to producers under the Milk Act of 1965 has made all of these improvements possible."

But the producers had just passed through some troublesome years. Wages in August 1973 were indicated as being 22 percent higher than in the previous year. The costs of electricity, fertilizer, petroleum products and building repairs were up 10 percent.

The farm input price index for eastern Canada was 27 percent higher in the third quarter of 1973 than in the comparable period in 1972. So the board made up its mind to bring about an increase in the price of class one milk.

At the same time, the federal government was considering providing some price relief to fluid milk consumers. There was talk of a consumer subsidy.

On September 6, 1973, the board received a telegram from the Honourable Eugene Whelan, minister of agriculture for Canada, which was designed to "provide amplification of the federal government's decision on a consumer subsidy for fluid milk." The body of the telegram stated, "The federal government intends to pay a consumer subsidy of five cents a quart for fluid milk. The objective is to contain and roll back fluid prices. The intent is to pay the subsidy directly to processors, who will be expected to pass along the benefit to consumers. The subsidy will be paid with the clear understanding that there will be a containment and rollback of the retail price of the product. The subsidy will apply to partly skimmed milk, that is, two-percent and skim milk, but not to such products as flavoured milk. There will also be a 20 cents per pound subsidy on skim powder marketed in consumer-sized packages."

The board was upset and angry. In this high-cost period the producers needed more money. The board had no objections to fluid milk being subsidized for the benefit of consumers, but did object to its pricing authority being usurped by federal authorities. Nor did it appreciate federal meddling in provincial matters. The board reacted: "This blatant political manoeuvre has placed the board in an untenable position with a proposed policy that would mean about $40 million of federal money going to Ontario consumers."

There was real concern because the federal intention was clear: "Once fixed, the price must remain at that level for twelve months." There was no explanation of what would happen at the end of the twelve-month period.

The Milk Commission of Ontario had made it clear that the board and the Ontario Dairy Council must reach an agreement acceptable to Ottawa so that Ontario could receive the benefit of the federal subsidy, which was now estimated at some $42 million.

The board objected, "To agree to a twelve-month price freeze, without any freeze on input costs, would be suicidal!"

There were heated arguments between the board and the processors. The board would not accept the proposition of the Ontario Dairy Council that price discounts given by processors to retail stores should be considered part of their operating costs. The board deeply resented the implication that producers should accept prices low enough to permit the processors to give wholesale discounts at their own discretion.

On September 26 the board and the Ontario Dairy Council did reach an agreement based on the fact that both groups required increased returns. Their proposal provided for a one-half-cent per quart relief to consumers, with the rest of the money divided between the processors and producers according to their agreement. The federal cabinet flatly rejected the idea, insisting on a one-cent per quart reduction of the consumer price.

The federal presence in fluid milk pricing had an unsettling impact on the general marketing situation. The federal government moved to withdraw the subsidy in October 1974 in five stages. The board insisted on two, and in February 1975 the federal government finally discontinued its involvement with fluid milk.

The federal foray into the class one market had not been welcomed. When they learned the government was backing off, the board was relieved; its reaction was summed up in George McLaughlin's comment: "The whole handling of the consumer subsidy was a disastrous experience. We certainly hope it will never be repeated."

Both the board and OMAF wished to bring about the production of milk of uniformly high quality in Ontario and all produced on grade "A" premises. The only difference in thinking was the rate at which these things should come about.

The board wanted improvements in quality as quickly as possible, while the ministry was conscious of the changes that would have to be made by a significant number of producers, and at considerable cost. The ministry wished to allow adequate time, among other things, for these producers to decide whether they wished to make the changes or seek other agricultural endeavours. This led to some heated discussions.

The authority for the regulation of milk quality and farm premises rested with OMAF; it had not been delegated to the board. The board didn't think the ministry was moving quickly enough to bring about improvements in milk quality.

Existing ministry regulations provided for warnings and the eventual shut-off of producers who continued to produce milk of undesirable quality. The board wanted to "hit" such producers faster and in a way that would make an immediate impression in their pocketbooks.

The board had been considering the matter of quality for some time, having discussed it with George McCague of the milk commission and Jack Palmer of the Milk Industry Branch.

George McLaughlin recalls, "OMAF had been planning a program and for some reason it was put on the shelf, so we decided we'd carry out our proposed program anyway. The program had been endorsed through the milk committees by what we considered to be a majority of producers. But we were ordered 'not to do it' by the ministry."

The chairman also recalls that George McCague said, "You know, you guys are trying to force the government into a program with your pricing authority, but the government doesn't think it's time for that yet."

"You people are supposed to be protecting the consumers," McLaughlin replied, "and I don't think you're doing a very good job."

"We're protecting the consumers by shutting the milk producers off," said McCague.

McLaughlin remembers, "It was a real blow-up, and our people were mad. We had spent a lot of staff time and money working out the program. There were a lot of producer meetings and then we're told not to do it! We didn't even get it off the ground. But Bill Stewart was still concerned about allowing sufficient time for producers to upgrade their production facilities. I remember a small group of us meeting with him. He banged the desk with his fist and made it quite clear who would be making the decisions on milk quality."

"Bill Stewart never talked about this, of course," said someone later, "but it's possible he thought McLaughlin may have been getting a little too big for his britches and decided to clip his wings a bit."

Discussions continued between the board and the Milk Industry Branch regarding the elimination of the existing shut-off procedures and replacing them with a scheme involving pricing penalties for any producers having low grade supplies.

The board continued to work with OMAF into 1974 in developing a program of payment deductions for producers who shipped low grade milk. A simulation of the program did commence on December 1, 1974, for a trial period of six months.

On June 1, 1975, the new milk quality payment program of the board commenced. A study just completed had indicated there would be substantial savings if all bulk milk had a uniform quality grade and milk no longer would have to be segregated for delivery to milk processors and distributors.

The need to continue the transport of milk in cans was becoming a cost and administrative issue with the board and a political issue in rural Ontario. Many milk producers were also concerned about the cost of switching from cans to bulk. Transporters could see their routes and businesses disappearing because less transport would be needed. As well, high costs would be involved in acquiring bulk milk transport.

In 1973 there were still 5,569 producers shipping milk in cans. There had been steady conversion to bulk, but many milk processors were becoming impatient and had indicated specific dates after which they "would refuse to accept milk in cans."

The board was also applying pressure for change, and even formed a "can to bulk conversion committee." As of April 1, 1974, the differential between can and bulk shipments was increased from ten cents to 18 cents per hundredweight. The milk commission had passed a regulation which was to be effective October 1, that "New producers may ship milk only from farm bulk tanks." Everyone wished to speed up the rate of conversion. In 1974 some 86 percent of the total milk supply was marketed in bulk, compared to 64 percent in 1968. Times were changing.

Can routes were quickly becoming less efficient. Trucks transporting cans now had to travel extra miles to make more pickups in order to maintain reasonably sized loads. Many routes were becoming so long that it was difficult to effect further route consolidation to maintain load size and offset higher transportation costs. As a result, the group two pool producers shipping milk in cans found their transportation costs increased by 36 percent in one year.

By the end of October 1975, board staff were strongly recommending, "A deadline should be set for conversion to bulk tanks." By this time only nine and a half percent of the total milk in Ontario was marketed in cans, though this did represent some 3,500 producers.

The industry was now faced with increasing transportation costs for cans and extra costs at the plant for receiving such milk. The costs had become prohibitive. The board had to deal with the situation.

The whole issue had now become even more political. To complicate matters further, there was a change in ministers: Bill Newman was now the provincial agricultural minister.

Early in January 1976 a committee of the board met with Newman regarding the whole matter of canned/bulk conversion. The board committee was not too pleased with the Newman meeting. The minister had insisted, "The whole matter must be taken to cabinet."

The board quickly decided that the situation was so sensitive that information meetings should be arranged as soon as possible with all party caucuses.

The board was becoming impatient. Eventually it decided that, "October 31, 1977, will be established as the date to end all marketing of milk in cans." Allen Ketcheson, one of the original board members from the heart of the cheese-producing area in Madoc, made the comment, "We haven't heard the last of this one."

"Some of you may not have a problem in your area with cans," Ketcheson continued, "but I certainly will have one. To the north of me they're still taking milk to cheese factories in large 40-gallon cans, and I know these people will never accept the deadline for conversion to bulk. They'll likely just carry on taking the milk to cheese factories in cans because I know the factories will be glad to get it. And another thing we have to remember when these factories go, these farmers won't have any market for their milk. Some may put in bulk tanks but I think most of them will stop milking cows."

Because of the perseverance of the cheese area members, cheese was usually discussed at most board meetings. They had encouraged a study on the cheese industry which had been completed in 1973. Among the findings it read, "A demand for natural cheddar has been and is strong and is expected to remain buoyant. The distribution system is adequate for consumer needs."

The report's findings, however, lacked an economic rationale to justify the development of a major business building program for aged cheddar for the Ontario industry. Ketcheson recalls, "I don't think we were ever able to persuade the chairman, the general manager and certain members of the board of the real importance of the board in maintaining a stronger position in cheese marketing."

There had also been concerns about surplus cheese, particularly as a result of the weakening of the U.K. cheese market. A cheddar cheese milk diversion program was still in effect in the winter of 1972-73. The purpose was to divert milk from the manufacture of cheddar cheese into the manufacture of butter. This did have a stabilizing effect.

The export potential for cheddar to the U.K. was now becoming uncertain, as that country had joined the European Common Market with its punitive levy policies. The board couldn't envisage any overall shortage of cheddar cheese in Canada, but at the same time was concerned that Ontario might lose its share of Canadian cheddar cheese production.

Fortunately, the price of cheddar cheese remained buoyant through 1974, and in 1976 the price of cheddar and the milk used for cheddar increased significantly. The board was doing everything in its power to have the 50-million-pound cheese import quota reduced by a significant amount, especially as Canadian milk producers were forced to limit their own production potential because of the significant loss in export markets.

Kraft Foods announced on April 24, 1975, that it would start bringing all its specialty cheeses into Canada from the United States: "On this afternoon trucks will start to roll."

There was a strong feeling of concern within the Canadian dairy industry.

"Action must to be taken against the importation of highly subsidized specialty cheese from Europe and what may prove to be uncontrolled imports of such cheese from the U.S.A."

A tough and urgent telegram was sent by the board to the minister of international trade and commerce, the Honourable A.W. Gillespie.

Peter Oosterhoff, a future vice-chairman, had been elected to take his position on the board in January 1975. He had an excellent knowledge of the European situation. He'd come from Holland with his parents in 1952 and since that time had been very active in the dairy industry, building a successful family enterprise. Oosterhoff understood the cheese market as well.

"When Hennessy held the hearings in Vineland," he recalls, "my father urged me to attend, though it was silo filling time. That was really my first formal introduction to milk marketing. I started on the milk committee in Region 7 in 1969 or 1970."

The board had maintained within their administration the Belleville cheese warehouse and the Winchester warehouse. There had been continuing debates on the merits of maintaining the warehouses, and the industry argued they were needed for storage purposes. In the spring of 1976, however, the board realized the net profit that would be received from the Winchester warehouse, even full of cheese, would not equal the interest return on an offer of $400,000, which they had received for it.

In 1973, a major concern had developed regarding an equitable arrangement for the movement of MSQ between provinces in a way that would correspond with provincial industry patterns. The first movement of quota was to take place between Ontario and Quebec on April 1, 1974. During the week of April 15, George McLaughlin and Lorne Hurd were in Three Rivers, Quebec, discussing interprovincial quota, MSQ and other matters. The telephone rang. They were suddenly faced with an urgent new experience.

There had been threats of a post office strike. The board had been assured there would be no problems and had dispatched some 17,000 cheques to the postal terminal in Toronto. Bill MacPherson, thinking everything was fine, had taken off for a holiday in England. On Wednesday, April 17, there was a sudden overnight strike and almost all of the cheques were stranded in Hogtown. Only a few had slipped through.

Fred Saunders, the chief accountant in the finance division, hastily consulted with Hurd and McLaughlin over the phone. With MacPherson and the general manager away, Saunders was faced with a real administrative crisis. The producers simply had to get their cheques.

It was decided to produce a complete duplicate set of cheques for use when and if it became evident that they would be needed. The duplicates were all ready on the morning of the 19th. No one knew when the strike would end. Telephone discussions with the chairman and the general manager had concluded with, "Let's get the new cheques moving." The decision was made to get them to the producers through the plants and transporters.

Through Friday and Saturday, head office staff sorted the cheques manually. On Sunday, April 21, the board's marketing officers picked up some of them, and others were sent to the marketing officers by bus. Cheques began to be delivered by transporters on Monday, April 22, and the job was finished on Wednesday, April 24.

"I missed the 1974 strike, as I was in England," Bill MacPherson recalls vividly, "but I can imagine what it was like. We had the first strike in 1970. I remember heading east on the weekend with the family. We had left with the back of the car filled with boxes of cheques. I dropped these off at the Belleville office where they were sent in turn to Winchester to be given to transporters for the east.

"When I got back from England, Saunders told me we used the field men to distribute the cheques to the transporters and used the transporters to distribute the cheques to the farmers. We carefully included the distribution of billings to the plants, of course. It was quite an organizational task.

"The plants played a role in handling and sorting the cheques so that they could be divided among the transporters. It took a lot of cooperation and a great team effort on the part of all members of the industry to make the exercise successful."

The banks didn't appreciate our situation. They were not prepared to accept stop-payment orders on 17,000 cheques! The duplicate cheque envelopes contained a request to the producers to "Return the cheque to the board should the original cheque be eventually delivered by the post office."

Needless to say, there were numerous complications, such as the cashing of both cheques, and many adjustments and reconciliations were made over a period of time.

"It likely took six months to clear up the whole situation," MacPherson estimates. "But the task was accomplished and the producers got their cheques."

From the beginning, within the national milk marketing plan there had been real desire, particularly on the part of the Canadian Dairy Commission and certain officials of Agriculture Canada, that there be a formal means of moving industrial quota between provinces. This had been a major concern in 1973. The first movement of quota did take place on April 1, 1974, between Ontario and Quebec. Ontario surrendered more on April 1, 1975. Most of this again went to Quebec, with a small amount moving into British Columbia. Ontario still had adequate amounts of MSQ to cover any increases in milk production.

The agreed-upon policy at the time was relatively simple. It concerned only production. A certain latitude was allowed. For example, if that latitude was 10 percent and Ontario produced 16 percent below its provincial quota, then the difference of six percent was to go to the provinces that were overproducing their provincial MSQ.

The government in Quebec was actively encouraging the expansion of the industrial milk production in that province. The expansion of the co-operatives, particularly Granby, was reported to have involved significant subsidies. Farmers had received subsidies to upgrade their dairy herds, and they had come to Ontario and purchased cattle and industrial quota. A 25-cent milk subsidy was under active consideration in Quebec.
The board was worried and went to see Bill Stewart in December 1974. They talked about the possibility of an Ontario subsidy to match that in Quebec.

"I suspect the Ontario Government won't be attempting to compete with Quebec on the matter of financial assistance to their respective farmers," stated Bill Stewart.

The whole matter was settled later between ministers when it was agreed that a national program for industrial milk couldn't possibly work if there were competing subsidies within the provinces.

No more quota was moved interprovincially, however, because of the drastic cuts imposed by the Canadian Dairy Commission as a result of serious overproduction of industrial milk in the mid-1970s.

There were continuing complaints from industrial milk plants regarding inadequate supplies of milk. In 1974 George McLaughlin had worriedly stated, "The rapidly declining supply of industrial milk is a major concern. It has to be addressed. Governments must treat this situation as a priority. Producers are leaving the industry."

Producers had been feeling the high input costs, and others were reacting to the anticipated costs in becoming grade "A" producers.

The chairman was concerned that since the fluid milk market was the most lucrative market, and with an increasing demand for fluid milk, the board might be accused of being unconcerned about the fate of the industrial milk section of the industry. Some comments had been made suggesting that the board's perceived lack of attention to industrial milk production was a deliberate ploy intended to keep the percentage payout in the pools as high as possible. In later discussions this was strongly denied by former board members.

McLaughlin feared that the situation might create a poor public image for the board and result in government intervention.

"The maintenance and health of the industrial part of the industry in Ontario is critical for the agricultural economy generally and milk production in particular," he said. "Cream won't sit on the top unless there's skim to hold it up."

Board appeals to the federal government had met with some success, and there were product support price increases that had the overall effect of raising by about $1.00 per hundredweight the producer returns for industrial milk. In 1973 the Ontario government had introduced a loan scheme to assist farmers in buying additional industrial quota. It had also launched an Industrial Milk Production Incentive Program, which provided for guaranteed loans to qualified farmers to encourage milk production expansion.

The Canadian Dairy Commission had been pleased with the establishment of the Canadian milk supply management committee. The national milk marketing plan of 1970, which had initially been signed by Ontario and Quebec and the federal government, by the end of 1974 had all other milk-producing provinces as signatories. In its infancy, however, milk supply management appeared to be less than an exact science. There was still some lack of enthusiasm by certain provinces and processors when it came to their own particular situations. In the early 1970s glutted markets had disappeared. Input costs were high, and producers were being encouraged to produce more milk.

Suddenly the whole production picture changed. Milk overproduction and resultant surpluses were looming. The vagaries of weather and the traditional inconsistencies of economic forecasts resulted in difficult surprises. The Canadian Dairy Commission announced that as of September 1, 1975, subsidy would be paid only on 75 percent of the MSQ shipments. The 1975-76 dairy year was expected to produce that much more than domestic requirements for industrial milk.

It had been the CMSMC's goal to achieve an increase of about five percent for the national industrial market of 1975-76. But the milk shipments by the end of March 1976, on a national basis, were indicating an increase of 17.6 percent. A severe decline in world prices had also occurred, creating a state of shock at the CDC.

Yields per cow were up because of good weather and excellent feed conditions. Ontario production had increased by 13.5 percent by the spring of 1976.

While recognizing the need, the board was opposed to the drastic action decreed in the federal program. Industrial milk production was cut back by 18 percent in Canada and 15 percent in Ontario.

"Our board recognized that we should be taking quota out of the system, and we had gone to the CMSMC on two occasions recommending this, but they wouldn't touch it with a ten-foot pole," recalls Lorne Hurd. "Mr. Whelan was minister in Ottawa then. He recognized the dangers and finally had to issue an edict to the committee to take quota out of the system. Our board agreed with this, of course. Ontario had taken some out, so we were able to soften the blow a bit. If we hadn't done this our cutback would have been 18 percent. But it was a lesson the industry learned the hard way. It's never been allowed to happen since!"

The board had favoured a moderate and gradual adjustment. But there was nothing they could do to avoid the sudden severe cutback in MSQ. The shock waves were felt throughout the whole milk marketing system. Producers' financial planning was disrupted. They became very concerned with personal situations. Confidence was shaken. Fingers of criticism were pointed at the board. The consequences were traumatic and appeared grossly unfair at a time when other segments of society outside of agriculture were obtaining income increases of at least ten percent.

This experience indicated how a sudden surplus situation could cause a drastic reduction in the returns of milk producers and a significant disorientation of the industry. The board reaffirmed its support of supply management and pursued the philosophy with vigour.

Eugene Whelan, federal Minister of Agriculture between 1972 and 1984, during difficult years for the national milk marketing plan, has been a stalwart supporter of the supply management concept in the dairy industry.

The board was willing that producers be responsible for the main costs involved in disposing of any surplus of dairy products in return for an adequate national policy. If milk supplies were not tied as closely as possible to the requirements of the domestic market, as the 1975-76 experience proved, the consequences would lead to chaos in the marketplace and sharp declines in the income of every milk producer. These are facts still ignored by the critics of supply management.

The trauma experienced in the mid-70s could not detract from the extreme importance of the commitment in 1975, made by the federal minister, the Honourable Eugene Whelan, to a long-term dairy policy for Canada. The minister was and still is an inflexible champion of supply management. An important feature was the introduction of a formula for establishing target returns for producers of industrial milk. This policy was put in place on April 1, 1975, and Harold Scott, a long-term board member from Stratford, had commented, "This represents a gigantic step toward the principle of ensuring a reasonable level of stable returns for industrial milk producers."

While recognizing there would be differences of opinion in policy direction from time to time, the federal minister's announcement was received by the board with great enthusiasm.

"The key element of a target returns formula is for the adjusting of the level of producer returns for industrial milk," said Whelan, "and the target support level will be adjusted each year at the annual review."

But he also advised, "It is the aim of the government to aggressively increase the share of producer returns coming from the marketplace. The government will not raise the direct subsidy payments for milk and cream or total dollar expenditures above the present level. The management of milk and cream supplies will be a very important part of this new policy."

Some board members, concerned with the implications of this statement, had expressed fears: "This statement seems to imply that the government may use dairy product imports as a trade-off in GATT negotiations."

The federal minister further clarified the long-term dairy policy. At the November 6, 1975, meeting of the board they were advised, "The government also decided, as part of the long-term dairy policy, that dairy products consumed in Canada should remain predominantly of Canadian origin."

But the statement also read, "In accordance with the decision of April 18, 1975, imports will be allowed to increase gradually over the next several years until they reach not less than the equivalent of 10 percent of manufactured products."

The board went into orbit. Letters were sent to milk committees advising them of the developments and requesting their help in arranging face-to-face meetings with their local MP's to oppose planned import increases.

George McLaughlin and a committee of the board met in early December 1975 with Ellard Powers, chairman of the Canadian Dairy Commission. Their briefs stated, "The board's faith in the federal government and the CDC has been completely shattered by such a deliberate attempt to shrink the size of the Canadian dairy industry by permitting increased imports of cheese, by the complete lack of any consultation with the dairy industry before the minister's announcement on dairy policy, by strong objections among producers to governments making any trade-offs with foreign countries to the detriment of the domestic dairy industry, by the reduction of subsidies to dairy farmers when anti-inflation programs are being constructed, by the apparent attempt to shrink the domestic dairy industry even further by raising dairy product prices that will result in reduced consumption, and by a complete lack of any cost/benefit analysis for any of the government policies. There is no rationale, therefore, for the federal government's attitude."

"The commission is doing its best to get its points across to the government," Powers replied, "and we hope an announcement will be made in two weeks time which will set the matter right."

Ellard Powers, from Beachburg in the Ottawa Valley, was a member of the board from 1969 to March 1970 when Bud Olsen, federal minister, appointed him to the CDC. He was still vice-president of the OFU but had a very personal commitment to the industry. He had succeeded Dr. Cliff Barry as chairman in 1973. He remained chairman until 1976, when he had to leave because of ill health. He freely admits, "I didn't get along with Grant Smith, and some on the board regarded me as a union spy."

A few months after the meeting with Powers, the board was given a document which indicated that the accumulation of skim milk powder stocks by the CDC was approaching 300 million pounds and that the anticipated surplus production for the 1976-77 dairy year would amount to an estimated total holding of more than 500 million pounds of skim powder.

The CDC was faced with large and continuing losses in export sales. It was estimated that the massive short-term rate of disposal could involve losses amounting to more than $575 million. There were discussions about long-term food aid in skim powder and a stronger commitment to the world food program.

In 1976 the annual report of the board stated, "The matter of the level of the within-quota and over-quota levy rates became a burning issue. The over-quota levy was established at $8.60 per hundredweight. The federal authorities insisted the levy should be applied in full even when the net return from the sale from over-quota milk after the deduction of transportation charges was insufficient to enable the producer to pay the $8.60. Your board has resolutely refused to follow the federal dictates in this area."

There was also federal insistence that the over-quota levy be applied on the five percent "sleeve" in each producer's MSQ. The board had refused to implement this directive, but the provincial government had stepped in and guaranteed to pay the federal authorities the difference between the over-quota levy and the within-quota levy produced within the sleeve if it was not required by the domestic market. The board had enthusiastically and publicly expressed its gratitude for this provincial action. "The result was that your board was able to release 16.8 million pounds of MSQ to those producers with the greatest need, alleviating in the short run at least the serious financial difficulties," the report read.

During this period "a quota policy" was a continuing challenge to the board. Quota was a necessary part of supply management. There were concerns regarding the value placed on quota and the development of an efficient and acceptable quota transfer system.

Quota prices had indicated that they were sensitive to factors both within and outside the dairy industry. For example, in October 1974 the average price for group one quota in the southern pool fell to $3.64 from $11.00 per pound in 1973. It was concluded that this was likely due to the cost price squeeze being experienced by milk producers as well as the availability of alternative opportunities in other sectors of agriculture.

There was still the problem with the so-called "hunt and seek" system of finding quota. The board had attempted to control prices by setting a price above which no quota could be approved by the board for transfer. The so-called quota price freeze, however, was not working.

"We're attempting to control the price, but we can't do it," said Grant Smith. "We can't stop the under-the-table payments."

"We have to get a better quota policy or our graduated entry program is going to grind to a halt," pointed out Alex Bell from Smiths Falls. "I'm getting complaints all the time from farmers in eastern Ontario who can't buy enough quota because they can't find someone who's selling quota. They don't know what's happening in western Ontario."

The board really didn't like coming between individual producers in the transfer of quotas. They believed the individual producer was in the best position to judge whether or when he required more or less quota and how much it was worth. But there was still a publicly perceived concern about high-priced quota, and it worried the board.

It was obvious, however, that the milk producers were not happy with the "hunt and seek" quota system. The Haldimand County milk committee recommended in the spring of 1976 that, "In order to make group one pool quota freely available, the Ontario Milk Marketing Board should lift the freeze and allow quotas to fluctuate by supply and demand and that they no longer publish the price of quota."

An attempt was made at a lottery system for allocating quota. The policy provided that the group one quota be allocated to the purchaser on a first come, first serve basis according to a registration date. For those with the same registration date there would be a lottery draw.

The system didn't work, and staff reported difficulty with the group one pool quota in that at one point there were 2,777 producers wanting 313,389 pounds of milk. Only 8,034 pounds apparently were available at the time, however, which amounted to less than three pounds per farmer. The board decided that the whole matter should be referred for discussion at the Geneva Park conference in the fall of 1976.

The Kates, Peat, Marwick report entitled "Marketing Industrial Milk in Ontario" had been tabled in the Ontario legislature on March 27, 1972. As noted earlier, the report had been harshly rejected by the board. The major recommendation had been that the Milk Commission of Ontario should give more leadership to Ontario's dairy industry. The ministry report of

1972 had indicated the MCO should assume a more responsible role in the area of dairy policy and in the "monitoring of existing programs and policies in the long-range benefit of the industry."

In the report the MCO's responsibilities were referred to more specifically, indicating it would "...act as an appeal tribunal for the milk industry, it would be a supervisor of the Ontario milk marketing plan, and would develop and formulate a provincial dairy policy for government consideration."

In mid-1969 George McCague had asked to be relieved of the chairman's duties on the MCO, but he continued on the commission. His role had been critical and essential during the formative years of the milk board. A negotiator and a facilitator, he was tireless in his efforts to ensure that the board made as few mistakes as possible in its formative years.

McCague was succeeded by Dr. Ken McEwen as chairman. McEwen assumed his responsibilities when representatives of the industry were beginning to express strong reservations about the board's handling of the milk marketing situation and, in particular, the difficulties being experienced with industrial milk supplies. McEwen's approach reflected a policy that was more "arm's length" and significantly sterner as a result of the industry environment.

After ten years as premier of Ontario, John Robarts retired in early 1971. A great champion of agriculture, Robarts had taken very personal and supporting interest in Bill Stewart's objectives and plans for a stable and financially healthy dairy industry in Ontario.

After Robarts left, there were continuing, heavy pressures on the government and on OMAF from processors, politicians and others who were critically questioning certain policies of the milk marketing board. These included supply management and the perceived shortage of milk for cheese factories and other industrial plants, and what some condemned as "abuse and misuse of power by the board which had been granted under the Milk Industry Act of 1965."

Accusations were being made that the milk board had taken over policy-making decisions from the ministry and that something should be done about it. It was seriously suggested by some that the board's marketing powers be curtailed or removed or, at the very least, a vote of producers be conducted to clarify the whole situation. The board was being accused of arrogance. It was a very sensitive situation.

Dick Hillard was now deputy minister of agriculture for Ontario. Basing its actions on the Kates, Peat, Marwick report, the commission was proceeding to develop a policy research capability. A director had been hired and arrangements had been made for a presentation to Bill Stewart. The meeting had taken place in the minister's board room, next to his office at 1200 Bay Street. The presentation had just started and had stated, "This whole area of policy development is in the form of an outline of where the government should be heading in the dairy industry. As an example, we could use the can to bulk conversion that must be dealt with."

The meeting had ended just about there. The mention of can to bulk conversion had killed it. Politically, it was just about the most sensitive matter at the time. Bill Stewart glared and said, "I'll set the policy for this ministry. Nobody else will be setting it."

The meeting ended.

Mention of the policy role of the commission in the annual reports of OMAF disappeared quite quickly. There was some mention in 1976 of policy guidelines being considered by Bill Newman, but nothing after that.

While Bill Stewart was feeling the intense pressure and was certainly extremely annoyed with some of the activities and stances taken by the board, however, he still placed the development of a milk marketing plan very much at the top of his continuing list of priorities. He was convinced that regardless of the situation a vote of producers would provide a platform for opposition and rejuvenation for other smoldering animosities. He decided he couldn't risk taking the gamble. In actual fact, while recognizing and accepting the unrest and criticisms as the expected outcome of the changes taking place in the industry, he was convinced that the result would be a successful and efficient milk marketing system in the province. He told his colleagues just that, and they listened to him.

As chairman of the commission, Ken McEwen realized that because of the importance and the sensitivity of the appeal procedure, as a practice he should not express opinions to the milk board on planned policies that they were considering. He was convinced he could not do this and then have the commission facing an appeal by someone from the industry against a decision that had been made by the board. The board voiced strong criticisms to the effect that they considered the commission was attempting to set policy in some of the decisions that they had made on appeal. The commission maintained that this was not their intention, but that they were ruling on the board's application of a given, specific policy. The commission maintained that the appeal procedure was a very necessary and important part of the marketing legislation and that they were there to protect the public interest. In this they were supported by Bill Stewart.

Of course, the board was also experiencing pressures, many of them extreme at times. It was over-sensitive to anything that the members considered an interference in the authority granted to them under the legislation, unless it was considered that they were not treating producers and the industry generally in a fair and equitable manner.

On February 21, 1973, there was a meeting between the commission and the board. The board stated, "It would appear that the commission is taking more of an interest in board policy, which is further exemplified by the recent decision the commission has rendered on appeals. Perhaps the board and the commission should meet with the minister of agriculture and food to clarify once again the roles and responsibilities of the respective parties under the Milk Act.

The board was emphatic.

"The commission should not hear appeals regarding a policy of the board unless the appeals come from large groups of producers or it is a matter which has interprovincial significance."

Ken McEwen, chairman of the commission, pointed out, "The appeal procedure has been there for everyone's use. The Milk Act would not have been passed without it."

"With respect to rcccnt appeal decisions," retorted a board spokesman, "your letter did not provide reasons that were satisfactory as far as the board is concerned. It would appear that senior ministry officials want more involvement in Ontario Milk Marketing Board affairs. What would the commission's reaction be if the board were to ignore the commission's decision and direction on the latest appeal?"

Later the same day the group was able to see Bill Stewart. George McLaughlin had expressed his concerns.

"It's time there is another review of the respective roles of the two parties so that there is a clear understanding. What is the board's role on policy development, particularly as its role relates to government? The board thinks that as long as it has the support of the majority of producers in policy areas, the commission should not interfere, providing the board does not discriminate between producers."

Someone in OMAF had commented, "It looks as if George McLaughlin puts his own interpretation on the powers delegated to the board, as the occasion necessitates."

"Of late the commission has been acting more like a board of arbitration rather than an appeal body, particularly on appeals on price," McLaughlin complained. "The board is not opposed to arbitration, but if the commission is to be an arbitration board, then it must have the necessary resources to do a proper job."

"There has been no essential change in the role and responsibilities of the commission versus the board," Stewart responded. "The commission does have the right to review and comment on board policies as they affect the producer and the public interest. I'm very concerned about the public interest. The commission is answerable to me, and I hope the commission keeps uppermost in its mind the public interest aspect in all of its dealings with groups of persons or individuals who make appeals to it. Unless the public interest is paramount, the commission would not be doing a proper job, as far as the elected members of the legislature are concerned."

The minister went on to congratulate the board for its efforts in the role it was playing in establishing a stable and sound dairy industry. He emphasized that there would not always be agreement on all issues. He urged greater communication and discussion among the commission, the board and the industry as a whole.

(A few years later, when the appeal responsibilities were removed from the commission and placed under the new appeal tribunal, Ken McKinnon was appointed as the first chairman. In 1990 he still held that very contentious post.)

Stewart had made it clear that while he knew of and appreciated the progress and the accomplishments of the board, he was very much supporting the milk commission in their watchdog role over the public interest and their responsibility and authority under the Milk Act of 1965.

Tensions continued, however. The board learned of the intent of the MCO to convene meetings of the county and district milk committees. The declared purpose had been "...to become more intimately acquainted with the problems and desires of the milk producers."

The board was not at all happy with the commission's moving directly to county meetings with the committees, who were very much an essential and integral part of the board administration. The board had agreed, "No extra monies will be supplied to the committees for the purposes of these meetings."

In addition, there was a real problem in communications. The board considered that "edicts are handed down" by the commission. There was no doubt that the commission was reacting to extreme pressures resulting from the board's strong and unwavering position that it had always attempted to take within the board policy guidelines. The board believed "Consistency in the application of policy to every situation is essential, and any deviation from this would result in serious administrative consequences."

The commission's administration also believed it should remain somewhat aloof from the board, particularly since it had the responsibility of an appeal tribunal. In addition, the government administration was reflecting some real public concerns and reacting within its envisaged responsibility while the board was following an unwavering straight line of determination to develop a much needed milk marketing system in the province. It was very much a part of how the system was evolving and should be remembered as such.

George McLaughlin recalls possibly his most serious disagreement with Bill Stewart. In 1967 the direct election of board members commenced with producers electing an election committee, which in turn selected a member to the board. The minister had decided in the mid-'70s that the system would be changed to one of direct election, in which each milk producer would have a vote.

"This was in 1972 or 1973," McLaughlin recalls, "and I remember the minister saying, 'You just don't believe in it, but it's a democratic process.' And I had replied, 'So is the present system.' The producers still make the choice. We wouldn't have some of the good people on the board if they had to stand for normal election and stump the country."

The system was changed, however, so that every milk producer had an opportunity to vote on the board member who was to represent his region.

Murray Smeltzer of Rockwood, as chairman of the Cream Producers' Marketing Board, was appointed by the minister to succeed Howard Goddard of New Liskeard in 1975. It was the practice to appoint the chairman of the cream board. He was to remain as chairman of that board until 1982, the longest continuous term on record.

Strong new faces were also appearing in the administration. Wes Lane joined the board on August 1, 1973, as an agricultural specialist and given the responsibility of looking at farm production programs. Wes recalls that there was a farm management goal established at that time which was a particular project of George McLaughlin.

"There were concerns about the low level of butterfat test in eastern Ontario," said Lane. "We had pilot programs in the Quinte area around 1975 or 1976 that eventually led to the udder health program."

Lane moved to Board/Industry Relations in 1977 and later was appointed director of planning.

Phil Cairns, with a master's degree in economics, joined the board in December 1975. "The board had been frustrated regarding costs of production because of the lack of any good source of comprehensive

After exemplary service as Minister of Agriculture since 1961, Bill Stewart stepped down from his government post in 1975.

information," recalls Cairns. "The board was determined to ensure that producers got a fair and reasonable return. It was decided that there would have to be a system of collecting input costs and that they would be available for use directly in the pricing process."

John Karn, in 1990 director of the production division of the board, started as supervisor of the field staff in 1974. He had been an assistant agricultural representative in York County and was an animal science graduate from Guelph. He grew up on a dairy farm in Oxford County.

Al Hick, currently director of marketing, joined the board from Silverwoods in 1974 and started as director of planning. He had been the general manager of the Ontario operation at Silverwoods, and his responsibilities included eight processing plants and about 1,000 employees.

"I can remember well the apprehensions in management with regard to losing control of the purchase of our milk," Hick said. "But at the time of the inception of the board, all the managers received a letter from Gordon Silverwood advising that it was Silverwood's policy that we cooperate with the Ontario Milk Marketing Board. It was quite unusual to receive a letter from Mr. Silverwood himself."

Much happened during the years 1973 to 1976. There were many instances in which the board's authority was exercised, and many in which that authority was challenged. The board had been tested and had emerged with renewed strength.

But faces were changing. George McLaughlin was invited to become chairman of the Federal Farm Debt Review Board. He was later to receive the Order of Canada.

Bill Stewart had retired in October 1975 and was stepping over the threshold of a period that would bestow many honours and recognitions, including the chancellorship of the University of Guelph, an institution that he had helped to establish almost ten years earlier.

Stewart had been asked to accept the agricultural portfolio by John Robarts in November 1961. Over the years he had received suggestions to assume other portfolios, and there were many who thought during his political career that he could have attained the leadership of his party. He chose instead to devote many hard and dedicated years to agriculture and to rural Ontario.

George McLaughlin was the "man of the time," personally selected by Bill Stewart to lead the milk producers in Ontario out of confusion and relative disorganization. The minister's choice had proven out. By 1977 producers could truly see what was ahead of them. They were sure they had an organization to fight their battles, whenever the need arose, for an industry that had taken shape in positive and productive ways.

George McLaughlin had been a tough master of the subject, determined and sometimes described as autocratic, but always with the objective in focus, with the assistance of his board and staff, to develop an industry that would create a desirable environment for milk producers.

CHAPTER SEVEN

Supply Management

In which the board

- Greets a new chairman
- Looks at quota exchange
- Duels with Gilles Choquette
- Considers quota prices
- Considers northwestern Ontario
- Reaffirms importance of market development
- Talks about the dairy bureau
- Updates long range goals
- Continues transportation policies
- Brings in milk of uniform quality
- Assists the cheese industry
- Converts to metric
- Considers the decade of the 1970s

George McLaughlin carried out his last official act as a member of the board on Friday, January 14, 1977. With considerable emotion he expressed his appreciation to the members.

"There's been a lot that's happened since that first meeting on August 19, 1965. The pressures have been great. The temptation for the board to waver from its established policies has always been there. Many of our meetings have been stormy. There have been some violent arguments, and the odd person has even walked out of a meeting. But the board members all remained steadfast and united as they moved about the province. We all realized that from the beginning this was essential, and I've appreciated it.

"I've spoken privately with Lorne Hurd and his very capable and loyal staff. The board would not have realized its accomplishments without them. Harry Parker, our board secretary, has given much of his considerable talents; the board has benefited greatly from his many years of experience, both here and with the English board. We've been very lucky."

Ken McKinnon became the OMMB's second chairman in 1977. He had been a member of the orginal appointed board. He served as chairman until 1986 when he became vice-chairman of the Canadian Dairy Commission.

As a token of appreciation for his dedicated service, the board presented McLaughlin with the furniture from the chairman's office.

Ken McKinnon of Region 11 was next elected chairman, with Grant Smith of Region 8 vice-chairman. Smith was one of the three board members who had been first elected to the board by producers in the fall of 1967. The other two were Ray McDougall of Glanworth and Harold Scott of Stratford. Elphege Lefebvre of St. Eugene had not sought re-election, and Jean-Claude Dutrisac of Navan was now occupying his chair. Howard Sheppard had been elected to fill George McLaughlin's vacated position in Region 5.

Ken McKinnon had proven his leadership abilities. Before the formation of the board he had been extremely active with the concentrated milk producers and had been selected by the minister in 1965 to serve on the first board. Ken had already proven he was very much the farmers' man and could identify with them. Elphege Lefebvre, who also had the ability to get along with the producers of his region, had been heard to comment at one time, "Ken, he is very stubborn, like a bulldog."

Prior to the meeting on January 14, the new chairman had had an extended and detailed discussion with Lorne Hurd to compare notes on what was ahead for the board. As vice-chairman, McKinnon had enjoyed a close working relationship with Hurd, and they both admired each other. At the first meeting, McKinnon commented to the board, "We've established the policy and recognized the need to plan ahead. We saw early adoption of the policy of management by objectives. But there have been many distractions from long-standing, undesirable situations that had to be dealt with. There are still some of those around. But as we get closer to the '80s we must treat the matter of long-term planning very seriously. We should all think about it."

"We have to attack the matter of milk quality," McKinnon continued. "All milk should be grade 'A' and this goes for the premises too. This matter should not be open to compromise. The group two milk producers are now in pretty good shape, and we should give some thought to a possible deadline. We'll have to deal with the quota transfer situation too."

There had already been some serious discussion on the matter of quota transfer. Some members still thought that safeguards might be needed in the system to prevent high quota values from developing. Political and consumer opposition to high quota values weighed heavily on board members' minds.

"Public and political reactions are one thing," Grant Smith commented, "and it could create a real mess if we give those reactions prime importance. Our major concern must be to provide flexibility, efficiency and, most of all, stability for Ontario's dairy industry in any policies we come up with."

The board agreed that it had to develop a simple, well-understood quota transfer system that would remain stable and treat all producers equally.

Someone raised the idea of a quota exchange. This had been discussed on several occasions and had proved to be quite controversial. Peter Oosterhoff, a member of the board for about four years, had been close to the dairy situation for a long time. "Producers like negotiating among themselves," he volunteered. "What I see is that they want to decide whether the prices should go up or down. They like dealing with each other. At the same time we've got to take out the middle man in quota transfers. The exchange seems like a very good idea, but we'd better make sure that the producers understand it before we move too quickly. We must always remember to talk to the county committees!"

In early February 1977, Ken McKinnon advised the board that he had been talking to Ken McEwen, chairman of the milk commission.

"I don't like the noises I hear coming out of Ottawa," said McKinnon. "Gilles Choquette, chairman of the CDC, has expressed a view that provinces can't continue to protect fluid sales. It sounds as if he's suggesting that if provinces don't move quickly enough toward a single pool that includes industrial milk, some sort of system will be imposed on them. He maintains that surplus fluid milk is creating surpluses of skim powder and butter."

"Isn't this a matter for the Canadian milk supply management committee?" asked Ray McDougall of Glanworth. "They have the responsibility to manage milk supplies. I don't think Choquette should be making this sort of statement."

Fluid milk surpluses were now becoming an issue at the federal level. In March 1977 Gilles Choquette made a lengthy presentation in which he had attempted to justify a levy on fluid milk. He was suggesting a levy of 25 cents per hundredweight on fluid milk and insisting, "Fluid milk producers must look to a national perspective."

The board was extremely upset. They responded, "All producers in Ontario are eligible to share in the fluid market. Fluid producers have sacrificed a great deal of their incomes to industrial shippers at the start of the graduated entry program, and they've spent many millions of dollars to increase sales in the fluid milk market. Fluid milk is a provincial responsibility."

The proposed 25-cent levy was now very much of an issue. The board sought legal advice, which Edge Harris provided: "A new national agreement, or at least an amendment, would be needed to implement an export levy on fluid milk."

Board members were saying, "We're convinced that the CDC's statement contains many inaccuracies in both detail and logic. Staff should prepare a written analysis."

Feelings were running very high.

In May 1977 Bill Newman telexed Eugene Whelan, the federal minister, confirming that Ontario was opposed to the fluid levy. Whelan reportedly stated that he was bound by a cabinet decision that called for the collection of the fluid levy starting June 1, 1977.

Newman then telexed all provincial ministers, suggesting that they undertake to guarantee contributions to the federal treasury totaling $13.5 million, proportionately according to the industrial milk shipments in each of their provinces. The payments would commence June 1, and the whole matter would be discussed at the annual July meeting of the ministers and deputy ministers of agriculture. Whelan delayed the fluid levy for one week to give the provinces a chance to respond to Newman's telex. The response from the provinces was not encouraging to Newman.

On July 6 the chairman and Lorne Hurd met with Choquette and the Quebec milk producers in an attempt to seek a compromise solution. There wasn't one.

The board had made its opposition to the levy well known, and it decided to delay the paying of the within-quota levy, which was due on July 10 for May industrial milk.

The CDC sent a telex to the board on July 15, 1977, expressing its disappointment with the board's decision and asking them to reconsider. "In the meantime, until the levy money owing the commission, plus the accruing interest, has been paid, the commission must delay subsidy payments to the producers," the telex read. An invoice was later received by the board from the CDC for interest amounting to $1,202.59.

The board's solicitor wrote to the CDC and asked, "Under what authority are you withholding the 25 cents per hundredweight from subsidy payments?"

The CDC's reply stated, "Whether or not the levy is legal, the point is irrelevant because it could be made legal."

It was quite a statement.

In an atmosphere of extreme annoyance at the perceived arrogance of the CDC, the board did decide to make immediate payment of the within-quota levy money that had been held back. A letter was also forwarded reiterating the board's dissatisfaction. No interest was paid on the delayed payment.

The board also agreed, however, that, "Members should reflect on this interest question, as we always do on policy issues, for the customary 30-day period and make a decision at the August regular meeting." This seems to be an interesting practice.

The interest was eventually paid, but the board had clearly served notice that it would not hesitate to challenge, in the strongest way possible, any perceived injustice. In this case, the point in question was the arbitrary decision on the levy taken by the CDC without agreement from the Canadian milk supply management committee and the participating provinces.

To add emphasis to their stand on the levy matter, the board conveyed its position in detail to Gord Bennett, the Ontario deputy minister of agriculture and food, with the intention that it be discussed at the deputy minister's meeting, which was being held on October 27 and 28, 1977, in Ottawa.

At the board meeting on January 31, 1980, there was real concern, because they had heard Gilles Choquette speak at the annual meeting of the Dairy Farmers of Canada where he had raised the issue of quota values. The DFC had decided to write to John Wise, at that time the federal minister, detailing their fears and criticism.

The board's reaction was, "If the CDC is going to go public supporting a zero quota value, it would have been more prudent to first consult with the industry representatives at a private meeting. The meeting also learned of the Ontario minister Lorne Henderson's questions regarding the same topic.

Allan Ross of Harriston, who had been on the board for a little over three years, had originally been a concentrated producer and then a member of the Wellington County milk committee from the beginning. He commented early in 1979, "We have to get moving on this quota transfer system. It's vital to the whole supply management picture and also to get some order into what's happening out there in the country. I wasn't on a main road so, I guess, without being able to use the graduated entry program in 1970, I still might be producing industrial milk. These outside pressures are going to build, and the only way we're going to be able to deal with them is to have a firm policy in place that will stand up."

Professors Stuart Lane and Murray McGregor, from the University of Guelph, had been supplying research and study material to the board. The matter had been discussed at the 1979 Geneva Park conference, and the idea of a quota exchange was a key topic. Producers had supported it in principle.

Some worried about the need for restrictions and controls on producers who might buy and sell quota on the exchange for profit. But the majority thought, "There shouldn't be any problem as long as it doesn't take place on the same exchange day." However, the board did not forget the words of warning from the Geneva Park meeting.

In early December 1979, the board received recommendations from staff based on the principle of a market-oriented system, which would see quota transfer move on the basis of price. Grant Smith, vice-chairman, echoed the words of the chairman: "For the board's consideration it should not set an initial price on either group one or MSQ. There should be no limit on the price movement on the exchanges."

They both argued, "If prices are set by the board on the high side, this would quickly become the trading price. It's wiser to put the responsibility squarely on the producers' shoulders for whatever price prevails on the exchange."

"There are still a lot of concerns about the level of quota prices," a member volunteered. "But I guess, as Grant Smith has said from time to time, 'It's the system that's important, and also that it have the flexibility to look after the producers' needs.'"

Stuart Lane, from the University of Guelph, initially saw great dangers in quota prices but later concluded, "There has been concern over the years about high quota prices. I've looked at it over time, and the more I looked, the more I became convinced that perhaps it wasn't a real problem. It's more perceived than real."

The board had discussed in March 1979 a study carried out by McGregor and Lane for the five supply management boards. One conclusion stated, "The average producer will be guided in the purchase of quota by his production costs and the price he receives on the market."

One of their colleagues, Bob Marshall, had done a lot of work in the development of the mechanics of the proposed quota exchange. He didn't seem to have any problems with quota prices either.

"There are still quite a few producers out there who like to see the other chap's face," said someone else. "They feel that they can make a better deal. I guess it's a little more interesting. It's like a game."

"But they're not always face to face with the seller," interrupted Ken McKinnon. "We've had too much third-party involvement. I'd like to draw your attention to the policy statement the board made last year: 'The board would like to eliminate third-party involvement in transferring quota among producers with an equal opportunity to all producers wanting to buy or sell quota and provide an accurate market value and eliminate any possibility of exploitation for personal gain.'"

The board members gave their approval and decided that the quota exchange be introduced in March 1980.

The exchange was not an auction. It would provide more flexibility for producers. The producer wishing to sell or buy quota would list his offer on the exchange by telex and by the seventh day of each month. Using a computer, board staff would match the volumes of quota and price that had been submitted by potential buyers and potential sellers and thus establish a clearing price. This would be the price at which successful participants would buy and sell quota.

Field staff received training and instruction on the new system during January 1980. Reference cards were prepared for producers, and the system was highlighted with every issue of *The Ontario Milk Producer*. Meetings were held with federal and provincial government agencies, the banks, provincial party caucuses and the Consumers' Association of Ontario, to thoroughly explain the new system.

There were a few problems, the most common being that producers failed at times to indicate whether the MSQ they wanted to buy or sell was used or unused. Some also were waiting until the last moment to send in their bids or offers, thus creating an unwieldy workload for board staff.

In April 1980 the market clearing price for group one quota was $65.50 per litre, unused MSQ was 21.1 cents, and used MSQ was 18.3 cents. By November the group one quota price was bid at $114.00 per litre.

Meanwhile, a particular problem had been developing relative to the Algoma and Sault Ste. Marie market. Although fraught with milk marketing problems, as in most areas, and with a very adequate share of controversial milk headlines in *The Sault Star* and elsewhere, the producers in the beginning hadn't been very supportive of the introduction of the milk marketing plan. Just prior to the board's inception the producers had been able to negotiate a very satisfactory market agreement with the local distributors.

In Algoma producers were getting older. There were alternative work opportunities for the younger people. Quota was moving out of Algoma at a rate that alarmed the local industry. They wanted a freeze placed on the movement of quota.

On May 23, 1979, Algoma producers stated, "In recent years producer numbers have decreased, essential agricultural services are being seriously threatened, transportation costs are increasing and quota milk production is moving out of Algoma. We are requesting that Algoma milk quotas be confined for sale in Algoma."

Algoma wanted to supply their own fluid milk needs. High quota prices being paid by producers in New Liskeard resulted in most quota being sold out of Algoma with little if any opportunity given to Algoma producers to bid for the quota. They had stated, "We have 95 percent support of the 47 Algoma shippers. If this request is granted, any quota offered for sale by Algoma producers will be purchased within the area at fair and competitive prices."

The board placed a freeze on all quota transfers in Algoma during June and July 1979 while the situation was being evaluated. A Region 12 meeting in June didn't give majority support to the freeze. Algoma in turn had insisted, "This request is of concern only to Algoma producers, and the approval of the other committees in the region should not be required. Let us make up our own minds."

Bernie Gallagher recommended that a meeting of the Algoma producers be held on July 5, 1979, to get a final decision on the matter. But there were travel problems. Gallagher was traveling with Ken McKinnon, and they had to get a small aircraft from Orillia Airways. They had problems finding the pilot and so telephoned to say that they would be late. They arrived at the Sault Ste. Marie airport and then had to travel 40 miles to the meeting.

Gallagher recalls, "There were more than 40 producers there. We arrived at 1:00 a.m., and apparently only two of them had left by then. This indicates how serious the matter was."

Seventy percent of those present at the meeting had supported a 50 percent transfer assessment on any quota moving out, and they supported the withdrawal of the freeze, since it was realized it could have serious consequences and would set a precedent.

With effect August 1, 1979, the board advised the Algoma milk committee, "The board will levy a 50 percent assessment on any quota moving out of Algoma, and any quota accumulating from the assessment will be made available to Algoma producers with consideration of new shippers. Any balance will be distributed on an equal basis among existing shippers in Algoma."

Because of the size of the assessment, no quota moved out. There were a few problems, but the policy did maintain sufficient milk production in the district to satisfy the needs of Sault Ste. Marie.

From the very beginning, the board had been conscious of the absolute necessity of promoting milk and milk products. They had inherited the promotional bodies for milk products, the Dairy Foods Service Bureau, under the Dairy Farmers of Canada, and the Associated Milk Foundations. The latter had been a joint fluid milk product promotion sponsorship between the producers and milk distributors in certain fluid markets.

The board had been preoccupied in the early years with developing a sound marketing system for raw milk. Not until the start of the 1970s were they able to turn their attention to that essential part of marketing - consumption.

Fluid milk made up about 40 percent of the market in Ontario and brought the highest producer return. Under the established promotional systems fluid milk had been steadily losing sales for some time. The board decided the trend had to be reversed. There was no other choice; it decided to take on the task of fluid milk promotion. Consumer marketing experts were retained to develop advertising and promotional programs. New staff were put in place. They were specifically instructed to review and strengthen nutritional and educational work related to milk and milk products. All this with the objective of halting the long-standing downward trend of per capita consumption of fluid milk.

The board had moved aggressively in 1972. Detailed consumption statistics were collected. Lorne Hurd recalls, "We wanted to find out how much money we had to spend to halt the trend and expand the fluid market.

At the time this was estimated at 20 cents per capita. We learned 55 percent of fluid milk was consumed as a beverage and 15 percent was used as an ingredient in cooking. The other 30 percent was being used with coffee, tea and cereal. We decided to concentrate our promotional efforts on the beverage and ingredient markets."

Over the years target audiences were changed. Advertising was used to correct numerous marketplace misconceptions inhibiting milk consumption. Positive moves were made to correct milk's image with certain groups. Target audiences were switched to teenagers and young adults, with a more aggressive attack against competing beverages. This was in a period of rapidly changing life-styles. Nutritional benefits of milk and milk products were advertised and influential educational programs initiated.

"With the teenage target groups in particular," Hurd remembers, "we successfully developed and implemented a number of fluid milk campaigns to make milk an acceptable beverage in this age group. We were pitted against very strong peer pressure against milk within the group."

The result? The long-term decline in fluid milk consumption was not only halted, but turned around. Between 1970 and 1974 total fluid milk sales increased by 9.7 percent, per capita consumption by 2.8 percent. The trend continued until 1979 when downward sales pressures increased. Adverse consumption pressures were coming from an aging population, an increasing nonmilk-drinking immigrant population, and changing life-styles. Economic pressures were also visible, particularly in the 1980s. The board did not change its mind.

"In a market economy we must compete," one member said. "A very necessary part of that is products promotion and advertising."

Billboard campaigns were mounted. The board was even involved in the sponsorship of Olympic gymnastics in Ontario. This had a climax in a China/Canada demonstration in Toronto that was most successful in achieving mass exposure for milk.

TV was used as well, and milk calendars were distributed. A "Milk Top Bingo" contest promotion was test marketed in Kingston - unsuccessfully. "They liked the bingo games in the church basements better," someone quipped.

The board had four nutritionists active in interviews on radio and TV. The promotions were winning national and international awards, such as for milk commercials in Venice and the billboard campaigns in Canada.

Recognizing that promotion is a very essential part of marketing, the board started to talk about "fluid milk market expansion" in very positive terms. Lorne Hurd is very proud of the promotional team that he first put together and which has been built upon since then. The New Product Promotion Division was established in 1972 with Dick Hutchinson as director. When he later left for McKim Advertising, he was succeeded by Keith Cowley, who died prematurely.

Bonnie Lange, the next new director, became the spark plug in milk promotion, as witnessed by her awards, until Michael Pearce took over in 1979.

Pearce had joined the staff in 1978 as advertising manager and then took over as director in 1979, succeeding Lange. He was the fifth person to head the division office since it was formed in September 1971, when responsibilities for the advertising and promotion of fluid milk were transferred to the board from the Canadian Dairy Foods Service Bureau.

"I joined the board about the time we moved from the famous 'milk moustache' campaign," Pearce recalls. "Now you can't make much of a moustache with two-percent milk, and even less with one percent.

"Then we went to the campaign, 'Thank you very much, milk,' which was very successful and very controversial. It targeted teens and young adults. Not many farmers liked it and there was a lot of fuss at Geneva Park. They weren't in the target group, and I guess they didn't appreciate the message. Everything you do in a creative sense must appeal to the minds of your target group. Also, of course, there weren't too many teen farmers around at that time, and the younger farmers weren't yet represented at Geneva Park.

"'Irreplaceable milk' was back in the 1982 period, and I believe this campaign assisted greatly in avoiding the decrease in consumption that would have taken place otherwise. We had quite a thumping recession at that time. We suffered a fairly modest hole compared to other retail products."

The board advertising was paying dividends. The 1977 annual report indicated the per capita consumption of fluid milk had increased for the second consecutive year. This increase took place in the face of a stagnant economy and two increases in the retail price level.

In 1978 the board boasted, "Ontario continues to have the highest per capita consumption of fluid milk in Canada; total expenditures are about $3 million."

In 1979 there was another one percent increase in consumption.

The Product Promotion Division was strengthened at about the same time.

Marketplace pressures were building up, however. There were rising costs, an aging population profile, a declining birth rate, an increase in out-of-home eating and a growing proportion of immigrants from countries that lack the milk drinking traditions typical of Ontario.

Promotion staff advised the board, "One-third of every food and beverage dollar is being spent in fast food outlets, family restaurants and hotels. A dramatic change is taking place in the life-style of people in Ontario and Canada. There is a traditional resistance in the food service industry to fluid milk."

By 1980 the negative factors of life-style and demographic changes, as well as economic pressures, were taking their toll. Some of the gains in fluid milk consumption were lost. A litre contained 12 percent less milk than a quart, and this resulted in a sales volume decline because people still tended to buy on a unit basis. They were not buying as much milk in total for the home either. Families were smaller, and more working men and women were eating out more often.

Milk was competing against very big promotional budgets of other beverages and food products. The board attempted to meet competition aggressively, but inflation had been eroding the promotion budget.

On the other hand, there were encouraging developments. In 1979-80, 6,200 Ontario teachers showed up for workshops on nutrition education. There was a fantastic increase in the distribution of milk calendars, which had been received by 1.6 million households, with 1.1 million being retained. Sixty thousand copies of a diet plan, "The Great White Way," prepared for the late teen and young adult women's market, were taken up by more than 60,000 interested persons.

Alex Bell was a member of the board from 1970 until March 1981. Shortly after joining the board he became a member of the Dairy Foods Service Bureau. This became the Dairy Bureau of Canada, and Bell headed it up from the spring of 1974 through 1981.

"At the beginning, and for a number of years, funding was one of the major problems of the bureau," Bell explains. "We were able to negotiate support from Eugene Whelan for a joint publicity program until the dairy farmers were able to pick up the tab for themselves. I think the bureau has proven over the years that it's capable of improving the market through advertising.

"The Dairy Bureau has had the responsibility of promoting the consumption of cheese and butter within its own discretion. The OMMB has two representatives on the bureau board and contributes about one-third of the gross budget. The bureau does arrange for certain appropriate research as well as checking on some of the claims of competing products.

"The bureau used to tangle with the Edible Oils Institute all the way from Europe into America," Bell recalls, "and we used to refer to it as the edible oil Mafia."

Bell still thinks, "Sometimes the Dairy Bureau didn't have all the support it might have had from the board. It was always difficult to measure results. The board was putting a lot of money into the Dairy Bureau, and some members of the milk board thought they were far too removed from management, since the bureau operation was separate. Claude Chevalier was very aggressive too. He was ahead of us most of the time, and I made the statement when I retired, 'At times I had to hold on to his coat tails so I could keep up with him.' But he was very capable and able to attract good people around him."

On March 6, 1990, however, in an address to the Carleton County annual meeting, Lorne Hurd stated, "Turning now to national promotion efforts on behalf of manufactured dairy products, your board was very instrumental in the mid-'70s in getting the Dairy Bureau of Canada to revise and revamp its advertising programs to use a 'rifle' instead of a 'shotgun' approach towards activities, and to concentrate most of its expenditures on cheese and later the butter markets, where more than 80 percent of the manufacturing milk supplies are used."

Hurd advised the Carleton producers further, "Since the introduction of margarine in 1949, butter sales had declined steadily. Between 1968 and 1978 alone, per capita butter consumption fell by 38 percent.

"The CDC and the milk producers decided in 1978 to see if generic advertising and promotion could halt the decline. Government funds were used at first as a catalyst and then matched by producers. This was carried out by the Dairy Bureau of Canada, with the end result that the long-term per capita decline in butter consumption was halted and the level of per capita sales remained virtually steady until the last two years.

"There have been steady increases in the investment that producers have been asked to contribute to market expansion activities," Hurd continued. "I would simply remind you that this policy is based not only on positive results, but on the fundamental premise that the size of our dairy industry in the future is going to depend, to a considerable extent, on meeting and beating the competition for the consumer's food and beverage dollar."

Long-range planning had been very much a part of Lorne Hurd's administration and the board's planning policies. The 1979 annual report noted, "The past year is viewed as a possible springboard for the next decade. Many new programs are ready for implementation in the early 1980s." In January 1977, during his first meeting as chairman with the board, Ken McKinnon had made the same emphasis.

In 1979, priority goals were established. The board indicated its intent to minimize the cost of transportation through better use of equipment and facilities. The board believed it had a responsibility in having programs leading to improvements in productivity at the farm level and was giving attention to the dairy herd improvement program. The board also decided to reduce the incidence of mastitis through field activities with producers.

In 1980 two planning conferences were held and long-range plans were reviewed.

Some revised statements of objectives were adopted, including:

• To provide an opportunity for efficient milk producers to achieve net incomes from management, investment and labour equal to those of comparable enterprises.

• To maintain an environment of confidence and stability in the market for milk, and thus to supply the market demands for milk, including Ontario's share of the national requirements for industrial milk, to the mutual benefit of consumers and all dairy industry participants.

• To promote efficiency in the production and marketing of raw milk so that milk and dairy products will be as competitive as possible with other beverages and food.

In 1981 the board was busy developing goals for the 1980s. These included a financial measurement to determine the extent to which milk producers were receiving net incomes equal to those of comparable enterprises. They wished to increase the percentage of producer herds on milk recording to at least 70 percent of the total number of herds by July 1, 1985. They wished also to develop and recommend a program of testing fresh milk samples for paying producers and billing processors, and to develop and recommend a system of multiple component pricing in Ontario.

The board looked at the marketplace and recognized the fierce competition out there from the beverage industry and other competing products. It was "promote or perish."

Above all, the board decided, "Good long-range planning is essential if producers are going to favourably influence the course of their own destiny."

Conversion to metric was not an easy change. It was like a new language. The board's metric committee had been giving much attention and study to pending changes, and in November 1977 had agreed that the conversion factor for group one pool quotas would be that one litre equals 2.2700826 pounds. The complete conversion was a significant task for the industry.

Open discussion and cooperation among all facets, including government, resulted in a conversion from imperial to metric measurement on April 1, 1978. This involved the conversion of farm bulk milk tank charts, raw milk prices and the butterfat differential, transportation rates, fluid milk package size and units of measurement. The conversion to metric involved approximately 400 changes in the board's regulations.

Transportation was a matter that had received the board members' continuous attention since 1965. They had guided change, nurtured it, prodded when necessary, all the while attempting to give transporters fair and adequate returns. At the same time they recognized that the resultant savings and efficiencies would be measured in terms of dollars for the industry and for consumers.

The 1977 annual report noted, "While transporter input costs have increased by 80 percent in the past five years, the board's transportation expenses have increased only 50 percent, made possible through improvements in route rationalization and milk direction, route consolidation and increased volume per truck. The number of plants has decreased at the same time by 100, to 153. This means that it is necessary to transport milk longer distances and at increased cost."

In the late 1970s it was costing $25 million per year to transport producers' milk. One of the board's goals was to "Develop a program to minimize milk transportation costs to improve utilization of milk transport equipment and facilities." Studies were instituted in five areas of transportation. Joint study committees were established with the Milk Transport Association to develop ways and means to achieve transportation cost savings, computerized transport routing and milk direction.

"The big savings were in transportation, and measured to hundreds of thousands of dollars too!" recalls George McLaughlin.

Marked changes were taking place. There were larger trucks, conversion to pumpover depots, transport trains, increased double-tripping of equipment and greater use of tractor-trailer pickup units. There were some problems with inadequate access conditions to some producer milkhouses and to plant receiving areas. It was decided that cooperation would be required in the improvement of farm yards and lanes if transportation economies were to be truly realized.

Transportation had been a continuing problem in northwestern Ontario. The Kenora-Fort Frances milk committee wanted one primary transportation rate for all producers in the Dryden, Kenora-Rainy River pool and the same rate charged regardless of the producer's location. Staff provided an analysis of the history of transportation costs in northern Ontario.

The board considered the possibility that transportation charges for Kenora-Rainy River and Thunder Bay be pooled over a three-year period to commence July 1, 1980. The northern Ontario pool was not included since analysis indicated this would not benefit the Kenora-Rainy River producers and would increase the Thunder Bay charges even more. In April the Thunder Bay District milk committee asked for a delay in the implementation of the proposed pooling.

Due to legal advice the board had not pursued the proposal to pool transportation in northwestern Ontario. Such a change would not be permitted between separate pools under existing legislation. Existing pool areas would have to be totally amalgamated in respect to all matters. This would take place in the future.

It was pointed out to the milk committees that the question "...involved the amalgamation of several policies such as quotas and payment methods." As well, other affected parties would have to be given an opportunity to present their positions. Rainy River agreed the board should have time to examine all of the implications of the proposal.

Both OMAF and the board had as their objective a common goal - that the production of all milk would be of the same quality. The goal had always been the same, but there had been differences of opinion about the time frame involved. The ministry had been influenced by some real concerns regarding the speed at which milk producers could be expected to adjust and make the necessary expenditures to improve farm premises.

In any case, on June 1, 1975, a new milk quality payment program had been introduced by OMAF. Previously, the provincial regulations provided that producers of persistently low-quality milk would be shut off from the market.

At first introduction, the quality penalties applied only to the group one pool. The same penalties would be extended to the group two pool shippers on September 1, 1980. This was part of a planned process to move to the production of milk of a uniform standard.

In February 1977 the board had reaffirmed its policy that all milk of the same quality should be eligible for the same rate of return. "This area is not open to compromise," said Ken McKinnon.

Discussions within the board and at regional meetings continued, and in the summer of 1979 the milk quality goal of the board was re-emphasized: "The board intends to introduce a program that requires all milk to obtain a common standard for quality and farm premises."

In the meantime, some concerned farmers had been expressing fears to Lorne Henderson, the OMAF minister. During the fall of 1979 he had questioned the board's proposals regarding quality. He wanted some additional information on the proposed common standards for farm premises.

After reviewing the material supplied by the board, the minister was prepared to support the program but did express concerns about sufficient time for producers to comply. As a result, the target date for producers to meet the grade "A" requirements was changed to September 1, 1981. Agreement was reached that board personnel would proceed with discussions with OMAF staff to develop implementation procedures.

The 1981 annual report of the board included a comment from the chairman, Ken McKinnon.

"The attainment of a single quality grade for all milk, from both the bacteria and premises aspects, is an event of enormous significance, not only from the point of view of improving our products for the consumer, but also from the viewpoint of enabling the board to refine its marketing and transportation programs."

Leland Wannamaker, from just outside of Napanee, joined the board in 1980. Wannamaker had been a cheese milk producer until 1950, when he had started shipping fluid milk. During his seven years on the board he gave strong support to cheese concerns and took much delight in debating the many issues.

"In my opinion the biggest enemies of the industry are not the consumers, but (1) the academics; (2) the bureaucrats; (3) the politicians; and (4) the other segments of agriculture," he said bluntly.

"When I came on the board, small cheese factories, including those around Napanee, were short of milk. It took about five years to resolve the shortage. I fought some real battles over that. I also battled about the selling of the Belleville warehouse, and they used to talk about it on the board to get a rise out of me."

The cheese situation continued to enjoy its share of attention and discussion on the board. The board members representing the cheese areas were aggressive. OMAF received continuous pressure from cheese area MPPs and cheese factories themselves. All of this was felt by the board.

An industrial milk marketing method review committee was established in 1979 to examine pressing and plant supply quota policies for industrial milk and to make recommendations to the board. The committee was assisted by OMAF and the University of Guelph. A package of proposals was developed with objectives of ensuring that milk would be supplied to protect growth areas, so that producers could achieve the best returns for their milk, and as well, that the smaller cheese processors would be protected from further milk supply reductions.

From time to time, accusations were angrily made at board meetings that some of the members, including the chairman, didn't understand the importance of the cheese industry among the board's responsibilities. George McLaughlin replied at one time with pointed humour, "I may not understand it, but I'm certainly aware of it. Cheese milk producers have some difficulty in separating their thinking from the end product cheese. We're a milk marketing board. You've had some different approaches over the years in marketing cheese and paying for milk.

"I well recall when we first visited a cheese factory meeting not too far from Kingston, when the producers first saw the butterfat tests coming from the board. There were individual variances. The plant had been paying the patrons on a flat 3.4 percent. I had to go down to a meeting there, and there was no way that they would believe there was so much difference between herd tests. We checked the overall plant average, and it was about 3.4 percent. Collectively, the plant wasn't cheating them, but over the years apparently the wrong impression had been given regarding milk tests; they all thought they were producing 3.4 percent milk."

The review committee proposals were discussed with the Ontario Dairy Council, but a consensus could not be reached. Too many plants had their own particular needs and ideas about policy.

During the late spring and early summer of 1980, discussions were held with Lorne Henderson and his officials. Henderson had succeeded Bill Newman as Ontario minister of agriculture and food. As well as a desire to find ways and means of helping the cheese plants with their milk supply, the board was considering selling the warehouse at Belleville. There was less demand for storage space in it, and the board had agreed that they couldn't afford to continue operating the warehouse at a loss.

The Ontario Dairy Council supported the board's proposal to discontinue its cheese export marketing activities but had no objection to the board's retaining the marketing powers.

The Hastings County milk committee asked that the board delay any decision on the cheese industry until some consultation had been had with interested parties. They had submitted their concerns by letter, "...so we can be presented with facts relevant to the case rather than trying to deal with rumours."

The Hastings County council contacted the board, expressing concerns about the possible closing of the Belleville warehouse. The board replied, "We aren't thinking of closing, but rather selling or leasing the facility, but all of the views of the industry will be taken into consideration in any decision."

There was a real concern about the declining volume of residual milk, which was going to butter and powder plants. The discussions had gone on for about two years and the cheese industry was getting impatient. They were concerned about milk supplied and the board's attitude toward cheese. In the spring of 1981, there were 43 people at a meeting in Trenton, including producers and cheese processors from central Ontario including Harrow, Black River, Eldorado, Harrowsmith and Maple Dale. A board spokesman stated, "We will attempt to operate the warehouse for another two years and at that time the warehouse business will be reviewed. The board doesn't intend to be in the export business but will retain all of its cheese marketing powers."

The board was having some difficulty reaching a decision. Leland Wannamaker was concerned.

"There has to be a decision on ensuring that these smaller plants get sufficient milk. There should be some minimum quotas for these plants which will take some priority over quota-free milk for industrial purposes. I like the idea of a minimal guarantee of milk for the small cheese factories."

"We have to move on this," suggested Ken McKinnon. "I suggest that we regard this as an interim solution for cheese and that the overall problem continue to be evaluated. Would you consider, as well, a date of August 1, 1982, for the implementation of a new policy?"

After considerable discussion the board agreed, and the cheese plants welcomed the new plan. It involved a minimal guarantee of milk for smaller cheese factories. It was relatively successful. Some of the plants would have liked a little more milk, but they now had a specific minimum guarantee that gave them more security for planning and management.

While Bill Newman was still minister, he had witnessed strong pressures to maintain the market for cheddar cheese in the U.K. He had also been attempting to meet the shortage of milk in the smaller cheese factories by another means. He'd appealed to the federal minister for additional MSQ.

On June 22, 1978, the chairman and the vice-chairman, Grant Smith, met with Newman. He asked them to try, over the long term, to maintain the U.K. cheddar cheese market. The board agreed to try to procure cheddar cheese for export.

The board staff advised that a premium on cheese, together with quota-free milk, would bring forth enough cheese to meet the U.K. requirements. Staff thought that the plants wouldn't be interested unless the premium and additional milk supplies were tied together. All this had been reported to the minister on June 22.

In the meantime, the Ontario Dairy Council was appealing the board's proposed cheddar cheese export program to the milk commission. The commission had granted the council's appeal. They had not been aware of Bill Newman's request to the board.

The members exploded. They couldn't understand. They had been advised by Newman to proceed with the program, and so Grant Smith was requested to immediately contact the minister's office for his advice and clarification of the milk commission's decision. The advice came back, "Request another 14 million pounds of MSQ from Eugene Whelan, the federal minister, to make enough cheese to export to the U.K." Newman was upset.

The board was bewildered. They were aware of the tensions among the cheese factories, and they had been intending to explain the current cheddar cheese situation to the county milk committees, but had been hoping for a solution before writing to them. They were suddenly enlightened and thrown into the public spotlight.

Joe K. Raison had written to the premier, to Bill Newman, the OFA and various newspapers. His letter stated, "Because of a sincere and profound concern for the present status of our dairy industry in general and the cheese producers in particular and the direction in which we are heading, the chairman of the board should resign and be replaced, and over the long term the board should be disbanded."

The newspapers printed Raison's letter. A furor was created. Bill Newman was upset because he was getting queries from Premier Bill Davis, his cabinet colleagues and many MPPs.

The board realized that they had erred in not getting more information out on the cheese situation earlier. They couldn't wait any longer, and four press conferences were called to explain the problems associated with cheese milk supplies.

When Bill Newman retired as minister in August 1979, he took home with him a gift that I had presented when he left the Ministry of Environment to go to Agriculture and Food about five years previously. He'd always jokingly maintained that he kept it in the centre drawer of his desk where, I had told him in jest, Bill Stewart had kept a similar instrument.

Stewart's cabinet colleagues always admired his facility for handling delegations in his office. Bill Newman had asked me more than once about his methods, and of course, when he was asked by Bill Davis to go to Agriculture and Food, he was even more curious.

As was the custom when anyone was leaving or retiring, middle and senior management and others gathered in the large board room located on the 14th floor of the Ministry of Environment's offices at 135 St. Clair West in Toronto. As deputy minister I had the responsibility to chair their meeting and make a few remarks on behalf of the staff.

In my concluding remarks I'd commented, "Mr. Minister, you're going to Agriculture and Food. From time to time you have expressed some interest in Bill Stewart's techniques in handling difficult delegations from marketing boards and other organizations. I'm going to let you and this group here today in on a secret which until now has been carefully guarded.

"During my more than 11 years in the Ministry of Agriculture and Food as deputy with Bill Stewart, I've seen many delegations go into his office. Some have come out looking rather shaken and subdued. With such difficult groups Bill Stewart quite often, without comment, would remove a particular instrument from the centre drawer and carefully lay it on the top of the desk. Bill Stewart is leaving and I'm sure he won't mind if you have the benefit of knowing at least one of his secrets of success."

I'd spent $28.00 a few days before and bought a shiny stainless steel set of burdizzos. Bill Newman opened the box and laid his gift on the table. He seemed to get the message and made a few appropriate remarks.

Practically all of the Ministry of Environment's staff were from the urban environment, male and female alike. They had never heard the word "burdizzo" before, let alone seen a set. Very intrigued, they pressed around Newman, asking questions. I left the minister to explain the intricacies of that particular utensil and the specific farm practice involved.

As a guide in establishing the price for milk going into fluid milk products, the board had adapted the formula used under the Milk Industry Act of 1957. It was based on the indexing principle and was not a direct reflection of actual farm input costs.

Inflation had been relatively high in the early 1970s. Farmers were not completely satisfied with milk prices, and the board had no means of accurately determining farm costs. This became a real concern when wage and price controls were brought in during the mid-'70s. The board had been completely frustrated because of the lack of any good source of comprehensive information.

Costs were increasing. The board was determined to ensure that producers got a fair and reasonable return for their labour and management skills. The first use of farm costs by the board was in 1974 when information that had been gathered by the economics branch of OMAF was used to determine the cost formula. Not satisfied, however, the board looked for alternative sources of information and data. It was decided to create a project that would have as its primary objective the collection of production cost information.

The Ontario Dairy Farm Accounting Project, or ODFAP as it was soon called, was born out of a series of industry discussions in the summer of 1975 and made its start in 1976. It was a cooperative effort among the board, OMAF, the CDC and Agriculture Canada. Agriculture Canada was interested because it wanted more exact figures for the target returns formula that it had developed in 1975.

Phil Cairns, senior economist on the board's staff, explains, "The project is based on 150 randomly selected participants. Currently, individuals are asked to stay for a period of five years. They're then dropped and replaced by another person. One of the matters that has received much attention recently is the fundamental approach of collecting data on labour hours with particular reference to cost. We've started to use time sheets with farms coming on in 1990. Ontario, Quebec and New Brunswick have been attempting to harmonize the method of collecting data so that we would be comparing apples to apples and not apples to oranges. This has become necessary because of the importance of the data being collected and the very high visibility of the numbers. The Ontario data on costs has been invaluable for board purposes."

In the fall elections of 1980, Bill Schouten joined the board from Region 4, Jim Tunney came in from Region 5 and John Core, a future chairman, from Region 9. The board was continuing its momentum and ensuring its future strength with each new face appearing around the board room table.

The Challenge of Achievement

The Ontario Dairy Council had maintained its strong voice on behalf of the processors, but from time to time had problems as it attempted to present a consensus of a membership that represented many separate and competing operations.

Following Gord Bennett, Ken Lantz became OMAF's deputy minister in 1978. He had been an ag rep in southwestern Ontario in the mid-1960s. Lantz smiles as he recalls, "We had some wild times and wild meetings. I remember some reports of threatened physical violence. The younger milk producers won't remember, but maybe their fathers will. These were interesting, exciting and sometimes frustrating times, but through it all there was great reason within the industry for real satisfaction and pride in setting a new course. This course must be maintained."

In 1979 Orville Sinclair, the ODC's executive secretary, was getting ready to retire. He had been a milk distributor in London and a past president of the distributors' association. He had been executive secretary of the council since its beginning. As the council's chief administrator he had given balanced and sympathetic leadership to the changes taking place in the industry.

"The times were tempestuous and hectic, but very exciting," he said. "The changes had to come, but they hurt at times."

The decade of the '70s was over and the board had crossed the threshold of the 1980s. The board was looking back with pride, which was shared by the committee men and many others. The board and its staff were looking forward with confidence.

There had been many accomplishments during the previous decade. Many of them had balanced on the fulcrum of supply management. They had been introduced, challenged and tested. Supply management was now the philosophy and credo of the vast majority of milk producers in Canada. It had been accepted as policy by the governments of the milk-producing provinces and by the government of Canada.

CHAPTER EIGHT

The Channel Islands Saga

In which we see

- Reflections on the start of two-percent milk sales
- The organization of CIBMPA
- The Channel Islands challenge
- Interbreed competition and confrontation
- Channel Islands milk promotion
- Channel Islands producers and Hennessey
- Legal battles and the OMMB
- The acceptance of legal inevitability

It was March 1, 1985, 4:00 p.m., and the sun was still shining on a day that had otherwise been gloomy for Francis Redelmeier. Redelmeier was one of the early elected members of the board and a member from 1968 until 1979. He was now president of the Ontario Channel Islands Breeds Milk Producers' Association. He had just finished chairing a meeting of the organization, which had not met since 1981. As he swung his car out of the United Breeders in Guelph he thought rather sadly, "This will likely be the last meeting for some time."

There had been only one item on the agenda: "The future of the CIBMPA." The organization had been formed in 1956 by a group of very aggressive and enthusiastic young milk producers from the Jersey and Guernsey breeds. They had embarked on a milk marketing program for Channel Islands milk, which as early as 1956 was meeting with some success. As well, improved milk sales were increasing the demand for Jersey and Guernsey cattle. All this happened some ten years before the introduction of the Ontario Milk Marketing Board.

As Redelmeier turned his car toward Highway 7, heading for his farm at

Maple, his mind went back over the many years of association with the milk business. His family had come to Canada before World War II and had established a substantial farm at Maple. Coming from Holland, they quite naturally might have established a Holstein herd, but inquiries indicated that the dairies in Toronto had all the Holstein milk they wanted. There was a demand for Jersey milk, however.

Jersey and Guernsey breeders had always been interested in selling milk because they recognized this was important since it created a demand for cattle. Jersey breeders always said, "If we can sell milk, we can sell cattle."

Redelmeier had been active in the Toronto Milk Producers' Association as well as the Ontario Whole Milk Producers' League. He recalled that his election into the league had been done by mainly Holstein breeders, who were the majority in his region.

He had always believed that controversy never did anyone any good, but controversy came.

Back in the early 1950s everyone was getting very concerned about cholesterol and heart disease. As well, at this time the public, the media and politicians were very conscious of the price of milk. Back in early 1952 there was an increase in fluid milk prices, and in order to cushion the price increase Colonel Tom Kennedy, the Ontario minister of agriculture, recommended regulations allowing partly skimmed or two-percent milk. This milk would be sold at a cheaper price than regular milk and, it was hoped, would soften the blow of a price increase and the traditional front-page headlines in the Toronto media, which appeared every time there was an increase in milk prices.

Jersey milk had been sold as a specialty product. There was even a special bottle with a bulb on top to facilitate the collection and pouring off of the cream. Butter had been rationed during World War II and as a result cream was not allowed to be sold, and this had apparently increased the popularity of Jersey and Guernsey milk. In the immediate post-war years, however, Channel Islands milk was losing markets, and interest in Channel Islands cattle was diminishing.

John Bull of Brampton was on the family farm of more than 1,000 acres and had a Jersey herd, all of which traced back to Jersey Island. He had picked up the challenge that the breed was facing in Canada. He believed that the Jersey milk, with higher solids than standard, would present a more attractive product to the consumer. Profiting from the experience in the United States, his enthusiasm provided the impetus for the launch of All Jersey two-percent milk. He managed to get a licence for his own dairy in Brampton in order to sell All Jersey products. His product base was too narrow, unfortunately, and his dairy was not a success.

The Channel Islands milk saga began to roll, however. There was great enthusiasm. The proponents and champions were young and with the complete determination to rescue the failing Channel Islands cows. Their effort was voluntary. They had no legislation to give them power and authority. The days were exciting.

In March 1954 Jack Pawley of Caledon Farms, and later an employee of the OMMB, was appointed chairman of a committee to promote Jersey milk sales in Ontario. John Bull was the playing coach.

A vigorous campaign was planned to market trademark Jersey milk, and producer participants were asked to contribute ten cents per hundredweight. By 1955 the All Jersey two-percent milk had spread to Ottawa and London, with work being done in Peterborough, Toronto, Barrie, Stoney Creek, Kitchener, Galt, Listowel and Midland. There were even some promotional programs on television and radio in London.

"There's unqualified enthusiasm from the distributors," stated Pawley. "Our London program has surpassed all of our expectations. The price of Jersey cows has gone up by $50.00 a head. New herds are being established to take care of the increasing demand. We're off at last."

The basic purpose was to sell more Jersey cattle. The Holstein breeders were not amused. The Jersey activities were also a thorn in the side of the Ontario Whole Milk Producers' League. Antagonisms built up and there were attempts to delay and obstruct the development of Jersey milk sales.

Jack Pawley reported to the 1956 annual meeting, "There are still many obstacles to overcome, but the highway to Jersey progress is at long last looking much smoother and brighter."

In 1956 at this same meeting in Woodstock there was a unanimous vote to pull out of the Toronto Milk Producers' Association and join the Canadian Guernsey Breeders' Association and create the Channel Islands Breeds Milk Producers' Association. They believed that with a new organization they could cooperate with the Ontario Whole Milk Producers' League and ignore any other fluid market organizations.

At the same meeting there was a veritable gauntlet thrown down in the face of the standard milk producers. Jack Pawley unveiled a program to "...invade the Toronto market with the new All Jersey two-percent homo." He gushed, "The high solid, lower fat and lower priced product is a product we've created for the consumer."

Battle lines were being drawn. Inspection of a new group of Jersey and Guernsey shippers, organized for the Toronto market, was not approved by the Toronto Milk Producers' Association. The Channel Islands producers withdrew from the Toronto organization, and Ernie Crossland of Newmarket was elected the first president of the CIBMPA. It was decided that political matters would be handled by the new organization and that the two breed associations would look after the organization and sale of their own milk.

The November 1956 issue of *The Jersey Breeder* reported, "The All Jersey programs in Ontario are successful even beyond the most optimistic forecast. We are now in 19 dairies in nine Ontario centres. There is a problem of supply. In Toronto seven dairies, which have taken on the program, need to get more Jersey milk."

By January 1957 All Jersey milk was in 21 markets in Ontario. The 40 percent surplus for Jersey milk shippers had suddenly changed to almost 100 percent at top price. The price for Jersey cattle was still increasing as well.

The Guernsey breeders saw an introduction of their two-percent product in 1957. They maintained that their sales had not decreased the sale of standard milk and had actually decreased the trend toward skim milk powder. Bruce Hodgins, secretary of the Canadian Guernsey Breeders' Association, argued that the swing to powdered products for fluid use had also been reduced.

The CIBMPA was now having some success in negotiating with the Ontario Whole Milk Producers' League. The league was the only fluid milk producer group recognized under the Milk Industry Act in Ontario. Jack Pawley, whose nephew later became the premier of Manitoba, was whipping up aggressive pride among the Jersey breeders.

"In our Jersey breed we have been lashed by the tongues of individuals drunk with the power of numbers and money, flaying unmercifully the individual who even attempts to support his favourite breed."

In 1957 the advertising agency responsible for the Jersey promotion, while talking about the remarkable acceptance of Jersey milk, also talked about "seeds of disaster." The speaker had recognized the promotion as "one of the soundest merchandising steps taken in the dairy industry in recent years."

The agency spokesman had asked, "Is it not reasonable to expect that faced with such an overwhelming demand for this product and with insufficient supplies of true Jersey milk with which to meet the demand, a distributor will feel compelled to deliver some kind of two-percent milk to his customer, whether it's called 'All Jersey' or not? Whether it carries the 'All Jersey' trade mark or not? Can we prevent him or blame him for calling it 'Jersey type' or 'Jersey content' whether it is all or partly Jersey or not Jersey at all? Where then will our Jersey milk be heading - inevitably back into the blending vat with the so-called standard milk? Supply is a problem."

Interest continued to grow in the Channel Islands milk program, however. *The Canadian Jersey Breeder* editorial of June 1958 stated, "Before the new AJ program took off, membership in the Jersey cattle club was dropping every year. It was beginning to look as if the Jersey and Guernsey breeds had seen their best days."

Reports from 1958 indicated that the Jersey AJ program milk sales had quadrupled in four years. Ralph Walker of Walkerton dairies took on the AJ program in 1957. Very interested in milk marketing, he was a producer/distributor who later challenged the authority of the OMMB before the Supreme Court of Canada.

Though the Jersey activities were more dominant, the Ontario Guernsey Cattle Breeders' Association was working enthusiastically. It was reporting that sales of cattle were breaking all records due to its active milk program. On February 3, 1960, Guernsey president Ernie Crossland exclaimed, "There are 15 dairies on the co-operative marketing program. Voluntary deductions have increased. I believe we've hit the jackpot!"

In the meantime, tensions were growing between the Channel Islands organization and the whole milk league. The league wanted the butterfat differential tied directly to the wholesale price of butter. The Jersey people thought this would be detrimental to the sales of Jersey milk. "The league does not represent the rank and file of producers," argued John Bull. "Perhaps the only recourse is to break away from the league and negotiate independently."

Irritations were growing. Gordon Greer of Carleton County, president of the OFA and already a recognized leader in the dairy industry, speaking to the annual meeting of the Dairy Farmers of Canada in March 1960, stated, "Two-percent milk is a danger to the milk industry in Ontario."

The Jersey people had responded by saying, "Greer is speaking the sentiments of the many pure-bred Holstein breeders among the standard shippers who load the annual meeting of the whole milk producers' league."

All sorts of accusations were floating around against the Channel Islands producers. They were being accused of being responsible for the drop in sales of standard milk. Speakers suggested they were largely responsible for the butterfat surplus. Comments were being made to the effect that in a short time the dairy cattle in Ontario would be predominantly Jersey and Guernsey.

Thinking people realized that most of the accusations had little basis in fact. With some exasperation many were saying, "Milk is milk and should be sold as such."

Thought was being given to milk composition. Some producers were beginning to recognize that milk components could be a merchandising feature. In September 1961 *Hoard's Dairyman* had stated, "Greater stress must be placed on solids-not-fat."

By the end of 1961 it was reported that chain stores in Ottawa and other cities were handling an increasing amount of two-percent milk. An Ottawa promotion was described thus: "An attractive young Ottawa housewife has been engaged to impersonate Miss AJ. She arrives unannounced and waits at the checkout counter in each store. She selects a customer with a supply of two-percent AJ in her cart. She approaches and comments on the AJ milk and then offers to pay the grocery bill. The customer is interviewed briefly regarding reasons for buying two-percent AJ milk."

The Channel Islands marketing efforts were becoming even more organized. The Jersey people had an aggressive committee consisting of Harold Butcher, Maurice Beaty and John Bull. Beaty was chairman of the CIBMPA and was later to become one of the appointed members of the Ontario Milk Marketing Board. The organizational strength was now such that the Channel Islands people were given a representative on the Provisional Marketing Committee Board appointed by Bill Stewart in 1962. Its failure had resulted in the appointment of the Hennessey committee.

By 1962 the CIBMPA had already expended several thousands of dollars in protecting their marketing efforts from attack.

"It's a strange paradox that we have expended these monies to protect our interest from the league, into which we pay dues," said Ernie Crossland. "It's supposed to represent us. It's in this area that we have the most thorns."

The Golden Guernsey Distributors Association was formed in 1962 to exchange ideas and purchase supplies cooperatively. The headquarters were in the office of the Guernsey association. These supplies included cup cards, folders, and bottle collars, all for Golden Guernsey milk.

In March 1962 John Bull reported on the speech that Bill Stewart had given to the Ontario Whole Milk Producers' League and the appointment of a committee to develop a marketing plan. "There was agreement that there be a provisional board, with three each from the cream, cheese, and concentrated, and four from the fluid group, one of which was to be a Channel Islands representative," stated Bull.

"We understand that the provisional board will administer the plan when it comes into effect," he said. "We're in favour of accepting this. We want orderly marketing. We're in favour of a plan, if one can be evolved, in which we can have a place to carry on our program. If a plan evolves that eliminates us, then we are against it. I'm suggesting we wait and see; we shouldn't criticize something we don't know about."

Because of the interest in milk composition, the Ontario Department of Agriculture was carrying out a study with broad aims. The departments of dairy science and animal husbandry and the Mastitis Laboratory at Guelph were all involved, as well as the ROP Division of the Canada Department of Agriculture. The study had started in 1961. The four dairy breeds were participating, with an involvement of five herds each, for a total of 500 milking cows. Some 21,000 individual tests had been completed by 1962 and additional tests were anticipated.

W.A. Savage, president of the Canadian Jersey Cattle Club, argued in 1963, "Surplus milk is going into powder. We have so much we don't know what to do with it. The federal government should introduce a policy requiring a minimum of solids-not-fat in milk and, if not available from cows, it should be added. Farmers should be paid on the basis of solids-not-fat. Butter could then be made competitive with vegetable oils."

Though terminally ill with cancer, John Bull was still the champion of the Jersey breed.

"The minister set up a provisional board, and a plan was developed that didn't get the support of the groups," he reported. "There were not sufficient hard facts. By opinions expressed at local meetings, farmers would not have voted in favour of the plan if it was submitted to them in 1962. Nothing has been presented that we could recommend to you.

"If all producers would promote and advertise and sell their product at a proper price, a lot of what's now called chaos in the industry would disappear ... This would be a better answer than marketing legislation that would give tremendous powers to a few who are not experienced in dealing with such a multi-million dollar business affecting so many farmers in the province. It could be a costly experience."

Later, at the 1963 annual meeting of the Channel Islands group, Bull further reported that Jim Baker, the dairy commissioner, was chairing a committee that included Emerson Farnsworth, Ken Gordon of Borden's, Orvil Guy and Sam Ault to consider marketing of concentrated and fluid milk. This committee had been formed after the provisional board was disbanded. Cheese had been dropped in frustration from the commmittee.

"They've had several meetings," complained Bull. "They've met with

Quebec. I know only what we read in *The Rural Co-operator* or the daily papers. We've not been consulted by government or the league. We no longer have the privilege of sitting in on the league's executive meetings. This was denied us on November 1st last. We don't know what's going on. It's not a bright picture I have painted of the future."

The CIBMPA had emerged as a strong, aggressive organization led by a number of relatively young breeders. John Kudelka of Glenville Farms in Newmarket was one such person. He was determined to sell Guernsey milk. His speeches and rapid-fire, colourful delivery left little to the imagination.

In referring to the Ontario Whole Milk Producers' League he had exploded: "A group of people out there are our so-called guardians by law and regulation, but their avowed purpose is to hurt us all. Our representations to this undemocratic, dictatorial and vicious organization have fallen on deaf ears. We do not think this vast, sprawling, unwieldy, undemocratic and socially unrepresentative league is fulfilling their function. The CIBMPA does not have any say in the operation of the league."

In 1963 the newly elected federal Liberal government had appointed Harry Hays, the representative from Calgary South, a dairy farmer, a beef farmer, an auctioneer and a former mayor of Calgary as the new minister of agriculture for Canada. There was considerable satisfaction among the pure-bred breeders, a great many of whom knew him personally.

The Hennessey report had not yet been released, and there was a feeling of expectancy; people were getting impatient. At the annual meeting of the Ontario Whole Milk Producers' League in 1964, Jim Baker was asked, "When will the report of the Hennessey Inquiry committee be available?"

Jim Baker had answered, "The report of the inquiry committee is imminent."

"What do you mean by imminent?"

"More imminent than it was a year ago."

D.A. Gilbert, general manager of the Retail Merchants Association of Canada, was about this time advising the annual meeting of the National Dairy Council, "The relatively new convenience stores' explosion - with 1,000 to 1,200 square feet and strategically located, with attractive colour schemes and open 9:00 a.m. to 11:00 p.m. seven days a week - is of concern. They feature jug milk at cut-rate prices. Dairy products make up 25 percent of the sales, and they're here to stay.

"A major concern of the retail industry is the dangerously low pricing level, which must be met by all competitors," continued Gilbert. "This will have the effect of reducing retail prices to a loss leader level which is not in the public interest. Another effect will be the elimination of profit in merchandising milk and the elimination of scores of retail outlets handling milk, to the serious inconvenience of the consumers and to the detriment of the industry."

In February 1965, at the annual meeting of the Ontario Jersey Cattle Club, president Frank Stenger reported that "1964 has been a most successful year and in many respects a peaceful year. Activities have been divided into two parts, breed promotion and milk promotion."

The group learned that there were 599 Jersey producers marketing milk to 35 dairies from Cornwall to Windsor and from Niagara to North Bay. Most of the milk was being shipped to the big three - Dominion Dairies, Silverwoods and Borden's. They also learned that problems were brewing.

The 15-cent federal butterfat subsidy had been removed, and this had reduced the distributor's return on butterfat sold for churning. This had become a major concern to a number of distributors. A number of AJ dairies were reporting unmanageable fluctuations in their supply of Jersey milk. Concerns were also being expressed regarding the matter of herd purity.

Jim Baker had been speaking to the Jersey breeders at the same meeting and had advised them that the Hennessey report, tabled on March 5, 1965, stated, "The relative merit of milk produced by the four principal breeds had been argued vigorously before the committee and elsewhere ... In summary we believe the differences between the milk produced by the Channel Islands breeds, that is, Jersey and Guernsey, and that produced by Ayreshire and Holstein cows are not sufficient to merit the separation of milk into two separate and distinct classes."

Bill Stewart was now moving aggressively to implement the new milk marketing board legislation. He had stated, "The OMMB will act on behalf of all milk producers regardless of the final destination of the milk. When in full operation the board will, in effect, buy the milk from the producers, sell it for the best price, and remit the proceeds to the individual producers concerned."

A recent estimate had placed the total number of milk shippers in Ontario - that is, fluid, concentrated and cheese - at about 30,000. In addition, there were 28,000 cream shippers.

John Bull had died on March 3, 1965, at the young age of 49, two days before the tabling of the Hennessey report. At the November 1965 meeting, while reporting an increase in the sales of AJ milk, the Ontario Jersey Club learned that while the momentum of promotion had continued, there was a wait-and-see attitude, and no new distributors had entered the All Jersey program. A few months before, John Bull had advised them, "The future is never guaranteed for people in any business."

The CIBMPA was making representations to Bill Stewart and to the milk board regarding Channel Islands milk sales. Maurice Beaty, a Jersey milk producer, had been appointed a member of the first board by the minister.

In February 1966, while addressing the Ontario Jersey Cattle Club, Beaty stated, "Whether or not one agrees with the changes under the new act, it will be difficult to say producers do not now have better equipment to meet their problems and improve their positions. It does seem that with the affairs of the producers being administered by one group, the results should be consistently better than having two or three working individually and often having a conflict of interest, resulting in somewhat strained relations. At producer level there must be more unification of effort and purpose.

"In the past, the relationship between the Channel Islands producers and the other producer organizations has not been the best," Beaty said. "There's been misunderstanding on both sides. Out of this has grown a biased thinking, which seems to me to have become traditional with some people. I hope the Channel Islands producers may now share the responsibilities with other producers in working toward an improved condition in all respects."

Jack Pawley, first chairman of the Jersey milk committee and an employee of the OMMB in the early years - he was the first director of the board's marketing system - reported at the same meeting, "The marketing of Ontario milk includes about 30,000 producers, 700 transporters, 250 dairies and 450 industrial plants. The initial grade 'A' pool will involve some 8,500 fluid milk producers."

The northern Ontario pilot pool, established to test the board's marketing plan for grade "A" milk, had become operative October 1, 1966, and the target for the southern pool was June 1967. In October the board announced its "Get up and go!" campaign. Launched on October 1, it would show up on 197 billboards in Ontario. It would also appear on radio, in 40 dailies and 85 weeklies, plus a series of TV flashes. The new board had grabbed the momentum of change provided by the new marketing legislation.

But by January 1967, the Jersey leaders were expressing concern.

"No policy has yet been announced on the handling of Channel Islands milk. We have been advised that an outside party has been hired to study all aspects of the Channel Islands position and report to the board. There are great uncertainties facing Channel Islands milk. The view of the board is that 'Milk is milk.'"

By March 1968 Frank Stenger, president of the CIBMPA, was reporting, "For too long the CIBMPA has been kept in a state of uncertainty. We've continuously asked for a separate pool. There have been voluntary deductions of over a million dollars spent on developing markets. The OMMB has turned this all down.

"We had proposed a separate quota and entry of new producers into the fluid milk pool according to demand. The board has rejected all proposals. We have appealed. Appeals have been denied, and we have now turned to the Supreme Court of Ontario."

In a 46-page judgement, Mr. Justice Lieff of the Supreme Court of Ontario dismissed the Channel Islands case. The CIBMPA decided to go to the Ontario Court of Appeal and at the same time to file an application with the Supreme Court of Canada. The Ontario Court of Appeal upheld the previous decision.

In the spring of 1969, George McLaughlin had alleged before the standing committee on agriculture and food of the Ontario legislature that distributors were guilty of irregularities and practices in the sale of Channel Islands milk and in the payment of Channel Islands producers.

In frustration the Channel Islands producers had stated,"No longer can we market our milk under a free enterprise system. We are forced to market under a socialistic government control system, a government who incidentally claims to be in favour of free enterprise. We are the only group of producers who are seriously challenging the trend of the times."

Consideration was being given to the possibility of selling milk outside of the jurisdiction of the OMMB. On May 2, 1969, it was announced that the application of the CIBMPA to the Supreme Court of Canada had been denied.

On that same day, Harold Crang, owner of Glenville Farms and Glenville Dairy, and a Guernsey breeder, was reporting that he had approached a group consisting of the minister, the deputy minister, the chairman of the milk commission and the chairman of the OMMB, asking for some consideration of the Channel Islands marketing problems.

"The group made agreeable noises but took no action," said Crang in disgust.

The decision was then made to bypass Bill Stewart and go directly to Premier John Robarts. But difficulties were experienced in arranging a meeting. Alan Eagleson, then president of the PC Association of Ontario, was involved and had apparently had been raising some dust around PC headquarters regarding the treatment of the Channel Islands breeds. They did get to see the premier at 4:30 p.m. on September 25. Unfortunately for them, however, Premier Robarts was completely supportive of the new milk marketing plan and the legislation.

On the other hand, attitudes were changing. By the spring of 1972, the authority and responsibility of the milk board were recognized by Frank Strenger when he stated, "The OMMB has a responsibility to market all milk in Ontario to the best advantage of all producers." This statement, of course, was made in the context of assuming fair treatment for the Channel Islands producers.

"The OMMB has appointed a committee to study multiple component pricing under the chairmanship of Dr. J.C. Rennie of the University of Guelph," Strenger further advised. "I hope payment on the basis of multiple component pricing may come in by May of 1976."

Francis Redelmeier had given a lot of study to multiple component pricing. He had been elected a member of the board in 1968, and by 1976 felt that multiple component pricing could have some advantages for the Channel Islands producers.

He continued to press the matter, and at the March 1, 1985, meeting of the CIBMPA in Guelph he stated, "Fundamental to our position is the principle that producers should receive compensation for their milk according to the value that processors extract from it. Multiple component pricing is vital to the health and stability of Ontario's dairy industry."

The Channel Islands saga, as some have called it, represents an initiative taken by young milk producers determined to promote their breeds and the milk from those breeds. Lessons can be learned from their singularity of purpose and the evidence of certain successes. Under law and through general acceptance they became part of the marketing system wherein "Milk is milk."

Frank Stenger has continued as a champion of the Jersey breed. In 1989, while discussing shipments of Jersey cattle to Brazil with me, he said wryly, "I suggested to the Brazilians that they get on with the sale of two-percent Jersey milk before they get a milk marketing board down there."

In May 1989, following a video recording dealing with the historical activities of the Channel Islands Breeds Milk Producers' Association, Ernie Crossland of Newmarket, a former Guernsey breeder, past president of the Ontario Guernsey Breeders and charter president of the CIBMPA, confided to me, "The creation and existence of the Ontario Milk Marketing Board has been the salvation of all milk producers in Ontario."

CHAPTER NINE

Achievements Challenged

In which

- The board enters the 1980s
- Milk marketing policies are attacked
- The board becomes image conscious
- There is a drastic cut in MSQ
- The milk transportation system is streamlined
- The cream shipper is recognized
- The Ontario Dairy Herd Improvement Corporation is established
- The Central Milk Testing Laboratory is pictured
- Multiple component pricing is adopted
- The board decides on specialty cheese milk
- McKinnon goes to CDC and Smith becomes chairman
- GATT worries worsen
- A presence is felt internationally
- New faces appear on the board
- There is a glimpse of northern Ontario

The board stepped through the portals of 1980 with a certain feeling of exuberance as it entered the year of its fifteenth anniversary.

"These last 15 years could be aptly described as a period of challenge and change," chairman Ken McKinnon suggested.

His photo showed a pleased look in the 1981 annual report, and his comment was, "The 1980-81 year has been exciting and challenging. Faced with a very tough economic situation and severe competition, the challenges facing the board and milk producers are daunting, but not insurmountable."

No one knew the extent of those challenges and how broadly based they would be! For the board, the 1980s were to present a real crunch in their challenge of achievement.

The year 1982 witnessed an economic situation that pressured most Canadians, including milk producers. There were rising costs and reduced milk consumption. Inflation became a fear, and interest rates were rising. Many would see the interest on operating capital at a cost of more than 22 percent at the banks.

Restraint guidelines, implemented by the federal government in 1982, had an impact on the fluid milk pricing formula and national support prices. The federal government was attempting to control wage and price increases in those areas where they had direct authority. Milk producers were beginning to hurt.

The beginning of the 1980s brought a realization to the board that outside of the dairy industry very few people understood or appreciated the benefits of the Ontario milk marketing system and, in particular, supply management. Opposition and downright antagonism on the part of many groups and individuals were not unexpected during the first several years of the board's responsibilities and development. Danger signals, however, were becoming very visible in a period when the board was well established, and board members were concerned.

"We just can't sit back and simply assume that everybody is going to agree with us just because we think we have a good system," said Jim McCague of Alliston, who had succeeded Francis Redelmeier in Region 6. "We're holding our own in the market, but there are people out there who think they'd be able to buy milk cheaper if we weren't here. This is something that we have to deal with."

The board proceeded to have some serious discussions within itself and with county and district milk committees. All of these discussions concluded, "This matter of communications has now emerged as an extremely important and critical activity, warranting the most serious attention."

"There's a real danger if the board doesn't move aggressively to recognize these danger signals," pointed out vice-chairman Grant Smith. "They're now going beyond the original criticisms, which were simply based upon change and fear of change in the industry. We're now getting reactions that are more broadly based, including among certain segments of the government and the general public.

"I think it was 1982," Smith recalls. "Things were rough; wage and price controls had just been introduced. The federal government was getting a lot of flak, and at one time we were having a little dinner party. Eugene Whelan came in and he looked in bad humour, 'What's on the menu?' he asked.

"'Beef,' someone said.

"'Beef makes me ugly,' said Whelan."

Smith recalls another time when, "The over-quota levy was high, and some producers had used up their quota early in the year, and they were getting IOUs from the board. Whelan made it quite clear, 'You're going to change your policy because there's no damn way I'm going to have producers getting an IOU from the board.'"

Milk marketing had certainly already received its share of attention from government and consultants. Back in 1976 the Food Prices Review Board had scrutinized fluid milk marketing in Ontario and noted the administered pricing and supply control. They suggested, "If society wishes to have a stable supply of high quality fluid milk available to consumers at stable prices, but does not wish to provide substantial monopoly profits to dairy farmers, these same policy tools can be utilized." The review did not necessarily want to interfere with the trading of fluid quotas, but they did conclude that if fluid quotas traded at too high a price, this would be a signal that the price of fluid milk was too high. As a result of these conclusions on the part of the review board, the OMMB moved very quickly to develop the Ontario Dairy Farm Accounting Project (ODFAP).

The board had also been concerned about the conclusions and recommendations of a 1978 study by Broadwith and Hughes, carried out for the Ontario Economic Council, which had remarked on the board's single stated objective, "To improve the income of milk producers and the market stability for milk in order that their net returns for management, investment and labour will be equal to that for comparable enterprises." The study had concluded, "The board has used its monopoly powers over fluid milk to raise prices above the level that would on average prevail in a competitive market."

The study recommended, "The Ontario government should amend the Milk Act to remove monopoly pricing and supply control powers from the Ontario Milk Marketing Board." The study's authors actually recommended that the board's regulatory powers be assumed by the Milk Commission of Ontario.

The national dairy policy was receiving a great deal of attention from an interdepartmental dairy policy review. As well, the Department of Finance in Ottawa had carried out an economic analysis of the national policy and in their conclusions had stated, "In summary there is a trade-off among objectives. The government cannot simultaneously ensure producers a "fair return," maximize economic efficiency, keep consumer prices down, and minimize the cost to the Treasury. The producer's gain is necessarily the consumer's or the taxpayer's loss."

In Ottawa, while an interdepartmental committee had completed a somewhat questioning review of the national dairy policy, in the same year, the Economic Council of Canada had released a report that suggested certain needed changes in the marketing of milk and dairy products, and that also criticized supply management.

Critical stances were being taken by certain economists regarding milk marketing and supply management, which seemed to be based more on personal philosophy than balanced economic facts. All of this reinforced the board's conclusions, that there was a lot of misinformation out there that had a negative impact on the board's marketing efforts.

The board deliberately subjected itself to a detailed self-examination of its perceived image with politicians, the media, civil servants, the producers themselves and the public at large.

It was concluded, "The board must maintain contact with its many audiences and it must provide accurate, honest information as openly and readily as possible."

In order to bring this about, the board decided to expand the Board/Industry Relations Division. The activities of this division involved media contact, government contact, publications, and the task of dealing with many hundreds of inquiries that came to the board concerning general questions about the industry and very specific ones on the many activities of the board.

As a result of this strengthened and reinforced attention, an agricultural reporter noted in 1982, "Politicians and bureaucrats are being kept fully briefed. Reporters get prompt, well-informed and complete answers to even the toughest and nastiest questions."

In 1987 Ken Smith became the director of the division.

"Rather than considering it as Board/Industry Relations, it's best described as the Communications Division," said Smith. "We now relate to the media, we publish the *Ontario Milk Producer* magazine, look after the Dairy Princess competition, work with the milk committees, orchestrate the annual meetings, the annual reports, and so on.

"The board has put orderliness and stability into the industry," he continued. "But we can't sit back just because we know we have a system that has benefited people. We have to do a better job of keeping people informed."

The year 1983 saw little relief from the economic pressures of the previous year. There were enormous stocks of butter, powder and cheese, particularly in the United States and the EEC. This caused price reductions and increases in levies for Canadian dairy farmers. There were cuts in MSQ.

The poor economic conditions adversely affected consumption patterns for fluid milk and manufactured dairy products. Producers were facing continually rising input costs and restricted income. Interest rates reached record heights. The pressure on milk producers was severe.

In Canada the supply management program was able to check the threat of sizable surpluses. The significant and aggressive advertising and promotion program helped to maintain fluid milk and milk products sales. But there had been difficulty at the national level during 1983 to balance supply and demand. This was aggravated by the world glut of dairy products, which resulted in a serious deterioration in world prices. There was a reduction of 4.7 percent in total MSQ. There were severe increases in levies on milk producers so that the costs of exports could be met. The pressures were being felt intensely by milk producers, but the system did prevail.

An important event for the board was the move to the new head office building in Mississauga on October 31, 1983. The Maitland Street property was 28 years old and in need of substantial repairs. To find parking was very difficult. The new office was the first building that really was customized for the board's perceived responsibilities and activities.

Alan Ross from Harriston, who had succeeded Harold Scott in Region 10, recalls, "It seemed like a great thing to have somebody come in virtually off the street and offer a couple of million dollars for a building you didn't like in the first place. It didn't take us long to make up our minds to accept that offer.

"I was on the site selection committee. We thought some land around the airport would be a good idea because of people coming from beyond Toronto to meetings. But there was nothing out there except small pieces under hydro lines, so we found a spot out in Mississauga. It seemed like a long way out at first, but I still think it was a good decision. It's close to Highway 401 and not far from the airport.

"We did have $400,000 in the building fund," said Ross. "The only additional sum we had to pay for the new building was for the installation

The third home of the Ontario Milk Marketing Board on Maitland Street in Toronto, above, served until the OMMB moved to its current building in Mississauga, below, in 1983. Minister of Agriculture & Food, Dennis Timbrell, left, and Ken McKinnon, OMMB Chairman, preside at the official opening of the Board's new facilities in December 1983.

of a new, modern telephone system. It was pretty hard to convince the producers out at a country meeting that it wouldn't cost more than that."

The new office site was situated on 3.6 acres in a light-industrial park, a stone's throw from the main highway on Campobello Road in Mississauga. The total cost of the new building was $2.497 million dollars. It was officially opened December 1, 1983, by the Honourable Dennis Timbrell, Minister of Agriculture and Food.

Even in the move to a new office building the board didn't escape the attention of reporters. John Schmidt, writing in *The Kitchener-Waterloo Record*, seemed to derive great satisfaction out of jabbing organizations and the government on a regular basis in his farm column.

From Alberta he wrote to me in February of 1989, stating, "In that March 27, 1984, column item I sent you, I said, 'A few columns back I nearly swallowed my tobacco...' I looked for that column - and had to go all the way back to January 7th, 1984, but I still could find no original column. Then I got mad and pulled out the 1983 file. There it was, dated December 23, 1983.

"It read: 'Thaddeus McMurphyvisk wishes he'd known the Ontario Milk Marketing Board needed a new board room table. He would have hammered together a few old crates and a couple of sheets of plywood for about $10.36. However, with the thousands of dollars the Ontario Cream Producers' Marketing Board is skimming off cream cheques, it spent $10,365 to buy a board room table for the Ontario Milk Marketing Board - you read it right: $10,365. The OMMB moved out of rented space in Toronto into a new office building in Mississauga recently and desperately needed a new table to assist it in tabling amendments to the amendments. The OMMB therefore tapped the cream board for $10,365, as it had been making office space available to the cream board for a nominal fee for years."

Though the dairy industry in Canada was hurting, it was surviving. This was due principally to the firm foundation of the supply management policy. There were apprehensions and second thoughts among some producers, however.

Board chairman Ken McKinnon was very concerned that producers might allow their well understood and rightful apprehensions over the size of the within-quota levies and the high costs of promotion to prejudice the long-term future of Ontario's marketing efforts and supply management.

"In the past two years the levy has risen by 25 percent," he noted in 1984. "We're attempting with some success to control our surpluses, but we're still feeling the pressure of depressed prices on world markets created from huge surpluses in the EEC and the United States. The within-quota levy covers the cost of disposing of skim milk powder produced from within the national market sharing quota. About twice the quantity of skim milk powder compared to butter comes from a given quantity of milk, resulting in a structural surplus of skim powder."

Some arguments were being presented both within Ontario and at that national level that, "Canada should consider eliminating the powder surplus by producing only sufficient milk for domestic powder consumption. Butter could be imported to meet the shortfall of butterfat."

Ken McKinnon, vice-chairman Grant Smith, and other board members had reacted very clearly and emphatically on several occasions, "This would bring enormous damage. Canada's milk production would have to be reduced by at least 25 percent in terms of the MSQ. The annual loss of income to producers would be at least $298 million. There would be a severe reduction in milk producer numbers. There would be a carryover into the processing sector, with a severe loss of jobs and economic activity."

Ken McKinnon urged producers to continue swallowing "the bitter pill" of high within-quota levies and bring production back to needed supplies.

Data coming from the office of Phil Cairns, the senior economist, had enabled Lorne Hurd to express some optimism to the board: "There's evidence that the increase in world milk supplies is leveling off, with the EEC and the United States attempting to bring supply and demand into better balance. There's hope that within two years the surplus of butter stocks will start to decline and prices will start to improve."

The clouds were starting to disappear and there was some light on the horizon. Board members wondered if the clearing economic picture would allow some relief to producers who had been bearing the high cost of within-quota levies and increased promotion efforts. This was treated very seriously because members recognized that many producers were hurting from a decreased net revenue squeeze.

Board members were saying at every opportunity, "It's necessary to be on guard to preserve the basic ingredients of the national dairy policy. The central structure of the CDC and its services must be preserved. We must continue to increase the already heavy investment in market expansion activities."

The board's twentieth anniversary was marked in 1985. They reflected on their accomplishments. "To achieve unity under a marketing board means surrendering some individual independence for the common good. It involves considerable self-discipline, especially to make a supply management program function efficiently." They also reminded themselves, "In celebrating our twentieth anniversary we must be conscious of a real need to avoid complacency."

The determination to make the supply management system work had paid off. Canada ended the 1984-85 dairy year producing 101.4 percent of the national MSQ. Milk and cream producers together in Ontario had shipped 101.8 percent of the province's MSQ. The board was able to refund $3.6 million of the total of $22.1 million collected as over-quota levies. Supply management was working to the benefit of milk producers and the taxpayers.

The board had continuing perceived problems with the Ontario Farm Products Appeal Tribunal. The appeal tribunal had been organized under provincial legislation on February 1, 1979, and had absorbed the appeal functions of the milk commission. Dr. Ken McEwen was the tribunal's first chairman.

The board was now expressing concerns that in hearing and ruling on appeals, the tribunal was exceeding its jurisdiction and interfering with the administration of policy established by the board. Protests were made to the minister, the Honourable Dennis Timbrell. Some board members were more concerned than others. "The tribunal's decisions were never very upsetting," one said. "They were always fair. There were a couple of price increases that weren't allowed. That was annoying. But it was generally recognized, particularly by those with problems, that 'there has to be a referee.'"

In December 1983 Rainy River appealed to the tribunal regarding "...the price of class one milk and the higher costs of transportation in this pool."

The tribunal directed, "The Ontario Milk Marketing Board (to) review the class one price for Kenora-Rainy River pool and immediately establish a price for class one milk that reflects the higher cost of transportation in this pool."

There was extensive discussion in the board regarding the tribunal's authority to make such an order. The board agreed to accept the order of the tribunal and comply with the directions. In accepting it, however, "The board (did) not necessarily accept the authority of the tribunal to make such an order."

In any case, the order of the tribunal was rescinded because the tribunal had not taken into account that other parties were involved, and they had not been notified of the hearings giving rise to the order. The tribunal also emphasized that the order had not intended to restrict the OMMB in any way in exercising its powers.

Bernie Gallagher left the board in 1983 after 15 years service to the industry. He was succeeded by Claude Chartrand of New Liskeard. Chartrand farms about 760 acres and, as well as dairy, has some cash crops. He had taken a great interest in the development of the milk marketing plan. "There were two things that changed New Liskeard," he readily states. "The first one was the milk marketing board and the second was tile drainage. The board changed us from industrial milk, and tile drainage allowed us to grow alfalfa."

Grant Cameron joined the board in 1984 representing Region 1. He had worked for ten years with the Carnation company and as an OMMB fieldman and had gone back to dairy farming.

It was the continuing determination and policy of the board to make every effort to streamline and create every efficiency in the milk transportation business. In 1983, concerns were being expressed at board meetings regarding certain inefficient milk transporters. The transportation committee at the board was stating, "We believe the termination of agency status for some transporters would have the advantage of reducing the cost of transportation and eliminating forever the inefficient transporter and improving the efficiency of other transporters. It would demonstrate to them and to producers that the board is playing a much more active role in the management of the system."

The committee proceeded to recommend that four transporters receive 60 days' notice to the effect that, "The board no longer requires their services, and that they will be given the opportunity to sell their businesses to a board-approved buyer.

The committee also advised, "The board should be taking a more active role with respect to selling the routes between transporters."

The board was concerned that many sales of transport routes were being completed before the board's staff even learned of a transporter's intention to sell. This was placing the board at a disadvantage in the administration of the system.

The committee further recommended, "...transporters be notified that if they wish to sell their routes or a portion thereof, they should first seek board advice as to which buyer would be approved, and failure to do so would result in the board's not approving the sale if they chose to sell to a nonapproved buyer. The volume would be reassigned to a transporter of the board's choice, presumably with compensation as provided for in the compensation agreement."

There was no doubt that in the exercise of its authority under the Milk Act, the board had moved a great distance from the day when the

Milk transportation in Ontario has changed dramatically along with the rest of the dairy industry over the past 25 years. Milk cans on open trucks gave way to bulk milk tankers and larger units such as this tandem pup milk transport owned by Ron Guest. This truck has a 40,000 litre capacity. Guest saw many of these changes personally. He began in the business delivering milk to homes in Port Credit.

transporter was a relatively free and blithe spirit, selecting producers for his route those who would benefit his transportation business, specifically while he was acting as an agent of some processor.

Rationalization and efficiency had been introduced into the milk transportation business in Ontario, and though the numbers of transporters had decreased dramatically and they were now agents of the board, most seemed to be satisfied that they had been treated fairly and that compensation was adequate.

In June 1990 John Wishart, of the Ontario Milk Transport Association, stated, "Looking back over the years, milk transporters experienced several significant changes in the way they did their business, both in the dairy industry and in the trucking industry. With the introduction of milk marketing, the business habits of producers, transporters and processors had to be merged into a common milk marketing scheme. Conflicts arose and were negotiated and settled."

"Transporters had to deal with route rationalizations, conversions from cans to bulk shipments, changes in destinations and increased truck sizes.

The industry matured, however, and changes became accepted. Today, milk marketing as we know it has brought stability to the milk trucking industry, and now producers and transporters work together to ensure a sound dairy industry for future generations".

The board had been firm in its determination to bring about every efficiency in the transportation of milk from the farm to the processor. It had been a very complex task when the original, virtually uncoordinated pickup system was studied in light of creating a rationalized efficiency. The development of one uniform grade for all milk did help facilitate the allocation of producers to more efficient routes.

The significant amalgamation of processing plants had assisted in transportation rationalization in some cases but had created problems in others. With larger plants the coordination of transport arrivals became more difficult. The board exerted increasing pressure and encouragement to have most plants receive milk on a seven-day basis.

Transporters were being bought out and larger transportation companies were appearing. Milk was being transported greater distances, and the larger transportation firms facilitated improvement with more efficient equipment.

More tractor-trailer units were seen on the road, and there was an increase in a number of pumpover trailers. The milk transportation system was becoming more sophisticated as was the extremely important role that the bulk tank milk graders/drivers were playing in the marketing system.

By 1987 pride was being expressed by the board, by producers, and the industry generally in the very positive image projected by the clean and efficient bulk milk tankers found every day on most roads in the province. Loads were increasing in size, and distances traveled per load were decreasing. There were now only 119 transporter/agents.

In 1988 the board was proudly reporting to its annual meeting, "There has been a 1.7 percent decrease in the cost of transporting milk compared to last year. Board policies have been encouraging transporters to become more efficient, and transportation costs are being held below the annual increase in consumer price index over the preceding five years."

The board expressed appreciation for the cooperation, understanding and effort of their transporter agents who had responded so well to the improved efficiency challenges. Transporters had recognized that though they had decreased in numbers they had grown in efficiency under the gentle, and sometimes not so gentle, rationalization and payment policies of the board.

Coming out of the shadows of the troubled economic times of the early 1980s, the board had entered the twentieth anniversary year of 1985 with great enthusiasm. The board shared with producers the message of chairman Ken McKinnon in the annual report, "United we stand; divided we fall. To achieve unity under a marketing board means surrendering some individual independence for the common good. It involves considerable self-discipline, especially to make a supply management program function efficiently. We've had our fair share of ups and downs, successes and disappointments. But we've maintained a record of fairness and equity for which we may be justly proud."

The cream producers of Ontario had been traditionally supportive of a milk marketing plan from the very beginning. They had played a significant role on the co-ordinating board, and though they had decided to maintain their own administration, there was an appointed cream representative on the OMMB from the beginning. Traditionally this had been the chairman of the cream board. Glen Cole was the first appointee of the minister. He was later president of the Dairy Farmers of Canada from January 1968 until January 1970, providing aggressive leadership to the industry.

Founded in 1946, the cream board represented at that time some 70,000 mixed farmers who were producing cream as one of their several sources of income. Over the years, many left the business and several had become milk producers through acquiring quota and using the graduated entry program. By 1990 fewer than than 1,300 cream producers remained in Ontario.

Having a cream representative on the milk board has allowed for better understanding and cooperation between the two boards. It is quite likely, however, that if the cream board had not continued, farm-separated cream would have disappeared by the late 1970s. The administrative offices of the cream board have remained in the OMMB head office.

Howard Wilson of Owen Sound was chairman of the cream board and a member of the milk board for six years before leaving in November 1988. He comments, "Cream producers are a different breed of people or they would all be milk producers. Traditionally, cream producers have been older than other milk producers. We do have some Amish and Old Order Mennonite people. Producing cream seems to suit their life-style better."

However, Wilson was advising the OMMB in 1984 that a request had been received from cream shippers expressing an interest in the possibility of marketing the skim milk portion of their farm separated cream.

In March 1985 a committee of cream producers appeared before the board, presenting themselves as the cream action committee. They maintained, "The only way to improve the cream producers' income is to sell skim milk instead of feeding it to livestock on the farm."

The proposal was for producers to sell the skim to milk processors. The committee maintained that 40 percent of cream producers would be prepared to meet all quality standards regarding the stable and milk house if they were allowed to ship the skim milk. The board was strongly opposed to the idea, and the cream committee appealed to the appeal tribunal.

It was a significant presentation, one that was attended by Grant Smith, the vice-chairman, and Peter Oosterhoof, a future vice-chairman of the board. The Ontario Dairy Council, the Ontario Milk Transport Association, the Canadian Dairy Commission, the Creameries Association and the Oxford County Cream Committee were all in attendance. There was little support for the proposal to allow skim milk sales by cream producers. The board maintained that permitting skim milk sales would cause more problems than solutions.

The OMMB did support the policy statement of the Dairy Farmers of Canada, however, "...that on the average cream producers' incomes were not adequate and should be brought closer to a comparable basis and more in line with the target level of industrial milk prices."

The board had always emphasized the importance of the efficient dairy cow. Very much a part of this philosophy was the policy to encourage producers to have their herds on test.

From time to time, concerns were expressed regarding the inability of the DHIA (later, DHI) program administered under OMAF, because of lack of adequate government funding, to be available to all producers.

Dwight Bennett of Kemptville, elected to the board in 1977, stayed on for two full terms. He supported the idea, along with others, of the privatization of DHI. Ontario was enthusiastic about the idea, as was Agriculture Canada. There was strong support from the AI units and the breed associations.

The Ontario Dairy Herd Improvement Corporation had been formed on April 1, 1981. It was supported financially by both levels of government and by user fees and an all-producer check-off. A further consolidation of the program took place, and its acceptance as the official milk recording organization in Ontario was recognized, when an agreement was signed amalgamating it with the federal Record of Performance (ROP) program effective July 1, 1985.

"The board has been involved in many activities directed toward improving the efficiency of producers," said Dwight Bennett, founding chairman of the Dairy Herd Improvement Corporation. "Because we have supply management, it behooves milk producers to be as efficient as we possibly can. The board felt that there were weaknesses in certain areas important to management. DHI was an example where possibly 50 percent of the herds in the province couldn't get on the testing program because of the lack of government funding."

The improvement of milk quality had been a long-term objective of both the milk board and OMAF. There had been a love-hate relationship. The ministry had the responsibility for milk quality but had some concerns regarding the speed at which producers should be forced to make changes in their production methods and facilities.

It was with some feeling of pride, however, that both were able to announce in 1981, "The attainment of a single quality grade for all milk is an event of enormous significance, not only from the point of view of improving our products for the consumer but also from the viewpoint of enabling the board to refine its marketing and transportation programs."

The first automated and computerized Central Milk Testing Laboratory in the world using infrared technology had been established by the Department of Agriculture and Food in Guelph in 1967. This, the beginning of the application of new technology, was due mainly to the perseverance of Jim Baker and the cooperation of the dairy staff of Guelph.

But technology was improving generally. The 1984 annual report of the board stated, "The world's most modern milk testing laboratory was dedicated October 25, 1984, in Guelph. It will take over the testing of milk for both quality and composition at a saving of approximately $600,000 annually. It makes use of the latest milk testing technology. The new instruments are capable of testing five times as many samples as before with the same number of staff. The new facility paves the way for a move to fresh milk testing which will commence in January 1985. Fresh milk testing will be a more accurate and credible system for both producers and processors."

The new laboratory continued to be operated and administered by the Ontario Ministry of Agriculture and Food.

The Ontario Milk Marketing Board had long cooperated with the ministry and, along with the Ontario Dairy Council and the ministry, had shared in the costs associated with all aspects of testing producer milk samples for the purposes of producer payment and plant billings. Costs associated with the regulatory function of the laboratory (i.e., quality testing and testing of packaged fluid dairy products) are borne entirely by the ministry.

The operation of the Central Milk Testing Laboratory has been hailed as an outstanding example of a practical working, cooperative effort of all parties involved in a vital part of milk marketing. A policy committee, under the chairmanship of the director of the Dairy Inspection Branch of OMAF, is made up of one member from each of the three participating groups.

The policy committee is assisted by a technical committee, again made up of representatives from the three participating groups as well as a representative from the Ontario Milk Transport Association. This committee continuously monitors the operations of the laboratory, including testing methods and control procedures as well as the investigation of any matter referred to it by the policy committee.

Every attempt has been made to maintain state-of-the-art equipment. All producers' milk is analyzed four times monthly for milk fat, total protein, lactose and solids-not-fat content. Regular somatic cell counts are carried out, total bacteria counts are made and producers' milk is tested twice a month for antibiotics. There are brucellosis tests, water content is checked, consumer packages are tested for flavour and volume determination, and the product is checked to ensure that there is no blending of milk from other species unless indicated on the label of the product being sold.

The taking of the milk sample at the farm by the transporter/grader, its care until it arrives at the lab, the rapid, multifaceted testing of the sample and the final use of the laboratory results for payment purposes by the board and for management guidance to the producer would make a fascinating story all in itself.

Over the years, the possibilities suggested by multiple component pricing had received a lot of interest and attention. Before the formation of the OMMB, the Channel Islands Milk Producers had seen possibilities for increased sales of Jersey and Guernsey milk because, as well as being high in fat, the Channel Islands milk also has a higher solids-non-fat content.

The introduction of IRMA, the infrared milk analyzer, and the tests carried out in the early '60s were a breakthrough in the determination of the basic components of milk,

In the early 1970s, an extensive study under Dr. Clare Rennie of the University of Guelph, dealing with milk composition, had been established and a report made. It created much interest in the industry as well as among the media.

Ken McKinnon, in an interview by Bill Dodds of the CBC in 1972, was talking even at that early date in terms of moving to some form of producer payment for milk based on a broader consideration of milk components. In the interview following the seventh annual meeting at which the study was announced, McKinnon said, "The study will be broad, looking at all aspects, but it will be thoroughly discussed with milk committees before we decide to go ahead with any form of multiple component pricing."

The inference was clearly left that MCP pricing was being seriously considered.

In 1990 Ken McKinnon recalls, "I admit my personal failure in not getting multiple component pricing into the industry 15 years ago. We had a fine opportunity around 1975, but there were other priorities. I guess the industry wasn't ready for it either."

MCP was a matter that did receive continuing attention, however. Francis Redelmeier and the Jersey breeders didn't forget about it; in fact, they pushed the idea at every opportunity. The decision was made eventually in 1990 that the board would move to a multiple component pricing system effective August 1, 1991. Many had expected that it would have happened at an earlier date.

Al Hick, director of marketing for the board, muses, "It's rather a revolutionary move. It hasn't had much use as yet and people haven't been moving to the system very quickly. A lot of processors still aren't too enthusiastic, and it hasn't been an easy sell. Over the years there's been a rather dramatic increase in the average BF test. It's up around 3.9 percent now. We have this trend to low-fat or lighter dairy products. The board and certain processors think we'd better get moving on it. We probably should have been in it four or five years ago."

For pricing purposes the board will be using fat, protein and other solids, mainly lactose and minerals. The board and the Dairy Farmers of Canada are supporting these three components. The intent is that with MCP, the total returns to the producers will remain the same, but prices paid for components will be subject to adjustment at some time in the future. It has been indicated differences in individual returns will be relatively insignificant.

Since 1985 the board had been visibly more aggressive in its consideration of multiple component pricing. It had reaffirmed its decision of 1979, that "...multiple component pricing of milk for both producer and processor be established for the long-term benefit of the dairy industry in Ontario and the consuming public. Discussions should be undertaken with all stakeholders with the idea of gaining industry acceptance. Producers should be provided with information on their statements and invoices showing how the MCP would affect them prior to full implementation of the program. There should be a national MCP liaison so that other provinces and the federal authorities are aware of what is being considered in Ontario."

All of this has been done.

"I think producers generally realize what's happening in the marketplace and are prepared to adjust," said Al Hick.

In 1990, Ken McKinnon, as vice-chairman of the CDC and chairman of the Dairy Industry Task Force, rationalizes, "I guess there's a time for everything. About the time the report came in back in the mid-'70s, we were in the midst of the most severe jolt that supply management had taken, with an 18 percent cut in MSQ nationally and 14 or 15 percent in Ontario. There was no way producers across Ontario wanted to talk about multiple component pricing. We couldn't get the processors to sit down anyway. In any case, we would likely have had problems with testing procedures in the 1970s."

In June 1990 Tom Kane, president of the Ontario Dairy Council, stated, "The ODC has identified seasonality and the composition of the raw milk supply (i.e., high levels of butterfat) as the two most important problems facing processors. Multiple component pricing, in the opinion of the ODC, won't address these problems. Therefore, the council is not prepared at this time to endorse MCP for processors. The council has asked the OMMB to prepare a package of information to educate processors as to the 'benefits' that the OMMB thinks are available to the processing community if MCP is introduced. In other words, the OMMB must 'sell' this project to processors."

Co-operative producer transports continued to operate successfully, though from time to time protests had been made to the board. In February 1984, the Blue Water Milk Transport Co-op of Wyoming asked the board's assistance in having the legislative liability removed which, they believed, compelled them to continue paying patronage dividends to members of the co-op who had been "arbitrarily" removed by the board from the co-op trucks. The board asked staff to attempt to obtain a resolution of the matter, but about the same time it advised the Federation of Co-operative Milk Transports, "The board intends to continue its existing policy to rationalize the routes of all transporters in the same manner."

The 1980s' illustration of the milk transport on the highways and in the rural concessions, with its very visible and fresh-looking "Milk" logo, has stood out and become a source of pride to milk producers. It is far removed from the "...seven producers along one road north of Brampton with five different transporters to pick up the milk" recalled by George McLaughlin.

By 1990, there were 109 transport companies in Ontario operating about 420 trucks. There were 435 individual routes. In that year most milk was picked up every other day, but some producers had everyday pickup. Milk was delivered to roughly 112 plants. Some 4,600 pickups were made each day by tankers responsible for the transportation of milk from about 9,200 licensed producers.

"On the average for the last number of years we've been losing about 300 producers a year," said Al Hick. "But our milk marketing figure has been running around 2.3 billion litres a year, and we've been pretty close to that figure for some time."

The Dutch auction clock crafted in Utrecht, Holland, with numerals carefully selected for use in selling cheese, has endured. It had witnessed the vibrant heyday in Ontario of the lively U.K. cheese market. It still operates every second Monday morning in its setting at the cheese exchange and warehouse in Belleville. It still brings buyers and sellers together. The board still wonders whether it should be in the cheese warehouse business. Opinions are still divided.

"Tenders have been called on the sale of the Belleville warehouse," said Al Hick. "Some bids have been received. The board could very well be out of the cheese warehouse business before the end of 1990. However, it has been very careful to make one of the conditions of tender the continuance of the warehouse for at least a year to allow time for the current customers to adjust."

Cheddar cheese plants, from almost the first time a cow was milked and milk sold for a price, have been an important community interest. "The factories were located at distances approximately equal to the distance a team of horses could pull a wagon and the milk cans and still get the milk to the factory in time for the cheesemaker to start the vat of cheese," recalls Leland Wannamaker.

With changing population backgrounds and market promotions, the popularity of specialty cheeses had increased rapidly.

It had been the board's policy not to subject the specialty cheese plants to the plant supply quota system. This allowed the specialty cheese plants to expand rapidly, and by 1985 Ontario plants were supplying about 60 percent of the specialty cheese market in Canada.

As the market for specialty cheese grew, and with decreased supplies of industrial milk, there was less milk for butter and powder and cheddar plants. The plant operators were complaining bitterly, as they had been for a lengthy period.

It was a difficult decision, but the board had no choice. As of October 1, 1985, specialty cheese plants became part of the plant supply quota system. They no longer enjoyed the freedom of "a milk supply priority." Their quotas were based on the historical amount of milk that they had received during the three-year period prior to 1985. This policy effectively put a lid on the growth of specialty cheese produced and sold out of Ontario.

This was not a hasty decision on the part of the board and it wasn't made in isolation. There were long consultations with the Ontario Dairy Council and processors, extending over several years starting back in 1979.

The change was to bring in less money, but the board believed that the class 5 plants were needed to get rid of the excess milk that was on the market at times and converted into powder and butter. These plants were needed particularly to handle the flush of milk in May and June.

Quebec was now able to go ahead and pursue the specialty cheese market with vigor, which they did. The controlling interest that Ontario had enjoyed in the sale of specialty cheeses across Canada had now dropped from 60 percent to about 40 percent.

Processing plants have believed that since they were in the business of manufacturing milk products, they needed more milk to meet their needs, and anything short of what they needed would be unfair to them. Producers and processors, however, were part of the milk supply management program. If the industry were not to adhere to the national MSQ, the potential exists for completely unmanageable milk product surpluses and resultant chaos in the industry.

"Ontario gets approximately 31.1 percent of the total MSQ," said Al Hick. "We simply have to take our share of the national pie. With the limited amount of milk we're able to market, the big problem is to try to keep all processors relatively happy!"

Discussions within the board had been long and heavy on the matter of the treatment of specialty cheese plants. One argument was, "We must remember that the plant supply quota policy and the channeling of milk into higher priced products has put untold quantities of money into the milk producers of this province." On the other side, "Certain plants are starved for milk. This may bring us less money, but on the other hand we have to be mindful of outlets for our excess milk during certain periods. If these plants disappear we won't have these facilities. As a board we don't have a choice."

In mid-1986, Ken McKinnon resigned as chairman to become vice-chairman of the Canadian Dairy Commission. He had emerged to national

Grant Smith became the third chairman of the Ontario Milk Marketing Board in 1986. He was one of the first elected Board members and continued to serve as a member following his decision to step down from the chairman's position in early 1990.

recognition as a leader on the dairy scene. He had proven that he could identify with farmers and their problems. His stubbornness when dealing with issues was well recognized, though the odd person felt it was tempered almost too much at times by his desire to ensure that situations and problems were well understood by board members and milk committees before decisions were taken. Others thought this wasn't a grave fault!

Grant Smith of Burgessville was elected chairman in July, 1986. John Core of Wyoming was elected vice-chairman.

John Core had six and one-half years on the board. He represented the new generation of milk producer. "I was growing up when the milk board was being put in place, but I grew up in a house knowing the kind of problems the dairy industry faced," said Core. "I can still remember my father on the day the small dairy we shipped to went bankrupt!

"But I'm not one to look back and worry where we've come from," added Core. "We've put together a very structured marketing organization that serves producers extremely well. In my opinion, it's the best marketing system that's ever been developed for milk around the world."

Grant Smith served the producers as chairman until 1990, when he stepped down and John Core took over the chairman's gavel. Smith had been one of the first elected board members, gaining a board position in 1967 when the policy was changed by Bill Stewart to allow producers to begin electing board representatives by region. Smith brought his own style to the board, as had McLaughlin and McKinnon. Howard Sheppard of Roseneath, a board member from October 1976 until March 1981, says, "Grant's a real good fellow. He always tells it the way it is."

Others say, "He's very businesslike and doesn't take too long to get decisions. He always stood up for the things he believed in. He can be crusty, but you know where he's coming from."

In the meantime, some of the heavy guns in the Ottawa bureaucracy were still being directed at the national industrial milk policy. The Neilson task force had been looking at ways and means to reduce the costs of federal policies. Options were being suggested that would result in possible savings to the federal treasury.

Recommendations were being considered which would see "...the Canadian Dairy Commission marketing operation costs discontinued and recovered from the consumers. The supply management system could be used to reduce production in even steps over five years to the level of skim milk solids self-sufficiency. It was assumed that butter would be imported to "make good the domestic production shortfall and that the profits on the resale of imported butter be credited to producers."

The general reaction of the dairy industry was very negative. "Such recommendations indicate a total lack of knowledge on the dairy industry and its economic importance to Canada," charged Grant Smith.

There were loud protests to the Honourable John Wise, the federal minister. He reacted by having an independent review of the national policy carried out under almost direct reporting to his office.

In January 1987 John Wise greatly heartened the industry by announcing that Canada's dairy policy, including supply management, would be continued without significant amendment. A year later he again touched on an important aspect of the national policy by announcing a new mechanism for the determination of target prices for industrial milk in Canada.

The board was not completely satisfied with the new pricing policy, as they thought it did not completely meet the needs of the late 1980s and was not completely fair to producers generally. It was accepted, however, because the philosophy and intent of supply management were still in place.

Acting on requests of the Dairy Farmers of Canada and the National Dairy Council, Wise moved to place ice cream and yogurt on the import control list under the then accepted authority of Article XI of the General Agreement on Tariffs and Trade (GATT).

Supply management policies generally, and to a lesser extent marketing boards, had traditionally been the target of the urban media, purists, certain economists and a number of bureaucrats. A new stage was provided by the Uruguay round of the GATT discussions, and critics now became more vociferous with the support of a generally receptive urban media.

"The academic and political critics want to drag down the supply managed sectors to the lowest common denominator," stated Grant Smith. "The MacDonald Commission on the Canadian economy in 1985 came up with a prize solution, that existing boards increase their production quotas so that quota values fall to more reasonable levels. The commission really thought that one of the arguments in favour of a free trade deal with the United States was that it would lead to the eventual elimination of supply management boards."

Milk producers across Canada were becoming disturbed and anxious. Smith pointed out at the 1990 annual meeting of the board, "The federal government put yogurt and ice cream on the import control list, and our Canadian trade gladiators marched fearlessly into the multilateral den of the GATT to negotiate a deal by the end of 1990."

As Federal Minister of Agriculture, John Wise, a native of southwestern Ontario, reaffirmed the national dairy policy for Canada in 1987, indicating his support of milk producer strength in the marketplace.

A panel under GATT decided that the import control action taken by Canada was not permissible under Article XI. The Canadian government reacted by stating no action would be taken on the implementation of the panel decision until after the Uruguay round.

The GATT discussions resulted in the world trade in dairy products taking on a worrisome significance. It was no longer a bilateral matter of free trade with the United States, but involved complex discussions of 97 nations.

Article XI was the concern. Expressed simply, the interpretation had been that it provided for import controls when a country such as Canada controlled production to essentially meet the demands of the domestic market and not contribute to world surpluses. The panel had ruled that in the case of ice cream and yogurt such a control was not within the spirit and authority of the general agreement. The apprehensions of the Canadian dairy industry were increasing.

There had been increasing concern regarding the negative vibrations that seemed to be emanating from Ottawa regarding supply management and dairy policies. The board and other industry spokesmen in Canada became more emphatic in their presentations, arguing, "Supply management was the solution, and not the cause, of the general chaotic and completely undesirable conditions in the international milk market."

Many in milk production circles were beginning to ask, "Looking at the relative buoyancy and economic well-being of the dairy industry in Canada compared with other sections of agriculture, why would anyone consider, let alone seriously discuss, any weakening of the supply management system for the dairy industry?"

In the spring of 1990, Peter Oosterhoof, vice-chairman of the board, was saying, "Many producers in my region are still skeptical about whether or not the government is going to support them in these trade matters. Some producers aren't making the production changes they have under consideration. They don't want to spend the money yet. They're going to ride this out and see where we're going. We've been telling them over the past six months that the federal government has been moving in the direction of pushing our interests in the GATT negotiations. They're still worried."

In the summer of 1990 this was the opinion generally reflected across Ontario.

During 1990 trade apprehensions were being expressed by milk producers across the province. They considered that their future and the prosperity of the industry were on the trading block.

Considerable reassurance came from statements attributed to the federal minister, the Honourable Don Mazankowski, who was stating on numerous occasions, "Canada's supply management systems may need changes. Marketing boards are not trade distorting. They don't contribute to a world surplus in agriculture. Canada wants to clarify and strengthen the wording of the current rules that permit supply management practices."

The minister had moved aggressively in 1989 to appoint a national dairy task force, under the chairmanship of Ken McKinnon, to carry out in depth an investigation of all aspects of the dairy industry in Canada and in particular its position of competitiveness with particular reference to the United States. Producers were beginning to feel that they would have a real voice in determining the direction of future dairy policy through the recommendations which would be going forward from the task force for the minister's consideration.

There was more optimism on the GATT scene with the Canadian negotiating team indicating Canadian support for supply management and the need for clarification which, it was hoped, would result in the strengthening of Article XI.

Producers had added confidence because the position paper had been drafted with significant input from the Dairy Farmers of Canada. But there was still concern and apprehension. The real answers would not be known until December 1990, and perhaps not even then.

At the very first meeting of the board in 1965, members had strongly agreed on the extreme necessity of playing a significant role in national dairy matters. Continuously, ever since, the board has given unwavering support to the Dairy Farmers of Canada. George McLaughlin was president of the Dairy Farmers from 1966 to 1968. Glen Cole followed him for the next two years. Jim McCague was there in the mid-'70s. Ken McKinnon held the office between 1977 and 1979. Grant Smith was the choice from January 1983 until January 1985.

The times and Smith's personality gained him visibility on the international scene.

It all started with his appointment by the Dairy Farmers of Canada as a delegate to the International Federation of Agricultural Producers. The IFAP meeting was in Delhi, India.

"The chairman of the Dairy Products Group was not able to be present and so I was asked to chair the first meeting," Grant recalls. "This was in 1984 and I ended up being chairman of the Dairy Products Group. I've been chairman for six years (by 1990), and I think I was elected because of the supply management policy in Canada. This group consists of 17 of the largest dairy producing countries in the world. This excludes Russia, because as yet they don't belong to IFAP."

Smith and Richard Doyle of the Dairy Farmers of Canada in discussion decided the group should be developing and endorsing a policy statement, as had been the practice of the Dairy Farmers of Canada. They didn't receive much encouragement; an official of IFAP even said flatly, "Well, it won't work." Exercising his prerogative as chairman, Smith said, "Anyway, that's the way it's gonna go.

"We had our meetings with the 17 countries and came up with a policy statement that set the tone for the meetings of the future," Smith recalls. "The basic idea of the statement was to suggest that each country be responsible for its own surpluses. We really wanted supply management around the world. And it worked.

"At the next meeting in Australia the statement was reworked and brought up to date. We're convinced that one of the results of that policy statement has been to help the surplus of skim milk powder in Canada come back to a normal level and to reduce our within-quota levy from about $6.00 to around $2.35.

"I remember when the price of skim milk powder on the international market was about $700 per tonne," Smith added. "And today, in the spring of 1990, it's close to $2,000 per tonne. There are about 22 or 23 countries in the world who have adopted some form of supply management. Our system was introduced in 1972, and these others went into place by about 1986. The policy statements of the Dairy Products Group have become well known. The one adopted in Adelaide last year has been accepted by the EEC."

Smith emphasizes, "This sort of world dairy association is very critical and important for Canada. We know all these dairy leaders on a first-name basis, and last summer when we needed support for Article XI, we got the blessing of Don Mazankowski to take a trip to the Common Market. We found we do have a lot of support in countries like Germany, France, Switzerland and others. One country not supportive is Holland. They're free-wheeling and they want to export in the world market. You can understand that with such a small, high-producing country, they need markets."

Lorne Hurd recalls that Grant Smith had always been very much aware of the importance of Canada's role on the international scene. In 1970 the board had received a request from the University of Guelph to pay the expenses of the university person to the International Dairy Federation meeting and congress in Australia. Smith commented to the board at the time, "If we're paying anyone's expenses to this, it should be the general manager."

"The IDF, organized in Brussels in 1903, is an independent, nonpolitical, nonprofit-making, international association of 36 countries," said Hurd. "Its aim is to promote through international cooperation and consultation the solution of scientific, technical and economic problems in the international dairy field. The congress is being held in Canada in 1990, with the congress itself in Montreal and the IDF annual sessions in Toronto.

"I went to Australia with Ken Savage, the senior dairy officer from Agriculture Canada," Hurd said. "It was the beginning of a long and very productive association. Agriculture Canada had been a member of the IDF, but Ken and I decided that it was an organization that Canada should be giving more attention. I agreed to talk to the producers, and Ken took on the provincial governments and processors. We had to organize a national committee, which we did."

This action resulted in a long and valuable association for Hurd with the IDF.

Hurd has been Canada's representative on the Supply Management Group. He has also made significant contributions to the world study of payment schemes for ex-farm milk and given leadership under the IDF in a two-year study on how to reduce tranportation costs from farms to milk plants.

"I've been a better senior staff officer because of my association with the International Dairy Federation," said Hurd. "For many years, I've known people from around the world. We can talk on a first-name basis. If you have to take, you have to give, and Canada has made its contribution. This association is very important, even critical, particularly in the present times."

The faces on the board were changing. Members representing milk producers who were looking to the 1990s and beyond were joining the board and mixing with the experience of the past.

Paul Henderson of Spencerville, representing Region 2, was one of these. Working with his father and brother on a family farm operation, Henderson and his family have lived on "the hill" for a little over 115 years.

"In 1965 a cyclone blew our barn away," he recalls. "Dad spent many sleepless nights trying to figure out how he was going to get enough money to put the roof back on. I was only 15 or 16, and I saw what things were like before the board came into existence. It wasn't good."

As a producer of the new generation, however, Henderson is looking to the future. His first board meeting was in 1986.

Gordon Coukell, representing Region 6, had bought a farm near Stayner in 1971. He became a board member in 1986. A dairy science graduate from Guelph, he had managed Walkerton Dairies and been a field man with the Dairy Branch of OMAF. He has a particular interest and expertise in milk quality.

"Probably the quota policies created the most problems and were perhaps the least understood," recalls Coukell. "I think the graduated entry program was the key to success of the board's earlier activities. It was certainly the key for ourselves."

His broad experience, which included being secretary of the milk committee for twelve years, and his extensive knowledge of the industry are allowing him to quietly assess the current challenges facing the board.

Bruce Whale of Alma joined the board in January 1986, and he succeeded Alan Ross in Region 10. In partnership with his father, Whale produces milk on a farm that has been in the family for more than 100 years. He is quite convinced that, "One of our challenges is the lack of understanding by some producers and by the public of the type of system that we're trying to operate in the dairy sector."

But Bruce Whale has other concerns. "I think some of the politicians don't fully understand that we have different costs than those of the United

States, New Zealand and Europe, for that matter. There are also different government programs in these countries. Climatic conditions are another thing. We grow our crops and feed cattle. They talk about sustainable agriculture. The livestock industry is possibly one of the most compatible industries with the environment."

Bruce Saunders is representative of the new faces on the board. A Guelph graduate in crop science, Saunders has been associated with the dairy industry for 20 years. He was president of the Junior Farmers of Ontario in 1976-77. He also succeeded Ken McKinnon in Region 11.

"I never had any doubts about producing milk," said Saunders. "Under the system you know what you're going to get for producing your product. We took advantage of the graduated entry program. This program gave farmers in our area an opportunity to share in the higher priced market. We were far enough away from Toronto that very few of the producers in Grey and Bruce had any fluid market."

Gordon Donnan of Stirling, representing Region 4, has been in the dairy business for about 35 years. He comes from the cheese county of Hastings and was president of the Ivanhoe Cheese Factory. As well as the experience of many years as a milk producer, Donnan also brought to the board a knowledge of milk processing and its associated problems. He thinks very much about the future but also remembers the past.

"The problems of the past may be history, but they brought us to the point where we are now," said Donnan. "Maybe the young producer doesn't appreciate it. But would we be where we are today if we'd not had the problems and hadn't experienced the difficulties and found the solutions?"

In 1990 Gaston Levac, representing Region 1, was starting his second year as a member of the board. Levac and his wife started farming on their own in 1956 with 100 acres and 18 cows. He is an example of one of the many success stories that have developed under the OMMB. A champion of the milk marketing system, he says simply, "I grew up with it."

Now incorporated with his wife and oldest son near St. Bernardin in eastern Ontario, Levac operates a farm of some 350 acres and a herd of about 100 cows. Of the situation in the spring of 1990, he says, "There are many questions from producers, but the questions are constructive. However, one can see that there's an uncertainty in the industry at the present time."

Claude Chartrand of New Liskeard succeeded Bernie Gallagher in Region 12 and attended his first board meeting in 1984. He says, "Distances are a problem in northern Ontario. Where I'm sitting here in my living room, my farthest producer in Rainy River is almost 1,000 miles away. Hearst is the farthest distance north, and it's 300 miles to the last producer there. From here it's 300 miles to Sault Ste. Marie. There are a total of ten milk committees in the north. It's very important in the north to have the milk committees, and they are doing a tremendous job."

Chartrand reflected on the vast expanse of his region: "Cochrane North, 500 miles north of Toronto, had a lot of very small producers when the board started, but farms there now are probably the biggest in all of Ontario. There are fewer producers but with larger units. The Verner area is very fertile and there are some 80 producers. Algoma has seen possibly the greatest changes. There was a lot of opposition there to the board in the beginning. Quota was moving out of Algoma, but the 50 percent transfer assessment stopped that. The producers in Algoma now are possibly the youngest in all of Ontario. They're very interested in milk production. They've actually been buying back quota from the New Liskeard area.

"Manitoulin Island has had a very stable production," Chartrand continued. "I call it the banana belt, and there's a young group of dedicated producers there. The Powassan area has been holding steady. Dryden has only six producers left. There are none in Kenora. Rainy River production is very important, and it's an excellent producing area. The Manitoba milk problem has been solved, and we hope that the problem of an industrial milk outlet will be taken care of next year with the plans for an installation of a cheese plant there. When you think they're getting about $47 for their surplus milk and then having to pay $15 a hectolitre for transportation, it doesn't leave much for labour, expenses and management.

"Timiskaming is an important milk producing area, and it has changed from industrial. It's a relatively small valley 40 miles long and 20 miles wide."

Since the first cow was milked in Ontario, farm wives have played a critical role in the farm operation. They are, in fact, a sort of superhero on the farm scene. They have raised their families, kept their homes in operation and done chores in the barn. They have milked the cows and still do. More recently they have fulfilled a very essential responsibility in looking after farm records and accounts. They have been very involved with the farm business activities. But under the milk marketing board women have emerged as licensed milk producers. Many are partners in the farm production enterprise or members of an incorporated production unit. A significant percentage avidly read the *Ontario Milk Producer* and are completely knowledgeable of milk production problems and situations.

Gladys Helin is one of the dairy farm women of the north. She has been secretary-treasurer of the Cochrane South milk committee since the beginning in 1965. She is a member of a family partnership supplying milk to Timmins, the largest market of the north, with a population of 65,000. She recalls, "When the board started there were 136 producers. Now there are only 51 producing about the same amount of milk."

In 1990, about 25 women were members of milk committees and seven were on the executives of milk committees. They regularly attend the Geneva Park conference and join in the debates and discussions. They are saying, "It's only a matter of time until a woman is elected a member of the board and occupies that special chair."

Helin is very satisfied with the milk board, but along with the other producers in the region, she worries about the possible results of the current GATT negotiations. Time will determine if those worries are warranted.

Grant Smith worries about the trade situation. "The United States has $25 billion and 70,000 civil servants to help them expand their markets, and this includes agriculture. We need Article XI to have some support at our borders. I'm optimistic regarding the discussions on Article XI, but I'm not sure the final results will be as good as we have today."

Circumstances had chosen Grant Smith to be the official spokesman of the board as it completed the decade of the 1980s. In early January 1990, in the Royal York Hotel, he had put everything in perspective: "The early part of the decade witnessed the deepest recession we've seen since the great depression. This recession contrasted vividly with one of the longest periods of economic expansion in our history, lasting for the final seven years of the decade. The headaches of spiraling inflation, high interest rates and heavy unemployment gave way to rapid growth, spending sprees and huge budget deficits.

"The trade wars of the early to mid-'80s were notorious for battles over market shares between the United States and the EEC," said Smith. "The huge costs of agricultural subsidies appeared to lead them to a more sensible management of production of some commodities in relation to available markets.

"There are now 2,500 fewer milk producers in Ontario who produce 74 million more litres of milk in a year from 65,000 fewer cows than was the case ten years ago. Expressed another way, 20 percent fewer milk producers now produce three percent more milk from 13.25 percent fewer cows."

The man from Burgessville later summarized his speech, with an unsmiling direct stare, in front of a TV camera: "The 1980s have been a decade of accomplishment for the board, the milk committees and all producers. This has been a direct result of a deliberate planning process that began almost 25 years ago. We must regard the decade of the 1990s with optimism, but with the complete realization that perhaps there are more dangers and challenges out there now than have ever faced the board in its history. To have any other attitude would be completely irresponsible."

CHAPTER TEN

The 1990s and Beyond

In which we consider

- The 1990 GATT situation
- The U.S. farm bill
- The federal minister's support of supply management
- The level playing field
- U.S. posturings
- Sales losses by the northern pool to the United States
- Competitiveness in the dairy industry
- The plant as a competitor
- New milk products
- The role of new technology
- Quotas and supply management
- The family farm
- What lies beyond

The July 4, 1990, issue of *The Globe and Mail's* business section headlined an article, "Summit Leaders Facing Critical Trade Issue." The article began: "From the Canadian prairies to the French dairy farms to the rice fields of Japan, the political stakes are high when it comes to talk of governments reducing farm support programs at next week's Houston economic summit.

"Currently the seven richest industrial nations, whose leaders will gather in Houston, are at an impasse over farm trade, although they acknowledge that a resolution has to be found if the Uruguay round of world trade talks is to proceed toward a successful conclusion in December."

The Uruguay round of the GATT discussions had been going on for about three and a half years, with little significant progress being reported from the negotiators representing the 97 trading nations. Time was getting short, and progress was being anxiously watched by farmers around the world and, in particular, the dairy farmers in Ontario and the rest of Canada.

It had been hoped the leaders meeting in Houston would be able to find a common ground, which, according to the article in *The Globe and Mail*, would give "a political push to the trade negotiators. If the negotiators don't get that, they'll just spin their wheels."

On the matters of agricultural trade reform, the United States and the European Common Market had been faced off for some time.

The stated objective of the United States was to eliminate all price supports and all subsidies over time. That nation had taken strong exception to the "trade-distorting policies" of the Common Market. The U.S. was also not happy with Canada. They regarded Canada's system of marketing boards as a barrier to their exports. They were particularly concerned about the supply management programs practised by the poultry, egg and dairy sectors.

The Canadian situation appeared to be somewhat difficult for the Canadian negotiators. Canada did support freer trade for such products as grain and beef because it was thought that without the export subsidies, Canada could compete. On the other hand, the Canadian government was strongly committed to the philosophy of supply management for certain products on the domestic scene, with an import control system to help maintain the domestic production and marketing balance.

The twelve-nation European Community was protecting its Common Agriculture Policy (CAP), which was of particular benefit to French and West German farmers.

The United States had accused the EC of creating overproduction by the use of high domestic subsidies. They maintained that in certain cases the European price supports were twice as high as world prices. The European Community had offered to cut their supports by an "aggregate measure of support." They argued that they could achieve an overall reduction by decreasing support for their internal production, import barriers and exports. Some countries, including the United States and Canada, had reacted by saying, "The policy is too vague and would result in insufficient cuts in support."

The GATT administration placed farm price supports and other forms of subsidy in the agricultural trading world at a total of about $250 billion (U.S.) a year. But estimates were confusing. Other studies suggested only

$141 billion (U.S.) for 1989. It was still a lot of money. A significant portion of this was in the EC, where there are still memories of food shortages. The situation was being watched very anxiously by the developing countries who wished to strengthen their economies through an improved export environment in the industrial world.

Some believed time was running out for the Uruguay round. On July 4, 1990, *The Globe* article reported, "Six weeks ago at the meeting of the Organization for Economic Cooperation and Development in Paris, the divisions between the United States and the EC ran so deep on the farm issue that the final communique only stated the two opposing views."

Dale Hathaway, a Washington consultant and former USDA official, was not optimistic when he stated, "Either the U.S. drop its demands or the Europeans go back for a new mandate on agriculture. Neither is going to happen politically at this point."

In Canada during the early months of 1990, accusations were coming from the Dairy Farmers of Canada, which took issue with the United States' negotiating stance. "The U.S., like other major trading blocs, seeks freer trade for other countries but not for itself. The world's three powerful economic blocs, the U.S., the European Community and Japan, are bent on shaping GATT policies to their own needs." Farmers were urged to mount major pressure against Ottawa's politicians.

At about the same time, quotes were being attributed to Harvard-based Robert Paarlberg: "The Bush administration may be pushing for a new GATT agreement that would kill international food subsidies, but on Capitol Hill, Congress thinks the U.S. Farm Bill has worked so well they'd like to sign up for another five years of extensive price supports and farm payouts. President Bush is being asked by Congress to approve a budget that would boost export subsidies from last year's $560 million to $900 million for 1991. Congress is the place where farm policy is actually made. The Congressmen are in no mood to dismantle the Farm Bill.

"For 1990 spending should be just $9.2 billion under the Farm Bill," said Paarlberg. "However, the U.S. now spends three times as much on food stamp programs as it does on farm supports."

Whether or not the political economist is accurate in his forecasts, he concluded in May 1990, "I have to suspect that the Bush administration's GATT strategy will come to very little this year. They'll be left with an unsatisfying outcome of the GATT negotiations and also with a new layer of U.S. protectionism."

A few weeks earlier, on March 14, 1990, International Trade Minister John Crosbie, Agriculture Minister Don Mazankowski, Minister of State for Agriculture Pierre Blais, and Charles Mayer, minister of state for grains and oilseeds, were announcing a new proposal for strengthening and clarifying Article XI of GATT, which "allows countries to control imports in support of effective domestic production or marketing control programs for agriculture." The three ministers were saying:

- Strictly define what constitutes effective government supply-control measures;

- Determine the products eligible for import quota coverage in terms of those made, wholly or mainly, from the fresh product under domestic supply control;

- Clarify the application of import quotas, including the levels of access of foreign products to the domestic market; and

- Place limitations on exports of supply-managed products when import quotas are in effect.

The proposal was seeking a change to clarify Article XI to rectify the interpretation rendered in the GATT panel on ice cream and yogurt.

This was a necessary and critical change. The concern was that the interpretation used in this case could be used against other dairy products. If accepted, the proposal would clearly determine the products eligible for import quota coverage.

Meanwhile, the Cairns group had met in Santiago, Chile, from July 4 to 6, 1990. This group of 14 countries - Argentina, Australia, Brazil, Canada, Chile, Colombia, Fiji, Hungary, Indonesia, Malaysia, The Philippines, New Zealand, Thailand and Uruguay - "has been pushing for a reform of agricultural trade rules since the launch of the Uruguay round of multilateral trade negotiations (MTN) in 1986."

The ministers at the Santiago meeting had welcomed the overall thrust of the proposal for an agricultural "profile" put forward July 2, 1990, by Aart de Zeeuw, chairman of the Agriculture Negotiating Groups of GATT.

His text called for specific commitments on four essential elements - internal support, border protection, export competition, and sanitary and phytosanitary provisions. Ministers agreed on the importance of strengthening GATT rules and disciplines and making them operationally effective.

As for Canada, Trade Minister John Crosbie stated, "Although Canada has some important concerns with the text, on balance it provides a reasonable framework to carry the negotiating process forward."

Both Mazankowski and Crosbie had strongly reiterated, "Canadian negotiators will be instructed to pursue our concerns regarding supply management and export subsidies in Geneva."

Regarding supply management, Mazankowski said, "The chairman's text calls for strengthened and more operationally effective GATT rules, but the text is not explicit enough on GATT Article XI issues. A number of countries have supported Canada's position on Article XI, and Canadian negotiators will continue to vigorously pursue this objective in the final months of negotiations."

John Crosbie had underlined the urgent need for countries to demonstrate "...the political will to bring about real reforms to agricultural trade, particularly in regard to export subsidies. We recognize that phasing out export subsidies raises difficult problems for many participants. Finding solutions will not be easy, but it must be done."

The ministers' comments were reflected by the Canadian negotiators on July 13th, when they emphasized "the importance of the elimination of government-funded export assistance" and that they were committed to the proposal "...for the clarification and strengthening of Article XI. Given the support we have received, we expect the Canadian proposal to be reflected in the results of the negotiations."

In the meantime, on June 25, Carla Hills, the U.S. trade representative, had told the Institute of International Economics, "The U.S. needs to see a sharp decline in the area of export subsidies and market access barriers."

She differed with the European Community's proposal to deal with export subsidies and market access indirectly by lowering the internal support prices. "This will not help such countries as Brazil, Argentina, Canada, Australia, and New Zealand, which lose sales when the EC 'bribes' the marketplace with export subsidies instead of having its entrepreneurs win ... on the basis of price and quality," Hills said.

But she failed to mention U.S. export subsidies and other policy activities. *The Globe and Mail* of July 4, 1990, suggested, "Despite its purist views, the United States is a sinner too, with an elaborate and expensive system of restrictive quotas, export subsidies and production incentives."

"The removal of agricultural trade barriers would not have to happen overnight," stated Hills. "The U.S. has proposed taking roughly a decade."

Hills' assessment was, "It is possible to reach an agriculture agreement in July."

This notion was contradicted by Dale Hathaway who stated, "A miracle was required to produce a text for the agricultural framework agreement by the end of July."

It didn't happen.

"The absence of a framework in July will not be enough to force a change in the political position of the key participants," said Hathaway. "In all likelihood the December ministerial meeting in Brussels will begin with the major agricultural issues unresolved.

"A Uruguay round without significant results in agriculture is a possible outcome," Hathaway continued. "It would follow previous rounds of multilateral trade talks which began with a resounding declaration regarding the intent to reform agriculture and ended with the U.S. abandoning its demands for reform and postponing them to the next round of multilateral talks. Final decisions on whether to abandon the round or compromise on agriculture will be made after an evaluation of the overall package that has been negotiated. That is unlikely to happen before early 1991."

Hathaway maintained that failure to reach an agricultural agreement, if it did not destroy the Uruguay round, would mean the world would go on much as it is, with agricultural trade being a constant irritant, especially for smaller, lower-cost exporters.

"A minimum outcome would be close, but not identical to the current EC position, concentrating on modest cuts in support and protection using an aggregate measure of support. It would involve some product-specific minimum access commitments but would not involve rebalancing. It would also not require the phasing-out of specific policies, but would mean some 'tinkering' with Article XI (2)(c) on allowing quotas and with Article XVI (3) on subsidies. Such a minimum deal may raise the level of tension over agriculture in GATT. It would not significantly improve world resource allocations or trade distortions and would require dispute settlement over a whole gamut of issues.

Hathaway, the former USDA official, had argued, "The maximum agreement would include complex calculations for many countries and commodities. If there was agreement to convert import barriers to tariffs, the complexity of the issues will be multiplied and there will be endless possibilities for disagreements. It will be most interesting to watch the dispute settlement process. If the U.S. violates a commitment on target prices for wheat, who gets to complain, who is the injured party, and how is the compensation calculated and avoided?"

John Phillips had made some interesting comments in the April 24,

1990, issue of *Farm & Country*. "Managed trade is a fact of life," he suggested. "The European Community now has a love affair with supply management largely because it's been so successful in milk," wrote Phillips. "Western Europe had grown under a Mount Everest of surplus butter, powdered milk and cheese. Handling excess stocks played havoc with the EC's farm budget, a budget which took more than 70 percent of the group's entire budget. The EC's surplus poured onto world markets, causing major disruptions in Canada as well. The EC countries certainly do not wish to endure another round of uncontrolled output that results from a 'free market.'

"European governments have a social policy that involves ensuring the maximum number of efficient farm families living in nonurban areas. West Germany today has 665,000 family farms while France has 982,000. Canada's down to 200,000. Twenty years ago each of these European giants boasted close to 1.5 million farms. Consolidation took place.

"Today's French farm averages 72.5 acres and the West German farm averages close to 40. Most are highly efficient units, producing two or three crops a year on the same field. A political fact of life is that these millions of farm families still have enormous political clout."

On July 30, however, the GATT table was startled to learn that Ray MacSharry, farm commissioner with the EC, in a private meeting with agriculture ministers from Canada, Australia, Japan and the U.S.A., had challenged world trading partners to cut farm subsidies by 30 percent by 1996. The kicker was that the proposal would have to be approved by the EC commission in September before it could be presented to GATT. The United States stated that it would not officially respond until the proposal was officially presented at the GATT discussions.

Interpretations placed on the commissioner's statement by European observers indicated, "It confirms the Community is only prepared to concede reductions that reflect the scale and extent of its own domestic policy reforms. They do not intend that modifications of domestic policy be dictated by any GATT agreement. The Uruguay round has achieved very little in getting the Community to move from its entrenched defence of an unreformed CAP."

During the Canada-U.S. free trade discussions and debates, the term "level playing field" was coined. Everyone can envision a level playing field that provides no advantage to any participant; the original simplistic thinking was that subsidy support, if any existed, should be equal on both sides of the border.

Dairy farmers in Canada are convinced at this time that the so-called level playing field has a very distinct and definite advantage for the United

States. Through contacts with U.S. producers, they know that certain government programs have been available to decrease milk production. They know the milk price support programs support the price of milk by government purchase of surplus dairy products from processors at a purchase price reflecting processing costs and a profit margin. They see many other situations between the two economies and policy areas that they think weigh the scale to the U.S. advantage. This includes not only subsidies, both direct and indirect, but the perceived higher cost of certain production inputs, such as fuel, interest rates, taxes, and pesticides.

There is also the argument as to what actually constitutes a subsidy. GATT signatories apparently have been unable to agree on a precise definition or set of criteria to strictly define the circumstances that would justify the imposition of countervailing duties. This has been and will continue to be of major significance and concern in U.S.-Canada trade relations.

Some in Ontario and throughout Canada think that possibly the milk production industry and the dairy industry generally are overregulated. Whether or not the Canadian penchant for solutions to problems - to "make a law" - has been overzealous, perhaps should be scrutinized. The Ontario product is of top quality. The OMMB is proud of the product it is marketing.

Milk producers in Ontario's northern pool have had their own vision of the level playing field with the United States. In 1990, consumers understandably are traipsing across the border into Sault Ste. Marie, Michigan, on a regular basis to fill up with gasoline - and also to pick up milk and other retail products.

The producers and retailers on the Ontario side are feeling the result. Significant sales of milk have been lost. Concerns have been expressed at other border points in Canada as well.

Stu Greig, OMMB marketing officer in the North Bay office, in July 1990, said, "About three percent of a month's production in the northern pool is being lost. Cheap gasoline currently at about $1.08 to $1.10 an American gallon is the big attraction. It's about half the price of Ontario gas. People go over to buy gas, and then they buy milk and other groceries."

Stu recalls there was one service station that featured "discount milk" as a further attraction to buy gas. "There was a gas price war on the Ontario side two or three months ago, and the sales of milk here jumped considerably. There's a big food outlet on the U.S. side, and at times 50 percent of the cars in the parking lot are from Ontario. It's a real concern."

Meanwhile, when the northern pool producers discuss the level playing field, they say, "Among other high input costs, we'd sure like to get some of that cheap gasoline up here."

Retail milk sales in the Sault have dropped from 10.2 million litres in 1984 to less than 7.8 million litres in 1989, with a 1990 forecast of 7.2 million litres.

The Ontario four-litre bag, which corresponds to the U.S. gallon, has lost 23 percent in sales in 1990.

The local solution, some say, lies in the notion that "...gasoline is the problem. The government should let the Ontario gas stations compete at border points through lower taxes. In the current situation the government is losing the money anyway."

Studies were carried out under the federal dairy task force to determine the competitive situation and balance that existed in 1990 between Canada and the United States. The findings must be treated by everyone concerned in an objective and rational way. The level playing field involves more than just government subsidies.

There is, for example, the whole matter of differences in government-imposed costs. Differences in input costs, including labour, must be scrutinized. The June 1990 report of Ontario's Industrial Restructuring Commissioner points out, "There are pronounced interregional differences (not to mention a large degree of foreign ownership in Canada) undermining the possibility of a 'team Canada' approach to trade issues. The Americans, for their part, have little difficulty in deciding when the playing field is not level and when foreigners are unfair traders."

The dairy industry is very much in a competitive environment. It competes for the food dollar, and in doing so, it competes with other food products. Fluid milk competes with soft drinks and other beverages. To continue to exist, the dairy industry must continue to recognize the critical necessity of dealing with the competition, meeting it and beating it.

The task force on competitiveness in the agri-food industry, established by the federal minister, Don Mazankowski, used the following working definition: "Competitiveness is the sustained ability to profitably gain and maintain a market share on domestic and/or in export markets."

A June 1990 study carried out by management consultants Deloitte and Touche, entitled "Factors Contributing to a Competitive Agri-Food Sector," suggests how this can be done by an industry. The study emphasized that competitiveness cannot be sustained without continually innovating and increasing productivity.

Deloitte and Touche maintain competitiveness can be assisted through vertical cooperation, understanding of the nature of demand for the product, awareness of the competitive environment, and bringing the consumer to the product. Generic industry promotion is essential, as well as the exploitation of the natural endowments of a product. The attitudes within an industry are important, and the definition of innovations must be all-inclusive, including the best use of the latest technology, cooperation of the interested parties and marketing techniques.

Within the early history and development of the milk industry in Ontario, fluid milk distributors were restricted to specified geographic regions. There was little, and in most cases, no incentive to innovate. The system did not allow for competitiveness in the real sense. Plants were generally small and usually couldn't innovate because of lack of adequate financing.

There was vertical cooperation, but for the wrong reason. The processors tended to dominate the individual producer, and to a marked degree this held true for the truckers as well. There was little future if the producer was not part of the system. And becoming part of the system was not always easy.

With the arrival of the Ontario Milk Marketing Board on the scene, the situation changed. The dominant role of the OMMB for the past 25 years has come from the strength of the producers' bargaining position, abetted by legislation, strong leaders, a highly qualified staff and adequate financing.

Though the processors have presented a united front through the Ontario Dairy Council, to some degree the council has had to face the problem of the individual economic considerations and needs of the members. But the Ontario Dairy Council has allowed for good horizontal cooperation and leadership at processor level.

A strengthening of the vertical cooperation is required in the future. Milk producers and the board must recognize, even more than presently, that the future prosperity of the industry will result to a marked degree from the recognition and acceptance that to be successful and maintain a competitive position, as just defined, will require the ultimate in cooperation and mutual efforts on the part of the whole industry.

Tom Kane, president of the Ontario Dairy Council, in June 1990 suggested thoughts along this vein.

"The Ontario Dairy Council supports the concept of supply management for the dairy industry, though it would encourage introduction of some changes to the current system that would permit increased flexibility and market orientation. The Ontario Milk Marketing Board is the sole buyer and seller of raw milk in this province, and as such needs to continuously work with its customers (the processing companies) in order to determine if the product is meeting the needs of those customers. The infrastructure for communications and working relationships is present, and in recent years has been actively utilized, but there is always room for more improvement. The mandates of the two organizations will mean that total cooperation is highly improbable in some areas; however, there are many projects and programs that are being jointly worked upon and can be mutually beneficial to both parties. Continued good working relationships will depend on the willingness of both processors and producers to develop policies and procedures that enhance the usage of dairy products and reward the efficiencies and competitiveness of the industry."

In July 1990 in Geneva, the United States was saying, "Unless Canadian restrictions on imports of yogurt and ice cream are removed, Washington will retaliate this fall by suspending trading concessions on some Canadian exports."

In response, Canada's ambassador to GATT repeated, "Canada would implement the changes demanded in a GATT report but only if required to do so by new rules established in the current Uruguay round of world trade talks."

It was suggested that the odds of the American threat being carried through were quite slim, since a GATT consensus was needed in order to approve such a step.

In this example situation, competitiveness ultimately rests on the attitudes of the processors, the producers, transporters and government, with each reflecting its own constituency pressures. The service industries who depend on the health of the domestic market for their economic well-being are part of the marketing team. The consumers are critical to the whole picture.

The matter of competiveness is dynamic. There is no plateau that the dairy industry may reach and therefore rest on its laurels. It must maintain continuing efforts of change and innovation. This is merely the way it is in the current marketing environment, both domestically and internationally. Be that as it may, the definition of what constitutes a level playing field is critical and may be difficult to find.

This continuous movement for change is fed by technology, the restlessness of the industry, the almost universal desire for growth and expansion, and the pride of accomplishment.

In Ontario, with the average age of the milk producer around 43 years, a dynamic market atmosphere is being demanded. In 1990 there were two prominent and interesting scientists working close to each other in the general area of the campus of the University of Guelph.

Dr. Morris (Moe) Freeman is general manager of Semex Canada, which represents the member artificial insemination organizations in some 66 countries of the world. He is a very experienced animal scientist. The other is professor W.D. (Wally) Beversdorf, who chairs the department of crop science at the University of Guelph.

One presently serves the crops industry, and the other the dairy industry. Their responsibilities and interests are very much related, and conversations with them etch a pattern for the future of the dairy industry that is very challenging.

While possibly not by deliberate design, the developments in plant breeding and the potential results of emerging new genetic technology place the plant as a strong potential competitor of the future for the dairy industry.

The expression of agricultural scientists and plant breeders of yesteryear was "to make two blades of grass grow where one grew before." More recent progress in plant breeding has been much more dramatic than that. In three decades the yields of grain corn in Ontario have been increased by about 280 percent as a result of genetic manipulation alone. Most of this startling improvement has been due to the reshuffling of genes.

Plants have some advantage over animals because they have a shorter generation time. Plants have the ability to inbreed and stabilize types more quickly.

A number of crop species have the ability to move genes quite freely. There is some ability to modify proteins as well as fats and oils produced by plants. This can also be done with starches. Animals convert fixed carbons or carbohydrates into muscle matter, and plants convert light and carbon dioxide into carbohydrates and protein. Animals are convertors of chemical energy, and plants are creators of chemical energy.

From a global perspective, plant protein is very important. Wheat is the single most important source of protein for human consumption around the world. Over the long term and on a global basis, plant protein may become the world's most important source of protein and fats. It is already the primary source of carbohydrates. Technically, scientists can do almost anything they want to do in terms of modifying plants genetically. As well, plants have the ability to inbreed and stabilize types very quickly, certainly more quickly than animals.

Almost any protein that an animal produces can be reproduced in a plant. What scientists can do technically, however, doesn't mean it's going to be done. Wally Beversdorf says, "Consumer preferences are far more complicated than that. A major consideration is cost of development. While biotechnology can do many things, there's not the economic climate or the economic means in Canada to take advantage of all of these. For example, the corn root worm, which presently requires significant quantities of costly pesticides to control, could be eliminated by using genetic technology, but this would require $25 or $30 million in development costs over a five- or six-year period. Presently there is not the economic will to do this. There is the technical capacity but not the economic framework."

Canola is held up as an outstanding example of a plant's being modified to take a very significant place in the food market. Rapeseed was an oil producer, but the oil was at first unsuitable for human consumption. Scientists at the Agriculture Canada Research Station in Saskatoon and the University of Manitoba modified the plant to remove the erucic acid. This not only resulted in a plant food source for people, but also one that would grow in the colder regions of Canada. Canola oil is now the most important oil in the margarine industry.

Research is under way that will result in modifications to the oil produced from canola and allow it to be used for deep frying and at the same time improve its apparently desirable health attributes. Presently some 70,000 acres of canola grow in Ontario, producing about 30,000 tonnes of oil.

Dr. Beversdorf, the crop scientist, hastens to say, "Our role is not to displace the animal industry; we know that's fundamental to Ontario agriculture. But we do look at opportunities to move new crops into the cropping pattern and strengthen agriculture generally. Over time other crop areas will emerge to help displace imports. An example of this is soybeans, historically an imported crop. Currently a little more than a million acres of soybeans grow in Ontario, and the province is practically self-sufficient."

Beyond question, the plant is a potential competitor of the dairy industry. Soya oil, with its many diverse uses, became an important ingredient of margarine before the introduction of canola. It played a significant role in the marketplace in competition with butter.

For some time, technology has been available to produce substitutes for dairy products using a vegetable oil and a plant protein or a vegetable oil and milk protein. Such products have not been allowed in Ontario, other provinces and certain states of the U.S. This legislation is in place because of the economic significance of the dairy industry and its fundamental importance as part of the livestock industry to agriculture. The legislation, therefore, is not intended to protect the dairy industry in a maternalistic sense, but rather to preserve an important ingredient of sound agricultural production as we know it. The legislation is not there to protect inefficiencies, but rather to ensure that farming goes forward and is allowed to have an essential means of ensuring a sustainable agriculture for the future.

But the possibility of not achieving this realization and encouraging its acceptance as a viable and necessary policy by governments of the future must remain a continuing priority for dairy industry leaders. If the legislation were removed, it is certain that a new industry would emerge. Products could be produced at a fairly low cost considering the price of soybean protein and soya fat versus milk fat. Soybeans in the summer of 1990 traded at about eleven cents per pound.

The plant industry must be regarded as a potential competitor of milk products, but thought must also be given to its impact on meat. Even with the reduced number of dairy cattle in Ontario, dairy herds still supply 15 to 20 percent of the beef going to market.

If meat substitutes emerge with the texture, aroma and taste of the natural product, they could have a significant impact on the meat industry. Certainly pressure, sparked by ecological concerns, is mounting in this direction, and innovations are taking place, exemplified in the wide variety of palatable soybean meat substitutes that such companies as the California-based Loma Linda produces. But the basic importance of livestock in the agricultural system in Ontario must be remembered. Developing and maintaining a cognizance of this principle in the minds of the policy makers and the general public is a challenge that must be met. Policies supporting the viability of the livestock industry are essential in meeting certain environmental concerns, such as water pollution, and supporting a sustainable agriculture in Ontario and elsewhere.

North America and Europe historically and traditionally have enjoyed an animal protein-oriented consumer. This is not true in many other parts of the world, where vegetable protein is a part of the food culture. As immigrant cultures integrate with others in Canada, we must anticipate that the total Canadian use of animal protein could be diluted. The dairy industry could receive a smaller percentage of the consumer's dollar, but at the same time maintain its position in product demand. It should also be able to anticipate some growth. This will depend to a marked extent on the industry's willingness to compete with every facility at its disposal.

A scrutiny of the Canadian population is interesting. Demographers suggest that it should stabilize by the year 2006; that is to say, births, deaths and immigration will balance out unless immigration policies change. Some suggest that it will be impossible for Canada to maintain such a stability in the face of a forecast world population stability not being reached until 2070. During this time, the world population will double. The current world population is nearly six billion people, and with a doubling there could be a dramatic change.

Be that as it may, these are the current figures, and so it can be argued that planning should be based on these. It is important to note that the great population increases are taking place in the world under cultures in which meat and dairy products have not been an essential part of the diet.

Dr. Moe Freeman, the animal scientist, recognizes the challenges presented by the plant industry. He is an aggressive champion of the dairy cow. "The dairy cow will survive in the world, and she is a viable vehicle to feed humanity."

But Dr. Freeman doesn't pull any punches either: "If changes aren't made in the dairy industry, it's going to lose more and more of its share of the market, and who says what has happened to butter couldn't happen to fluid milk? The future is there for the dairy industry if it concentrates on products that the consumer wants and the health authorities say are good ones."

That's the challenge. The consumer influences the final balance wheel of market share. Everything else facilitates.

While recognizing that livestock and poultry, compared to plants, are inefficient producers of protein, Dr. Freeman argues that within the poultry and livestock industry the dairy cow is the most efficient. Data from the department of animal science at the University of Guelph indicate that a cow producing 15,000 pounds of milk will produce 27 percent of her total protein intake. In other words, 27 percent of the plant protein that goes into the cow comes out as milk.

Dr. Freeman thinks the dairy industry must be looking at more alternative products that will be acceptable from a health standpoint, but that will also be acceptable to the consumer.

The young farmer today who is looking ahead must be concerned about dairy products of the future.

Milk producers must ask themselves the questions, What products can we sell? How do we keep our share of the consumer food dollar? If these questions aren't handled right, the dairy industry will be relegated to a smaller and smaller portion of the consumer's dollar. The situation must be considered to be very critical to the future of the dairy industry.

Dr. Wally Beversdorf is impatient: "We're in an anti-technology culture right now. It's baffling because we need to be technologically competent so that we can be economically competitive. Everyone wants to have a higher standard of living, and they want to work less. The two just don't add up, and they won't unless there's the technological exchange that allows for increased productivity with less work. People seem to want the simple life."

Yet, in 1990 trade discussions had gone on with possible policy decisions that would test the competitiveness of Canadian industry and in particular the dairy industry.

The report made at the end of the summit meeting in Houston indicated that the leaders had sent the farm trade dispute back to their negotiators for resolution in further anticipated tense negotiations. July 23 was set by the leaders as the deadline for the first signs of progress. The day passed with no apparent progress and still wide gaps remaining in the leaders' thinking.

French Prime Minister Francois Mitterand was skeptical: "The differences between Europe and North America on agriculture are organic and structural and cannot be resolved by good balancing of a few diplomatic sentences."

The impasse between the U.S. and the EC over farm subsidies, and whether or not they should be cut, and how far and how fast, was threatening to scuttle the round of trade talks being conducted in Geneva under the GATT. The U.S. was still calling for an elimination of subsidies. The Europeans ridiculed this as "utopian"; they wanted a gradual reduction.

The Uruguay round of negotiations involved trade in items ranging from textiles to computer software. But the U.S. and a number of the developing countries have said they would not agree to the deals on these issues unless there was also a significant deal on agricultural trade. France repeated the EC view that farmers need to be subsidized for social and environmental reasons and not just for purely economic reasons. "It's a matter of a style of life, a social organization, and a culture."

The U.S. knew the original intent of Article XI GATT and apparently accepted it for a while. The U.S. has appeared to be less than consistent in its interpretation of certain trade matters. The question will be whether the government of Canada will allow itself to be bullied into submission by the United States on these trade matters, though the United States has not been, as someone said, "lily white."

Then there is the matter of milk quotas and quota prices, which some have attempted to make an issue. As of July 1990 the price for group one pool quota was about $249. It was as high as $305 a litre in September,

1986. The highest for unused MSQ was reached in July 1985 at $1.50 a litre, and used MSQ in July 1986 was 76 cents a litre. A large percentage of the trading has been within families, but new shippers have been coming in.

The price of quotas has not necessarily been indicative of profits enjoyed by milk producers. It does indicate a stable market and certainly the production of a product that does enjoy a more profitable return than certain other agricultural commodities. Much of the efficiencies developed by Ontario milk producers, however, have been passed on to consumers through lower priced products.

Tobacco is an example of how a quota price reacts to the stability of the market. In 1985 tobacco quota traded as high as $2.70 per pound. In 1990 the price was as low as 29 cents, and it wasn't too easy to sell. The drastic reduction in quota price was a result of a sharp drop in demand for tobacco, because of health concerns and government taxation policies, as well as having too much unused quota available for sale.

The organized dairy industry in Ontario, particularly in fluid milk, was built around the quota system. The system was accepted and encouraged by governments as a reasonable method of sharing a limited market.

Reputable economists and others have concluded that a quota policy goes hand in hand with a supply management system. A plant supply quota regulates milk processors. Producers have the right to produce milk within a specified quota. Plants receive a supply of milk based on a national milk supply quota system.

This right to produce or receive a specified amount of milk automatically takes on a value, depending on the circumstances of the market. This is no different from taxicabs, restaurants with a liquor licence, or even some residential areas whose desirability may be protected by a zoning by-law. In all cases, this right or privilege takes on a value and avoids what could otherwise be a chaotic situtation.

Logical reasoning therefore suggests that as long as there is supply management in the dairy industry, there will have to be a quota system. As long as there is a quota system, quotas will have values, and in the case of milk this will directly relate to the conditions of the market for milk products and to some degree on economic conditions in other sectors of agriculture.

It is within the capability of governments through trade agreements and associated policies to severely weaken and even destroy the current marketing system for milk in Canada. There will be continuing stresses ahead for industry and government leaders in these matters.

John Core, shown here speaking at the 1990 Dairy Farmers of Canada annual meeting, became the OMMB's fourth chairman when he was elected to the post in January 1990.

At the same time, it is inconceivable that any government, provincial or federal, would allow the weakening or the eventual destruction of a marketing system that has proven so effective in Canada and has been recognized by milk producers outside of Canada as workable and realistic. It can't and won't happen. Don Mazankowski and the responsible Canadian ministers appear too determined in their support of supply management to allow it to happen.

A strongly positive indication of their intentions is included in the Free Trade Agreement with the U.S. One of the agricultural objectives stated in the FTA is "to preserve Canada's agricultural policy instruments." Supply management is one such policy instrument.

With this scenario, however, goes a responsibility for the Canadian and Ontario milk producer. The industry must accept the challenge of the marketplace and deal with it using all the technologies that are available.

John Core and the 1990 OMMB are looking to the future. Bruce Whale, one of the younger producers on the board, says, "We have to plan for the future. That's better than reacting to something that happened yesterday and trying to come up with a solution tomorrow. This is impossible in such an industry as complex as ours today."

While at the same time John Core states, "Producers have become used to having a market for their milk every day. They're used to the stability of milk - it's picked up and delivered regularly, and a cheque arrives the middle of every month. It's critical that the younger generation realize why we have the marketing system we have, and what we would face if we ever were to lose that system."

The challenges in 1990 may not be more difficult, given the times, than they were in 1965. But they are more complex. They go beyond the provinces and beyond Canada, and rather than being restricted in their discussion and solution to provincial boundaries, they had reached a negotiating table representing 97 nations.

Milk produced in Ontario is worth about $1.1 billion at the farm gate. This translates into about $5 billion for the Ontario economy. In return, the Ontario and Canadian economy should be capable of adequately supporting the dairy industry in the marketplace without benefit of a consumer subsidy.

The dairy industry in the Ontario market environment can be entirely self-sufficient. In the markets it should be generally financially independent of governments. For the future well-being of the industry, this would be a very desirable situation. The marketplace in Canada should be capable of purchasing dairy products without subsidization. The consumer will buy dairy products providing they are the right ones, presented and adequately promoted to meet the competition.

"One of the greatest and most far-sighted actions taken by the milk board was to establish the 'dairy chair' at the University of Guelph," said Dr. Moe Freeman. "The industry must get these new products for the market, and they will get them. We can produce milk protein, but what kind of a product are we going to put on the market that will cause the consumers to say, 'I like that and I want to buy more of it'?

"We've never been able to tap the luxury beverage market. We've never had a product that we could sell against Coke or Pepsi. What do you have with your scotch? It's certainly not milk. You drink milk because it's good for you. You have to come up with a product that has more appeal than just being good nutritionally."

In 1990, the efficient and well cared-for dairy farms stand out proudly on the rural Ontario landscape for all to see and enjoy. They stand out in a very positive way, indicating the pride of the families living there. The message comes across load and clear, "We've accomplished a lot in 25 years. We're proud of it. We dare anyone to try to take it away from us."

There is no longer any place in the Ontario agricultural vocabulary, at least in the dairy farm vocabulary, for the term "family farm." The term has been around for a long time, and it's redundant. It's a "negative" for Ontario agriculture and particularly the Ontario milk producer.

It's not a question of how rural Ontario may feel about it, but rather it's a matter of perception by the urban media and the urban reader. It conjures up an image of a relatively small, inefficient social structure dependent upon government subsidies for its existence and far removed from the dynamic changes perceived as taking place in other industries.

The term "family farm" as used by the urban media does not reflect progress. In the minds of too many people it represents a way of life, rather than an up-to-date, modern, efficient and computerized business enterprise. The dairy farms or corporations in Ontario are still operated by families, but they are not a family farm within the meaning, understanding and intent of too many articles in the urban media.

The average age for Ontario milk producers in 1990 is 43 years. This indicates a confidence on the part of young families involved in milk production. Bruce Saunders, another young member of the 1990 OMMB, says, "I never had any doubts about producing milk. The system lets you know what you're going to get for your product."

Saunders, his wife Marg and three young children on their farm near Holland Centre, are looking forward to a future in the dairy industry. The future will be there for them, albeit with certain gradual modifications to the system that may be necessary from time to time, to fine-tune an industry that's going to be with us for a long time.

As one who is determined about the future of the industry, Gaston

Levac, the successful St. Bernardin dairy farmer, said firmly, "Confidence, we must have it. If one wants to succeed, one must be determined, to have confidence. One can't give up and not fight, because we will lose if we give up. We must protect our system or something similar to it."

John Core, the new board chairman in 1990, said, "I'm not much of a history buff. We have to look to the future!" He could be echoing George McLaughlin's words when he said in 1965, "The past is past. It's now our turn to make history."

With an eye to the future, the milk board is moving to multiple component pricing on the first of August 1991. It has been forecast that the current surplus of skim milk powder will disappear about the year 2000, when an equilibrium will be reached between fat and solids-not-fat.

With a fixed quota under a pricing system that emphasized butterfat, the producer recognized the only way to get an increased milk cheque was to obtain a higher average butterfat test. Presently in 1990, this is about 3.84 percent. If pricing starts to emphasize protein rather than butterfat, the milk producer's attention will be drawn to protein. As well, with the MSQ being expressed in terms of butterfat effective the August 1, 1990, producers no longer have the same incentive to increase their butterfat test.

It appears at the moment and for the foreseeable future that fat as a product is receiving less favour from the consumer.

This market trend has been visible for a long time in North America. It appears the time is long past that would allow it to be dismissed as a fad.

Europe is going very strongly for protein, much more so than North America. If they turn out to be right, perhaps North America will be bringing in their results, their cattle, their semen and embryos in the next 10 to 20 years.

The French milk board, Oni Lait, has been concerned about a "steady rise of butterfat levels in milk and falling protein levels." They have asked the dairy sector to reverse the trend.

The French concede, "There is no miracle solution. Genetic changes are a long-term work, but efforts must be made to ensure that breeding programs are oriented toward achieving higher protein content rather than increasing the volume of milk and fat."

Because of this perceived market demand, some wonder if the dairy cow should be de-emphasized as a high producer of milk fat. The whole question in the minds of many, as well, is whether or not this is a desirable course of action and even if it is possible.

Dr. Charles Smith, presently holder of the J.C. Rennie Chair in Animal Breeding Strategies at the University of Guelph, offers a clear view of the present and a professional outlook for the future of the productive dairy cow.

"Perhaps we overemphasize the impact of technology. I've been pushing embryo transplant for at least ten years. Slow to come along, it's only being used now to a limited extent. The cost of embryo transplant is still a limitation."

According to Dr. Smith, milk yield is improving genetically at the rate of 1 to 1.5 percent per year, so that in ten years there could be an improvements of 10 to 15 percent.

To this, of course, are added the impact of improvements in husbandry, disease control and other management considerations.

"It's almost an international game. We now have the ranking of bulls across countries so that, for example, bulls can be ranked in Holland and the U.K. against those in Canada. Bulls can be selected from any country in the world, depending on their merit. There's an international market, and it's very competitive."

In 1990 there is a large flow of semen and embryos from the United States into Canada. Europe and the world have bred very heavily to North American Holsteins. Canadian and American breeders are going to have quite a lot of competition from Europe, Australia and New Zealand, as well as other countries in the next five to ten years.

Dr. Charles Smith emphasizes that the 1 to 1.5 percent per year improvement through genetics is presently being achieved. "We could tighten up the present system. We could select bulls internationally. We could increase the rate of embryo transfers in females. Females could be selected at an earlier age rather than waiting for three lactations. They could be selected on first lactation records and pedigree information. This would allow us to turn over the generations more quickly and increase the rates of change.

"We could pay less attention to things like dairy character and type and go after economic efficiency. Economic efficiency is very difficult to define, and we're concerned about what it really is. We don't think it means milk yield. Maybe we'll give a negative weight to the yield of milk itself and concentrate on fat yield and protein yield.

"We also have to be concerned with herd life. It's important that cows get bred and last over the years, and so that's why we're trying to redefine economic efficiency."

And so we learn from Dr. Smith. Beauty is functional. The looks of the cow have to be evaluated and measured and determined as to their importance in the performance of an animal. More attention will have to be paid to herd life and whether or not the animal is temperamentally sound, whether the feet and legs last, rather than "wondering about the shape of her rump."

Currently the general opinion among scientists, it is also becoming so among technicians. They're worrying less about the fancy points of a cow and more about the economic aspects.

We learn, "It's quite difficult genetically to change the ratio between fat and protein. It can be done, but you would lose a lot of improvement in protein yield."

In France, meanwhile, Oni Lait proposes starting in 1990 to spend a lot of money in advisory campaigns. They plan to implement programs targeted at producers relating to protein and fat. Ways to revise the methods of calculating the milk price are being proposed for immediate study.

Dr. Smith says, "We'd have to change our whole philosophy so that instead of rating bulls for milk we'd rate them for fat plus protein. This would result in a different set of bulls. But it would take ten to 15 years before this would get through to the commercial population in any measure."

In breeding, concentration can be on protein rather than fat. If there were an increase in protein, however, there would also be a slight increase in the amount of fat because of the correlation, but still it will take some time to make a significant genetic change in the dairy cow.

Another problem bothering some milk producers: If you look 15 or 20 years down the road, you really don't know what the conditions are going to be like. What will be the public reaction to butterfat? What will medical people and nutritionists be saying in 2010?

Dr. Smith comments, "Cholesterol is not as bad a thing as it used to be. Things change."

Competitiveness in dairy cattle breeding will be very important in the next 10 to 20 years. Every country in Europe has its own breeding program. North America, Australia and New Zealand are also involved. All of these countries have had importations of North American genes and so they are all very competitive and will be mounting intensive improvement programs of their own.

"This means there's going to be a lot of duplication and redundancy," admits Dr. Smith, "but there will be a lot of competition as well. There are smaller herds in Ontario than in the U.S., and the production tends to be less intensive. Genetically there have been comparisons between the bulls being used in the two countries. Canada appears to be a little behind, about 200 kilograms per lactation, but within striking distance. This is equal to about five percent. We're improving about one percent a year, so this represents three years' genetic change."

Comparing practices in the two nations, consideration must be given to management situations and to the cost of inputs and such matters in both countries. There are opportunities, of course, with new technology, such as embryo transfers to increase the rates of genetic change in both countries.

Dr. Smith says, however, "Let's say we want to produce a herd that maximizes the efficiency of protein production. We could say fat isn't important. There's a group in Finland who are looking into this and the genetics involved. They're trying to set up a specific herd. They're not suggesting that they will attempt to change the whole country, but they could develop a special breeding unit."

And then there is genetic engineering. The possibilities of genetic engineering disturb many people. As opposed to genetic technology, genetic engineering tends to involve molecular genetics. It means that one gene may be taken from one species and put into the germ plasm of another species. There is replication in the new environment.

The researcher identifies a particular gene in which he is interested that has a desired trait, such as high protein. He takes it out of one species, clones it, multiplies it and introduces it into the other species. This is done by micro-manipulation. The outside gene becomes assimilated with the other genes. But there are still problems, and there is the whole matter of public reaction. There has not been any successful application to livestock as yet, however, but it will happen.

If it was possible to use genetic engineering to breed for milk and milk components, then there is the real possibility of speeding up the whole system. For example, it might be possible to clog up the gene that naturally produces fat, and there would be no fat produced. Protein production would be emphasized. This would be a very effective way of changing the components of milk produced.

Nevertheless, there is an abhorrence of genetic engineering. But let's say the United States started to use it and free trade were running full steam. Real problems would be created.

There is a real example of what can result if production policies have no economic basis. In Denmark a few years ago, for humane reasons battery cages for egg production were forbidden. But the Danes couldn't outlaw the importation of eggs produced from battery cages used in other countries. So their own poultry farmers were put out of business and now the eggs are coming in from Holland. A level playing field in trade has many considerations.

There has been much interest and controversy in both Canada and the United States regarding Bovine Somatotropen (BST) and milk yields. A recent Deloitte and Touche study with certain assumptions indicates, "Following current trends without BST, milk production for each cow is expected to climb 26 percent by the year 1998. Using BST, the economic studies suggest milk production will increase another three to eight percent for each cow in the same ten-year period, that is, 1989-1998."

The Deloitte and Touche study indicates, "Without BST use, the total number of cows would decline by 20 percent in the next ten years. With BST the cow numbers could be cut by another three to eight percent.

But some researchers suggest, "It seems to work, but it puts a heavier load on the cow. Increases in milk yield may not translate into economic efficiency. There is still some concern about herd life and the economics associated with the use of BST. Not all the answers are in yet."

There is also the whole matter of public perception and acceptance. The EC had an 18-month moratorium on the use of BST that remained in effect until the 1990 year end. The moratorium was based on socio-economic reasons; at the time of writing there was some suggestion it may be extended for the same reasons. However, some evidence has also been placed before EC Commission's Agricultural Directorate purporting to be relative to health concerns as well.

Again, what should Canada's reaction be if the growth hormone is permitted and accepted for use in the United States to produce milk products that could be sent to Canada in competition with Canadian production? It's the level playing field again!

Geneticists like Dr. Moe Freeman and Dr. Wally Beversdorf, however, while recognizing the possible potential of such a hormone, believe the genetic route is the most desirable.

There is no doubt that the future is alive and well for the dairy industry if it concentrates on producing products that consumers want and that health authorities confirm as nutritious and safe. The dairy industry must lead in this area, however, not follow the health people as they have been doing. Researchers working on rapeseed didn't ask the advice of the health authorities before they removed the erucic acid and renamed the new oil-bearing seed canola. The same aggressive action is required by the dairy industry.

"The technology is there to change the dairy cow, if it's desired to improve the protein content of milk," says Dr. Moe Freeman. "It won't be as easy as with fat because there isn't the variation in population and the heretabilities are lower than with butterfat.

"It's within sight, maybe within five years, where with embryo transplant and the perfecting of the sexing of the embryos, the farmer will be able to order an embryo, know that he's going to get a heifer, and what the milk yield will be on the first lactation. We can assume from this all other lactations as well."

A rapid rationalization in the number of dairy farmers in Ontario has taken place since the inauguration of the Ontario Milk Marketing Board on November 1, 1965. Generally speaking, this has been an evolutionary change. Certainly, following the introduction of the graduated entry program, it has been a change that has taken place usually because of a decision by a particular producer to stop producing milk. It has allowed the producer to leave the industry with dignity. Approximately 30,000 milk producers operated in 1965, and in 1990 there were about 9,300 licensed milk producers. On average, a milk producer licence represented 1.6 families in that year.

Latterly, there has been a reduction of about 300 licensed producers a year in the Ontario dairy herd. Using this figure as a projection to the year 2000, the beginning of the 21st century should see about 6,000 licensed milk producers in Ontario. With improved genetic technology considered, this number could be even lower.

While it could happen, the Uruguay round of trade talks will not likely be a complete failure. It appears there will be a start in the phasing out of export subsidies. The U.S. has talked in terms of ten years. The EC has suggested 30 percent in aggregate by 1996. Both must face political realities.

A doomsday scenario, in which zero progress could result in an all-out heavily financed export war between the U.S. and the EC, won't be allowed to take place. GATT import protection would be challenged further. Canada would be hurt.

Adding up the plusses and minuses, Canada supports supply management with the help of the European Community. Canada supports the elimination of export subsidies being demanded by the U.S. As of July 30, 1990, the EC made comments sympathetic to some export subsidy reduction. The mix is there for compromise and some agreement.

The Challenge of Achievement

If Article XI is not clarified, Canada, with the support of the EC, could possibly consider challenging the GATT panel ruling on ice cream and yogurt based on the original understood intent of the article.

On the other hand, the U.S. is a culprit under the GATT waivers and is seen as acting contrary to the GATT, since any import controls under the waiver are intended to be temporary. Canada can't export ice cream and yogurt to the United States. Canada, with the support of the EC, again would likely consider challenging the U.S. That country could then be open to more imports. This could be a bargaining tool for Canada.

Realistically, the U.S. can't give up all its farm supports too quickly. It has traditionally protected its dairy industry. It will settle for "more in the right direction." Article XI is being used as a bargaining tool by the U.S. The ice cream and yogurt action amounted to "sabre rattling." Canada could get the clarification of Article XI that it wants, and the contribution of supply management to world trade stability could be grudgingly recognized.

Canada has not put pressure on the international dairy markets either with product or price.

However, the consultative document of the task force on national dairy policy, July 10, 1990, was suggesting, "The (Canadian) dairy industry must recognize it is impossible to insulate itself completely from the world marketplace. Whether Canada wants to compete internationally or not, it appears that after the Uruguay round, its domestic markets may have to be more open than they are at present."

This could very well happen, but in a way that will preserve the integrity of the philosophy of supply management. Anything else would be politically and economically stupid.

Back on April 1, 1975, the federal government had said, "Imports will be allowed to increase gradually over the next several years until they reach not less than 10 percent of the manufactured products."

Producers protested. It didn't happen. The same pressures were being manifested again in 1990.

In any case, the deadline for approval by the U.S. Congress is March 1991, so the fine tuning of the final agreement could take until the end of February.

The Canadian dairy industry will survive. It may have to accede over time to certain controlled imports. Our dairy cattle will continue to stand up against those of other countries. Our geneticists at Guelph and other institutions are of world class. New market- and consumer-oriented products will be developed. These will be presented in well financed promotions. In Ontario and other provinces the economic and social fabric of dairy farms will continue to strengthen, supported by the abilities and youthful enthusiasm of the family-operated dairy farms.

The Ontario dairy industry will continue to be prosperous and efficient, an industry that will be greeted with positive optimism by the chairman of the Ontario Milk Marketing Board as he addresses the 35th annual meeting in early January in the year 2001.

EPILOGUE

An epilogue is supposed to give some sort of finality to a book. As the situation unfolds in late 1990, I find this hard to do in the case of the dairy industry. World matters and economies are confused. Currently there is real potential for armed conflict with Iraq in the Persian Gulf, and no one knows how that problem will be resolved without creating further difficulties.

The economic picture in Canada is turbulent. The CBC has referred to the current season as "the autumn of discontent." The United States is no less unsettled. The stock market has plunged.

On the economic and trade fronts, indecisive skirmishing to date is the picture in the GATT negotiations. All this is taking place with the feared spectre of the Canada-United States free trade agreement in the minds of a great many farmers. The GATT conclusions won't be reached until December 1990, if then.

Many young, aggressive milk producers and their families are eagerly and anxiously looking to the future. Most intend to make the dairy industry their life's endeavour. Quota values are reported to be dropping. "There is no question the industry is scared," says George Arnold of the Agriculture Service of the Royal Bank of Canada, adding, "The Royal in many cases no longer uses quota values as security because the value is no longer reliable."

There are still many unanswered questions swirling around—GATT, free trade, adequate net incomes, farm credit, farm costs and the very future of agriculture itself in this country. There are real fears and a very visible uneasiness on the farms. Challenges are facing governments to clarify and communicate their policies. Confidence is urgently needed to be restored to producers.

The answers won't be found in this epilogue, because the publisher is getting ready to slam his printing press onto the last of my scribblings.

November 1, 1990, has just passed by. Much has happened since the board had its first unofficial meeting on that hot August 19th in 1965. The appointed members of the first board were in their shirtsleeves, with an embarrassed Orm Coon among them, for that first photo of the board. They were all set for work, with the very positive objective of changing the marketing of milk. This they did, and much has happened subsequently, needless to say.

Several of those early faces are no longer with us. We remember them with fond appreciation and admiration:

Laverne Dyment, Dundas, died June 7, 1969.
Emerson Farnsworth, Huntsville, died April 1, 1974.
W. Ormand Coon, Elgin, died April 14, 1974.
Orvil W. Guy, Winchester, died September 16, 1983.
Elphege Lefebvre, St. Eugene, died February 23, 1985.
A. Sidney Pearson, Hickson, died May 28, 1985.
T. Glen Cole, Bewdley, died August 11, 1990.
Leland Wannamaker, Napanee, died September 29, 1990

To this list must be added the name of Edge Harris of St. Catharines, the board solicitor from the beginning, who died October 5, 1982. During his lifetime Harris gave invaluable service to organized marketing in Ontario and Canada. He guided marketing boards, the drafting of legislation and regulations, and he represented producers' marketing interests in the courts. Successful marketing was his specialty and dedication. There was no match for him.

Rob Wilson, of the same firm of Harris Barr, St. Catharines, has continued to serve the board as legal counselor since 1974. "Quite recently," said Wilson, "the Edible Oils Institute requested leave to appeal to the Supreme Court of Canada the decision of the Appeal Court of Ontario, which upheld the decision on the colouring of margarine."

The arguments were apparently to be based on the Charter of Rights and Freedoms. The request of the institute was refused.

Since the Ontario legislation was first passed in 1949, there has been a running battle between edible oil interests and the dairy industry on the matter of prohibiting margarine's being coloured the same shade of yellow as butter. It now appears that the latest decision by the Supreme Court of Canada should finally settle the issue.

Other changes have taken place. Effective November 15, 1990, the board will have sold the Belleville cheese warehouse, built around 1952. The buyer apparently intends to continue its operation as a warehouse. Its initial construction was greatly assisted by a grant of $500,000, approved by Col.

Tom Kennedy, left over from a hog improvement program. The sale of the Belleville warehouse practically wipes out the few remaining vestiges of the Cheese Producers' Marketing Board.

The Dutch auction clock, first located in the Seaway Building in Kingston, and later moved to Belleville, is all that remains of a unique cheese marketing system. The clock is still used to sell cheese. Charlie Heath, the former dynamic cheese board secretary, and I had given some guidance in Utrecht in 1952 for the modification of the famous Dutch auction clock for the purpose of cheese sales. It had been made famous through vegetable auctions and the well-known flower auction at Aalsmeer in Holland.

At 84, living in Tillsonburg and still fit, Heath mused, "So many memories. Cheese was the binding fabric of central and eastern Ontario for so many years. It was important. So many British buyers came to Canada. It played a major role in the war effort. Politicians paid attention."

In the fall of 1990 Canadian farmers are worried. Many believe their concerns are not heard or understood by governments in Canada. They think they have become less important in the eyes of some politicians and some bureaucrats. They're apprehensive about the future.

A report entitled "A Survey of Canadian Farmers," prepared for Agriculture Canada by the Angus Reid group, was released in July 1990. The report indicates very clearly what farmers are thinking. Generally, they're not exactly happy thoughts.

In 1987 37 percent of producers apparently believed they were worse off financially than the rest of the Canadian populace. In Ontario the figure was 41 percent. In 1990 57 percent of all Canadian farmers believed they were worse off financially than the rest of the populace, and the Ontario figure had jumped to 60 percent.

The report further indicates, "In terms of their well-being, farmers in general appear to be far more hopeful about the promise of GATT negotiations than they are about the impact of the Canada-U.S. trade agreement." Fifty-three percent of all farmers apparently believed that the agreement will have a negative impact on agriculture, while the fears in Ontario jumped to 64 percent of those surveyed. Sixty-six percent of the dairy farmers in Canada had a negative reaction to the agreement, grain farmers 51 percent, red meat 51 percent, and poultry 68 percent. Free trade seemed to be almost as important an issue with Canadian farmers as commodity prices.

In the midst of all of these concerns, in 1990 an extensive policy review is being carried out by Agriculture Canada. And yet the Angus Reid report suggests that 59 percent of Canadian farmers are unaware of the policy review. There is an awareness among 44 percent of Ontario farmers, but only 17 percent among Quebec farmers.

Eighty-nine percent of Ontario farmers, however, appear to be aware of GATT negotiations, with the number decreasing to 80 percent on a national basis. Fifty-nine percent of all farmers in Canada think the GATT impact will be positive, but dairy and poultry producers are more or less split on the matter, according to the report.

Seventy-four percent of Canadian farmers think the federal government is trying to reduce its support for farmers. This perception of reductions was more pronounced in Ontario (87 percent) and least pronounced in Quebec (55 percent).

Roughly half of Canadian farmers think that provincial governments are trying to reduce their support to farmers. But the survey indicated that 72 percent in Ontario think the government is trying to reduce support for farmers.

These survey results doubtless were reflected in the Ontario election of September 6, 1990, when the New Democratic Party swept so many rural ridings and, with general voter support at the polls, took over the government effective October 1, 1990. The Angus Reid report should prove to be a useful reference when future agricultural policies are being determined.

Ontario is reacting bitterly on more than one front. The Ontario Wheat Board charges, "The Americans are refusing to play by the rules that they say everyone else must accept. To them the word 'fair' means that the market has to be all theirs."

"The American principle," quipped a dairy official, "is that if they're not winning, the playing field can't be level." In late October the final results of the GATT negotiations are still unclear. A body divided, the European Community has still not agreed upon a common stance for their trade policy. Critics are getting impatient. The EC is being accused of "prolonging an excruciating agricultural soap opera with a humiliating display of political impotence within the Council of Farm Ministers."

Ray MacSharry, European agricultural commissioner, had suggested as a negotiating point a 30 percent cut in farm subsidies for the European Community. Fellow European commissioners wanted the cuts to go further, and MacSharry is being attacked. European farm leaders are advising politicians in their respective countries, "There will be hell to pay in the countryside if farm subsidy cuts go beyond those proposed by Mr. MacSharry."

In the meantime French farmers are demonstrating. An emergency aid program, intended to curb the wave of demonstrations and truck hijackings, is announced by the French agricultural minister. Premier Michel Rocard has to be protected by police who hurled tear gas grenades at protesting farmers who pelted the officers with eggs, tomatoes and bottles.

In the fall of 1990, John Phillips of *Farm and Country* is speaking rather harshly. "Whether we like it or not the key is Europe and more specifically a reunited Germany which is emerging as a kingpin in the EC. In Europe, preserving the family farm is a social and economic policy; "social" because the farm is regarded as the heart of any community and "economic" because industrial growth has been spread evenly across most of the continent, unlike North America where an obsession with economic determination produces a handful of bloated cities such as Toronto or New York and a depopulated countryside."

In the meantime the United States has been making conciliatory noises and softening its position on farm subsidies, proposing that internal subsidies and restrictions to market access be reduced by at least 70 percent and export subsidies cut more deeply.

Canada did meet the October 15th deadline which had been set to table farm proposals. Canada's offer was clear and supported the long-term interests of Canadian agriculture. It was put forward conditional on effective and equitable GATT rules applicable to all participants, reciprocal benefits for Canadian agriculture and a 10-year transition period.

Canada's offer in the agricultural negotiations is initial and conditional on other countries agreeing to negotiate a substantial agricultural trade reform package which has concrete benefits for Canadian agriculture. It is designed to achieve over a ten-year period:

- An end to the subsidy war through the total elimination of export subsidies.

- A greater market orientation through a reduction of up to 50 percent in trade-distorting internal subsidies.

- Improved market access through a reduction by one-third of normal tariffs.

- A greater security of supply management through a strengthened and clarified Article XI of the GATT.

Article XI of the GATT is used to establish import quotas in support of effective supply management programs. It is intended that the expression "wholly or mainly," used for determining the potential product coverage of

Bill Stewart, left, with Everett Biggs at a session for the series videotaped in connection with the Board's 25th anniversary.

import controls on processed products, would be defined by an agreed minimum percentage content by dry weight of no less than 50 percent of a fresh product under domestic control. It was made clear that this would cover all supply-managed commodities currently under import controls.

John Crosbie, irritated by the negative American reaction to the Canadian offer on agricultural trade reform, stated bluntly, "Canada intends to continue its supply management system. The Americans have had this fetish for a long time about supply management, and I dare say this will be irritating them for a long time to come."

Brigid Pyke from Wolfe Island, the fiery and effective president of the Ontario Federation of Agriculture, says, "Canada's GATT offer on behalf of the Canadian farmers contains much that farmers can support. Over all, the Canadian position positively reflects Canadian farmer interests. Now the hard part is that we pray our negotiators can deliver."

Much credit must go to Jacques Proulx and the farm leaders of Quebec. They have hammered and been critical of Ottawa and the GATT negotiation efforts. Proulx is president of the Union des Producteuis Agricole du Quebec and an effective and outspoken champion of supply management.

The headline in *La Terre De Chez Nous*, on October 18, 1990, following the Canadian offer on agricultural trade reform, said, "La formule "Alchimique' du Canada au GATT. The Canadian 'alchemy' formula for GATT."

The lead article went on, "No one dares to really say it, but everyone is

Lorne Hurd retired as the board's general manager October 31, after almost 25 years of service to the industry.

overjoyed or almost. It's a miracle. The position taken by the Canadian negotiators has succeeded in surprising even the most optimistic of observers. It's almost too good to be true."

Within the 14-country Cairns group, Canada is standing pretty well alone in its unrelenting support of supply management. Canada docs support the removal of export subsidies but on the important issue of supply management there is no agreement. The group is expressing disappointment at Canada's stance. Agriculture Minister Don Mazankowski is blunt: "The Cairns group has to come to terms with Canada's position. What's wrong with staking out a Canadian position? I thought we were sovereign in staking out our own trade policies. We did it with respect to the free trade agreement. And we are doing it now. We should be applauded for that."

The plaudits did come as *Farm and Country* reported on October 23, 1990, "Agriculture Minister Don Mazankowski and his officials seem to have done a topnotch job in defending marketing board structures to its many critics within GATT. Ironically one of the recent converts is an American, Mark Ritchie, an agricultural policy analyst at the U.S. Institute of Agriculture and Trade Policy. He has said in recent months "the Canadian system should be model for other countries."

With some reassurance milk producers in Canada and Ontario look anxiously to what the year end will bring. There is a real concern, but many now have a greater feeling of confidence in what the future holds. There is reason for optimism.

Lorne Hurd joined the board as its first general manager on March 1, 1966. October 31, 1990, after almost 25 years, saw Hurd's official retirement. As you recall, he had been selected after a careful and extensive search. He came with a background and knowledge of both producers and dairy processors, combined with a solid base of communication skills and administrative abilities. He very quickly moved to build a strong administrative team from whatever source he could find the best talent. The immediate delineation between policy making and administration resulted in an organization that was able to guide the board in the development of policies and to carry out those policies with dispatch and success. The imprint of Hurd's style and dedication will remain on the milk industry in Ontario and Canada for some time. His name is well respected in international dairy circles.

Ken Smith, who has been director of the Board/Industry Relations Division, became general manager on November 1, 1990. He joined the board in 1981 as marketing manager after spending some 20 years in the milk processing sector.

Smith is a communicator with a ready smile. He is direct and positive and dedicated to the role and responsibilities of the milk board. He has no doubts about a successful future for the dairy industry.

"Regarding the future, I think you can always take a situation and with the right planning come out of it a winner," said Smith. "We've had a lot of changes in the dairy industry, and there will be more changes, but these will take place over time. We have a marketing system that has benefited people, but we can't sit back. With the seriousness of the current situation, we must do the best possible job in keeping people informed both within and outside the industry."

Ken Smith is looking forward to the challenges of the 1990s. He is confident that they will be met and achieved.

Twenty-five years ago George McLaughlin was the first chairman. While discussing some of the problems of the past with the board, he stated, "All that is past. It's now our turn to make history." John Core of Wyoming, representing Region 9, is the board chairman as we enter the 1990s. Core was elected to the board in the fall of 1980 and elected chairman in 1990. He holds a master's degree in animal science and, with his two brothers, has operated the family farm since 1975.

Core represents the younger generation of dairy producers, whose successful future depends on a healthy dairy industry. And he too is looking to the future. Like McLaughlin, he doesn't intend to waste his time looking into the past. "It's where we're going that's important today. The younger generation of milk producers appreciates what the board has accomplished over the past 25 years. It wasn't easy. We've continually built on those experiences. But we have tremendous challenges before us. They will test the board's mettle as well as that of our county and district committees and dairy producer leaders everywhere. There's no doubt in my mind that these challenges will be met and dealt with in an adequate manner."

The Challenge of Achievement

And that's about it. The Ontario Milk Marketing Board has passed through 25 years of challenges, overcome them, and created a marketing structure for milk producers that is widely considered second to none in the milk producing world. From county and plant locals, a milk marketing system has been built that includes a networking of provincial, national and international concerns and efforts. Within Ontario, milk producers can be reassured that they have a marketing structure that has the strength and resilience to deal with the years ahead.

At board level and at the county and district milk committee level the necessary fortitude of leadership exists that will ensure a strong and healthy dairy industry in Ontario. With the continuation of the traditional role of the Dairy Farmers of Canada, there can only be a viable and prosperous industry in all of Canada.

Anything else can not be envisioned.

Appendix 1

List of Board Members

	Inclusive dates of Term on OMMB
Beaty, Maurice*	Nov. 1965 - 1969
Bell, Alex	1970 - March 1981
Bennett, Dwight	1978 - 1986
Cameron, Grant	1984 - 1989
Cazabon, Lucien*	Nov. 1965 - 1969
Chartrand, Claude	1984 -
Cole, Elgin	1989 -
Cole, Glen*	Oct. 1966 - 1971
Coon, Ormand*	Nov. 1965 - 1969
Core, John	1981 -
Coukell, Gordon	1986 -
Donnan, Gordon	1988 -
Duchesne, Benoit*	Aug.19/65 - Sept.19/65
Dutrisac, Jean-Claude	1977 - 1984
Dyment, Laverne*	Nov. 1965 - 1970
Farnsworth, Emerson*	Nov. 1965 - Sept. 1966
Gallagher, Bernard	1969 - 1984
Goddard, Howard	1971 - 1974
Guest, Robert	1970 - 1975
Guy, Orvil*	1972 - 1978
Henderson, Paul	1986 -
Ketcheson, Allen*	Nov. 1965 - 1980
Lefebvre, Elphege*	Nov. 1965 - 1977 (replaced B. Duchesne)

Levac, Gaston	1989 -
McCague, James	1978 - 1986
McDougall, Ray	1968 - 1981
McKinnon, Ken	Nov. 1965 - July 1986
McLaughlin, George*	Nov. 1965 - 1977
Oosterhoff, Peter	1975 -
Pearson, Sidney*	Nov. 1965 - Oct. 1967
Powers, Ellard	1969 - 1970
Redelmeier, Francis	1969 - 1978
Ross, Allan	1978 - 1986
Saunders, Bruce	1987 -
Schouten, William	May 1981 -
Scott, Harold	1968 - 1978
Sheppard, Howard	1977 - March 1981
Smeltzer, Murray	1974 - 1982
Smith, Grant	1968 -
Stewart, Alvin*	Nov. 1965 - 1969
Todd, Frank*	Nov. 1965 - 1969
Tunney, James	May 1981 -
Wannamaker, Leland	1980 - 1988
Whale, Bruce	1986 -
Wilson, Howard	1982 - 1989

*appointed Board Members

Appendix 2

List of Achievers

Over the past 25 years, many people devoted time and energy to the improvement of the dairy industry through County and District Milk Committees, advisory committees and other avenues of service.

The names of some of these people were provided by milk committees and are listed in alphabetical order. Board members are listed separately.

Thomas Aiken
Donald T. Arbuthnot
David Armstrong
Jack Armstrong
Gordon Atkinson
Sam Ault
Ralph Aylesworth
Martin Baan
Clarence Baker
Harris Baker
Stan Baldwin
Ryan Bangs
Edward Bell
Lionel Bercier
Allan Bernon
Robert Bolt
Harold Brown
Gerry Brugmans
Daniel Brunet
Hartley Cameron
Conrad Charlebois
Gérard Chartrand
Cameron Clark
Cyril Clark
Cecil Craig
Howard Crawford
Jack Crawford
Ralph Davis
Carmen Davis
Blake Dennison
Jake Doleman
William Doppenberg
Walter Drazecky
Earl Elliott
Mack Emiry
David Erwin
Laurent Farmer
Ernest Fleming
Albert Gauthier
Remi Gauthier
Heather (Innes) Golding
Jack Graveson
Gordon Greer
John Grieve

Koen Grootenboer
Simon Hallahan
Archie Hare
Roy Henning
Elmer Hill
Dougal Hobbs
Donald Hough
Jim Humphries
Jack Hunter
Harold Jenkins
Dalton Jermey
Grant Jermey
Klaas Kamstra
Wilfred Keays
Tom Keegan
Nelson Kennedy
Wallace J. Knapp
Noel Labrèche
Lloyd Lane
Noel Leduc
Harry Leekin
Wilfred Lefebvre
Warren Legge
William Loiselle
Willard Mackay
Arnold MacRae
George Marjerrison
Gerard Massie
Moris McArthur
Dr. R.J. McDonald
John Maxwell McIlquham
Arthur McKane
Sam McNally
Clarence Milligan
Charles Milton
Aubrey Moodie
Wallace Mooney
Charles Munroe
Stan Paisley
Rockwell Parks
Roy Peters
Peter Pichette
Armand Pommainville
George Powell

Preston Ralph
David Reid
Roy Rogers
Gaétan Rouleau
Robert Row
Bruce Sava
Gerald Seed
J.M. Senécal
Don Shore
Alfred Sloan
Allan South
Harold Smith
Arnold Stansell
Lorne Stencill
Art Stewart
Harold Stuart
Fraser Sutherland
Boyd Taylor
Donald Taylor
E. Tittley
Melvin Van Horne
Andy Van Kasteren
V. Villeneuve
Cecil Waddell
Richard Walker
Stewart Whyte
Clement Woolsey
Gordon Wright
Russell Yungblut